Detecting Corruption in Developing Countries

Detecting Corruption in Developing Countries

Identifying Causes/ Strategies for Action

Bertram I. Spector

Kumarian Press
An Imprint of Stylus Publishing

The text of this book is set in 11/13 Garamond

Editing and book design by Nicole Hirschman
Proofread by Kathryn Owens
Index by Bertram I. Spector

The paper used in this publication meets the minimum requirements of the American National Standard for Information Sciences—Permanence of Paper for Printed Library Materials, ANSI Z39.48–1984

Library of Congress Cataloging-in-Publication Data

Spector, Bertram I. (Bertram Irwin), 1949–
Detecting corruption in developing countries : identifying causes/strategies for action / Bertram I. Spector. — 1st ed.
    p.   cm.
Includes bibliographical references and index.
    ISBN 978-1-56549-479-4 (cloth : alk. paper) — ISBN 978-1-56549-480-0 (pbk. : alk. paper) — ISBN 978-1-56549-481-7 (library networkable e-edition) — ISBN 978-1-56549-482-4 (consumer e-edition)
    1. Corruption—Developing countries. 2. Public administration—Corrupt practices—Developing countries. 3. Corruption—Developing countries—Case studies. 4. Public administration—Corrupt practices—Developing countries—Case studies. 5. Corruption—Developing countries—Prevention. I. Title.
    JF60.S665   2012
    363.25'9323091724—dc23

                        2011028518

13-digit ISBN: 978-1-56549-479-4 (cloth)
13-digit ISBN: 978-1-56549-480-0 (paper)
13-digit ISBN: 978-1-56549-481-7 (library networkable e-edition)
13-digit ISBN: 978-1-56549-482-4 (consumer e-edition)
Printed in the United States of America

All first editions printed on acid-free paper that meets the American National Standards Institute Z39-48 Standard.

Bulk Purchases: Quantity discounts are available for use in workshops and for staff development. Call 1-800-232-0223

First Edition, 2012
10 9 8 7 6 5 4 3 2 1

To my family,
Judy, Sam, and Naomi

Contents

Illustrations and Tables

Acknowledgments

This book has been in the works for over 15 years. From a chance opportunity to conduct a rapid corruption assessment in Ukraine in 1996, I have been involved continually in uncovering the roots of corruption in countries around the world, developing analytical methods to process data and observations systematically, designing strategies to reduce or eliminate corruption vulnerabilities, and helping governments and civil society organizations implement major anticorruption programs. The techniques used to advance corruption detection and the approaches to control the spread of corruption have evolved over the years. Lessons learned from these experiences are incorporated in this book.

There are many people who have contributed to the development of ideas appearing in these pages. Principal among them is Elizabeth Hart, currently the director of the U4 Anti-Corruption Resource Centre and formerly the senior anticorruption advisor at the US Agency for International Development. She provided intellectual encouragement and support for these assessments, commented on many of the techniques, and participated in learning lessons from each of the pilot cases. My longtime association with Michael Johnston, Svetlana Winbourne, Emil Bolongaita, and Mary Liakos about corruption, corruption detection, assessment tools, and strategic approaches to deal with the problem helped to enrich the analysis.

Firsthand feedback from the members of assessment teams who piloted the new methodology was invaluable. These country and corruption analysts include Benjamin Allen, Edward Anderson, Eric Rudenshiold, Jerry O'Brien, Svetlana Winbourne, Michele Guttmann, Corbin Lyday, Margaret O'Donnell, Robert Charlick, Sheldon Gellar, Sergio Diaz-Briquets, Benjamin Crosby, Janet Tuthill, Bryane Michael, Tye Ferrell, Miguel Schloss, and many others. Their contributions to several of the chapters in this book are gratefully acknowledged.

Rebecca Regan-Sachs provided excellent research and support for the case study epilogues and fact checking.

Over the past 15 years, I have received continual support and encouragement from Larry Cooley and Marina Fanning of Management Systems International. MSI provided the fruitful breeding grounds for this corruption detective work. The US Agency for International Development provided much of the funding for the research and analyses contained in these pages.

Last but not least, I would like to acknowledge the encouragement and support of James Lance, editor and associate publisher at Kumarian Press.

The views expressed in this book are those of the author alone and should not be attributed to any sponsoring agency, the US Agency for International Development, or the US government.

1

Corruption Detectives

In good detective novels, the crime is typically solved through a combination of psychological drama and analytical process. The detective is singularly motivated to unravel the "whodunit" puzzle—uncovering the identity of the criminal *and* why he or she did it. There are always unexpected twists and turns, but by the end of the story—perhaps on the last page—the puzzle is solved. The style and methods that detectives use to solve the mystery are what make these novels so riveting—that, in addition to the eccentricity and brilliance of the detective!

Some fictional (and real-life) detectives use an inductive approach, collecting facts and evidence, conducting interviews with witnesses, observing the crime scene and the behavior of suspects, and then trying to connect the dots. Others—Sherlock Holmes is the greatest example—employ deductive reasoning to reach their conclusions from what appear often to be trifling clues. The deductivists subject the facts, evidence, and observations to the rigors of broader theories and hypotheses about how the criminal mind works to uncover their solutions.

One of the most insidious crimes affecting developing countries—and among the most difficult to detect—is corruption in the public sector. It involves secretive transactions by a very few who take advantage of their public office and power to benefit themselves at the expense of the wider citizenry. The professionals who search out such government corruption and bring public officials to justice when they abuse their authority are good examples of real-life detectives. These detectives often operate under the auspices of the police, prosecutor's office, auditor's office, justice ministry, and courts. They use the tools of induction and deduction to uncover corrupt behaviors when they occur, and they seek to charge and arrest government staff who can be proven to have abused their office.

Another type of corruption detective is actively engaged in investigating and preventing corrupt abuses in developing countries. These detectives operate on a more analytical, but no less important, level. They include international development specialists, policymakers, program and field officers, consultants, country experts, and researchers. In contrast with criminal detectives, these analytical detectives are more interested in understanding the *whys* of corruption in a particular country or sector than the *who* of corruption. They are particularly interested in uncovering the underlying causes of corruption: what the socioeconomic roots of the problem are, why people are attracted to such transactions, how they operate, and what keeps the code of silence operational, especially among those who are victimized by the transaction. By unearthing the causes of corruption, these analytical detectives can recommend or program anticorruption efforts that seek to reduce the opportunities for corrupt behavior, enhance transparency and openness so that these acts—if they do occur—can be subjected to greater scrutiny, and impose stricter controls to make authorities more accountable for their actions.

The work of these analytical detectives and the anticorruption strategies that emanate from their conclusions are the subject of this book. Their efforts may be conducted in offices, think tanks, and universities, but their findings can have widespread and visible impacts on people throughout the world, making them less vulnerable to corruption risks and allowing them to develop economically, socially, and politically in a freer, fairer, and more just environment. These detectives, by uncovering the roots of corruption, level the political and economic playing field by preventing the negative consequences of corrupt behaviors. Their methods have evolved over time. This book presents their detection methods, some examples of how they have been applied, and ways that these methods have been transformed into targeted solutions to remedy the problems of corruption.

Some Examples

The political, economic, and social fabric of a society can be torn asunder by corrupt behavior in the public sector. When excessive bureaucratic discretion, greed, and abuse of power for private benefit are widespread phenomena in developing countries, ordinary citizens can be victimized and left helpless. They can be deprived of essential services they depend on from government— health care, education, pensions, utilities, housing, for example—that are diminished in quantity and quality because public funds are siphoned off for private use.

The corruption phenomenon is complex. In many cases, corruption is viewed as a traditional or cultural practice and the customary approach by which things get done. Gifts are given to civil servants to obtain a service provided by government, a relative is hired for a public sector job to help out the family, money and influence are used to ensure that a favored business receives a government contract. These behaviors are often viewed as honorable and expected of those who have achieved high levels of authority or responsibility; it's a matter of "taking care of one's own." Those immersed in such cultures usually see no lasting harm in these actions. But far too often, even small acts such as these can result in major harm, even critical life-and-death situations. A few examples can illustrate this point.

On August 17, 1999, a 7.4-magnitude earthquake in western Turkey left few buildings standing and more than 17,000 dead. In many parts of the world, such devastating earthquakes are not so much *natural* disasters as they are *man-made* catastrophes. Construction codes may be adequate, but they are not enforced, or there are insufficient controls to ensure their effective implementation. Bribes or kickbacks are paid to get permits despite defective plans, materials, or building techniques. Building inspectors are bribed to turn a blind eye at construction shortcuts, omissions, or mistakes. Together, these practices make the general public a serious victim of corruption and its deadly consequences. According to one estimate, 75% of all deaths in earthquake zones can be attributed to corruption.[1] Of all the earthquakes between 1990 and 2005, if all corrupt practices had been eliminated, 6.5 million people would still have their homes, 7,750 would not have been injured, and 20,750 would still be alive.

Twenty-nine miners died on April 5, 2010, at the Upper Big Branch mine disaster in West Virginia. Soon after, the FBI began investigating allegations of bribery and payoffs involving the mine's owners and inspectors for the federal Mine Safety and Health Administration. The contention is that corrupt inspectors tolerated inadequate ventilation systems and firefighting equipment in the mine, thus allowing the strict mining regulations that are on the books to go unenforced.

In Iraq, the US military worked hard to ensure oil pipeline security, but ironically, millions of dollars meant to protect the pipelines were embezzled by Iraqi parliamentarians and channeled to insurgents who attacked the same pipelines. A member of the Iraqi National Assembly was indicted for corruption in this case.[2] In another case, a former Iraqi defense minister was charged with corruption for misspending $1.3 billion in military contracts.

In Ukraine, a nongovernmental organization that supports HIV/AIDS patients conducted a cost-benefit study in 2005 that compared the bulk purchase of prescription medications by the Ukrainian Ministry of Health and the Global Fund to Fight AIDS, Tuberculosis and Malaria for the same time periods. There were extreme cost differentials, with ministry procurements as high as 27 times the cost that the Global Fund paid for the same medications. The NGO came to the conclusion that kickbacks and collusion in the ministry's procurement process were at the root of the problem, directly endangering patients. In fact, a 2007 public opinion survey in Ukraine showed that over 13% of households gave bribes to officials over the course of a year, estimated to total over $700 million nationwide. This could have paid for six ultramodern children's hospitals, 18 fully equipped ambulances for every city in Ukraine, modern mammography machines for breast cancer screening in half of all rural district hospitals, or insulin supplied to every diabetes patient in the country for the next 20 years free of charge.[3]

These examples clearly demonstrate that corruption is serious business and can have major impacts on ordinary citizens. Corrupt practices not only line the pockets of abusive government officials but can also result in death and suffering for hundreds and thousands of citizens or prevent them from receiving critical public services they are entitled to or rely on. Even what seem to be insignificant bribes or turning a blind eye to regulatory evasion can have significant consequences for many in society, depriving them potentially of services and resources that they depend on. These corruptive acts can mean the difference between comfort and inconvenience, health and sickness, education and ignorance, sufficiency and hunger, life and death.

The cultural and traditional origins of much corrupt behavior are a confounding factor. But the inertia of these customs can be reversed, albeit gradually, if the negative consequences are demonstrated to outweigh the benefits. In Afghanistan, for instance, religious leaders throughout the country's 165,000 mosques often include anticorruption messages after Friday prayers to counteract long-practiced ways that promote corruption in everyday life. They and others believe that even culturally embedded corrupt practices can be eliminated with greater public awareness and if citizens are provided with practical ways to resist corruption.

The examples also reveal a few simple but disturbing facts. While corruption may run rampant in many sectors of everyday life, it remains a very hidden and secretive behavior. Because corruption can be a two-way street—it can benefit both the corruptor and the corruptee—little is often revealed about it, and even when there is a clear victim, there is typically insufficient hard evidence to convict the perpetrators. Because the parties engaging in it know that it is inherently wrong, they keep quiet and do their best not to leave a paper trail of their deeds.

People can experience petty corruption on a daily basis and know that it exists but may have only suspicions about grand corruption at higher levels, involving larger sums of money, power, and influence. Secrecy tends to be even more prevalent when it comes to grand corruption. Citizens may believe that there is widespread collusion, extortion, kickbacks, and outright theft of public funds and resources at high levels, but they often cannot prove it. The mass media can pursue investigative reports to track down evidence of misdeeds, and police and prosecutors can also seek evidence through more official means. All of these efforts typically result in heightened public mistrust of government and a sense of victimization.

The basic underlying causes of public sector corruption are identifiable: they generally originate in low-risk, high-gain situations where there are few control mechanisms, minimal accountability for the actions of public officials, and limited transparency. Essentially, corrupting influences tend to exist or thrive where there is little oversight of government, and the corruptors believe that no one is "watching the store." These environments are breeding grounds for greed, the abuse and misuse of power, and the use of excessive discretion that benefits entrusted authority at the expense of everyone else.

Corruption Defined

From a legal perspective, corruption is defined differently from country to country. Criminal and civil codes and public administration laws usually specify what is considered to be corrupt behavior, what are conflicts of interest, what are ethical standards for public servants, and what the sanctions are for corrupt behavior. Cultural and traditional norms may influence these laws and codes and can sometimes stand at odds with official legal norms. Corruption in any given context usually has both legal and sociocultural definitions, which are not always the same. But neither law nor culture is immutable, and anticorruption efforts may need to target one or both.

The commonly used behavioral definition views corruption as *the misuse of entrusted public office for private gain.*[4] It focuses on the proactive behaviors of public officials to extort or seek bribes for activities and services that they have been entrusted to perform, the use of personal influence or connections to get something accomplished outside of the legally sanctioned channels, and the breach of standards of conduct that may result in personal conflicts of interest. Corruption occurs any time public officials or employees misuse the authority placed in them as public servants for either monetary or nonmonetary gain that accrues to them, their friends, their relatives, or their personal or political interests. Even if public officials do not actively seek out corrupt transactions, a bribe or illicit influence attempt can be *offered* to them. They can be on the receiving end of corrupt behavior practiced by citizens or businesspeople who are seeking special influence over those who wield public power.

Corrupt practices and the sanctions against them are often referenced in a country's laws and regulations, but detection and enforcement may be weak or nonexistent. If appropriate controls are not in place or well enforced and officials believe they can act with impunity—in other words, if misuse of office is seen as a low-risk, high-gain activity—corruption can progressively degrade a country's governance structures and its ability to deliver services to citizens. It can also undermine the rule of law and legitimacy of government and thwart financial growth and investment along with a country's overall development objectives.

Simply, corruption can be viewed as wealth-seeking-power or power-seeking-wealth.[5] In the first case, the economic elite can use its money to seek public power and influence over the state's resources. The result is a form of *state capture* by which economic elites attempt to grab powerful positions to control the state to suit their private interests or "buy" the political elite to do their bidding. In the second case, political leaders try to take advantage of their positions to accumulate personal wealth for themselves, their families, and their kin. This can be seen as *state predation*, where political power is used to extract private financial benefits from a country's economic resources.

Detecting Corruption

To realistically tackle corruption problems, one needs to understand corruption, assess it, and devise a meaningful strategy and action plan that will attack and undermine its underlying causes, not just deal with its symptoms. Thus, one must accurately detect the corrupting influences and then design ways to overcome them.

A first step in developing a practical strategy to fight or prevent corruption must include creating a constituency for change. There have to be people and groups within government *and* outside government who are ready and willing to commit themselves to implement reforms and change the way institutions and procedures work. This is often called building *political will*. One way of mobilizing political will among important constituencies is to provide them with clear and indisputable information and evidence about the problem of corruption and the costs it imposes on society.

Conducting diagnostic assessments of corruption can help in this regard. They involve systematic activities to gather hard data, evidence, and facts, as well as perceptions, about the problem. Assessments try to find out how big the problem is in a country, where it impacts most, its causes, and its consequences for society, among other things.

But why do it? How can this kind of information help fight corruption? Diagnostics provide direction in the development of anticorruption strategies. They identify the principal domains where initiatives need to be taken, where corruption hurts the most. For example, should strategies target reforms in tax administration, customs, the court system, the delivery of public services, or somewhere else? The assessment helps to set the priorities for a new strategy.

Diagnostic assessments also provide baseline measurement of the problem. They can clarify how bad the problem is and how costly it is for society. Such measurement can also identify the degree of success of ongoing anticorruption programs and if they are having the intended effect. This information can be influential in mobilizing the political will of stakeholders and help them form cohesive constituencies for reform. These kinds of data provide the hard evidence that strengthens the conviction of individuals and interest groups that something really has to be done to change the system of corruption.

And these assessments constitute one demonstrable step showing that someone *is* watching the store—that corruption may be detected and possibly prosecuted, resulting in punishment. If there are predictable and negative consequences for committing an act of corruption, it may cause likely offenders to think twice before acting.

There are usually many obstacles in the way of conducting successful anticorruption programs: entrenched power brokers, cynicism, inertia, and weak institutions are among these barriers. But what about transforming political will? Sometimes political will already exists and just needs to be strengthened or channeled properly. But most times, political will is weak or nonexistent.

The data from diagnostic assessments can establish irrefutable information about the problem of corruption—and in so doing can help strengthen the motivation to fight corruption. It can help people understand the root causes of the problem and understand the real costs it imposes on society in terms of reduced economic investment, poor delivery of public services, and weaker governance. This kind of information can help mobilize people in all sectors of society to be more concerned and turn their words into deeds. Moreover, negative findings can shame leadership into changing its ways, enforcing rules of fair and just behavior in the public sector. These assessments can be most effective if they help transform a society's tolerance for corruption into outrage against corruption and, better yet, if it can transform outrage with corruption into practical and positive solutions to the problem.

There are five major types of assessment techniques available to diagnostic detectives. All together they can provide a comprehensive examination of the corruption problem in a country. First, there are *public opinion surveys*. Surveys provide data collected from structured face-to-face interviews with citizens, businesses, and government officials. The main goal is to show the significance of the corruption problem and the extent to which corruption has penetrated various elements of society using attitudinal and behavioral measurement. Beyond that, surveys can suggest where corruption has become a critical problem, for example, in dealings with police officers, doctors, and customs officials as opposed to teachers and bankers. In addition to asking perceptual questions, they ask experiential questions to measure the costs of corruption and corruption's impact on the quality of service delivery, the business environment, and public sector vulnerabilities. Sections of these surveys typically target corruption in various sectors—such as health care, education, and communal services—providing in-depth snapshots of high-risk areas, sector by sector.

When surveys are conducted regularly, year-to-year comparisons can be helpful in monitoring changes and can be extremely useful in developing or redirecting anticorruption reforms. The World Bank, Transparency International, USAID, and many other organizations and governments sponsor similar corruption surveys of the broad population or specific segments to detect changes in perspectives and what might be done to address the problem.

Another diagnostic technique involves *focus groups*. These are in-depth discussion sessions conducted with targeted interest groups in government and society. Using this technique, you can often get detailed information about what people believe about corruption and how to control and manage the problem. Interactive dialogue moves you beyond perceptions to some of the reasoning behind those beliefs. These sessions usually target the following types of questions: How big is the problem of corruption? How does corruption cause harm? What are its root causes? How effective are current laws and programs? What are possible solutions? What issues should be dealt with first?

In Romania, for example, focus groups were conducted with the business community and found that entrepreneurs were most concerned with corrupt interactions with the police, customs, and banks.[6] They were also very concerned with what they viewed as private sector corruption within large corporations. Focus groups conducted with government officials from departments that deliver public services indicated that there was a real need for greater internal oversight and quality control. There was also a need to institute serious civil service reforms and to develop standardized procedures on how to provide services to reduce the opportunities for corruption.

A third diagnostic assessment tool involves *legal assessments*. First, it is important to know what the laws and regulations on the books say—what officially constitutes a corrupt action and what are the sanctions for it. But, second, it is important to go deeper and analyze where the legal gaps are and if there are inconsistencies among laws. Certainly, anticorruption provisions can appear in many different laws—criminal and penal codes, civil service laws, public procurement regulations, financial disclosure laws, ministerial responsibility laws, and many others. These should all be consistent. Third, you need to look at how these laws and regulations are implemented and enforced in reality. Are these laws taken seriously? Are sufficient resources invested in their execution and enforcement? Fourth, it is necessary to evaluate what official oversight bodies do to make government officials and agencies accountable for their actions. Together, these findings can indicate whether a country's laws are adequate as they are written but also as they are put into practice.

The fourth assessment technique involves *institutional assessments*. Here, it is crucial to inventory what government agencies and departments are already doing to fight and prevent corruption and if they are having any success. But it is also important to go into greater depth within some governmental institutions to identify very clearly where the specific problems are. To accomplish this, a technique called *process mapping* has been used to analyze how the functions and procedures of governmental departments are carried out.[7] This mapping specifies how an organization does its business: what it does efficiently and inefficiently, where there are conflicts of interest, and where there are excessive opportunities for bribe taking and bribe giving. As a result of this institutional mapping, administrative process reengineering might be called for to improve control mechanisms and efficiency.

In Ukraine, for example, process mapping was conducted to analyze environmental inspection units and uncovered the need to introduce personnel rotation to reduce opportunities for corruption. Government procurement systems were also analyzed carefully, and the need for greater publicity and transparency of tenders and awards was identified. And the procedures by which communal property is privatized or leased at a municipal level were also analyzed. The results here showed that there was a need to simplify regulations, standardize procedures, reduce the number of documents required, and localize approvals.[8]

A fifth and more comprehensive assessment approach entails analysis of the *political-economic dynamics* in a country to evaluate the underlying causes of corrupt behavior and low accountability.[9] The politics and economics that have guided a country's development will have a definite influence on attitudes toward governance and the rule of law and its practical manifestations. One way of going about a political-economic assessment of corruption risks in a country is to observe the evolved dynamics of political and economic participation and political and economic institutions. Michael Johnston specifies a typology of *corruption syndromes* that defines different mixtures of these dynamics. The Drivers of Change model provides an alternate, less-structured approach to assessing political-economic dynamics.[10]

Where do all of the results from these corruption diagnostic assessments lead? They provide firsthand data for corruption investigations, but they also serve to bolster political will and the motivation for systematic change. They are most effective if they transform public attitudes of tolerance and acceptance of corruption into collective frustration and outrage against corruption and then from outrage to collective solutions to manage and control corruption. Diagnostic assessments provide the data that can help motivate these changes and build coalitions of interest inside and outside of government to fight corruption.

The strategy development process is informed by the data and priorities gathered in the detection and assessment stage. As anticorruption strategies are developed, all interested stakeholders—government reformers, NGOs, business, and the media—should get together to brainstorm what can be done. They need to do this in a nonconfrontational way. There is no room for finger-pointing. And they need to attack the problem of corruption from all perspectives—including law enforcement, preventive actions, and public education campaigns. In pulling together, these stakeholders can form a new and broad coalition against corruption, a new constituency for reform and change.

Once a strategy is developed, anticorruption activities must be implemented with rigor and consistency. The necessary resources—people, funds, expertise—must be assigned, political will and leadership at the highest levels must be mobilized and made visible, and the pace of activities and enforcement must be vigorous.

The message is that there are clear linkages between what diagnostic corruption detectives are looking for and the development of effective constituencies to fight corruption. Assessments provide a common foundation of information and understanding about the extent, nature, and impacts of corruption. In so doing, assessments can have the power to transform and mobilize the political will in society to find solutions. The process of detecting corruption, conducting corruption assessments, and developing strategies can open channels for communication and negotiation among governmental and nongovernmental sectors and provide a basis for active coalitions to fight corruption. These organized constituencies have the potential to effectively implement anticorruption strategies and to initiate real change and reforms for a sustainable fight against corruption.

Transitions in the Anticorruption Field

The global fight against corruption is facing a turning point. An article in *Foreign Affairs* asserts that the scaled-up rhetoric about corruption over the past decade has not been matched by adequate action, leaving little to show for it.[11] In fact, by some measurements the problem may be getting worse. But, the authors also argue that there are many opportunities available to decision makers to turn words into deeds that can have a real impact—by carefully monitoring the implementation of international and regional conventions; cleverly leveraging donor assistance, loans, and budget support; and targeting demand for greater compliance by multinational corporations.

Others, like Daniel Kaufmann, are less sanguine about the feasibility of these types of activities.[12] While his empirical research confirms the conclusion that past actions—largely focused on legal, judicial, and institutional reforms—have had insufficient effects on corruption, the implications he draws take a different turn. The problem is getting magnified because, in part, increasing trends of private sector influence on public sector governance—often producing intolerable levels of *state capture* in some countries—have brought proper governance to its knees. He suggests that what is needed are programs that exercise strict external accountability controls—monitoring and oversight via public watchdogs, parliamentary committees, e-governance tools, and the like—that provide for active and enforceable checks and balances on government decision making. These programs, along with ones that encourage greater political contestation, reforms to political financing, and increased transparency in the judiciary and executive branches, are the measures that are most likely, in his view, to produce real movement to curb corruption.

So, what works in the fight against corruption? Recent empirical analysis evaluates the impacts of a large number of anticorruption intervention cases.[13] It concluded that public awareness campaigns and initiatives against grand corruption may yield early positive results but are rarely sustained. A common element of these programs that often mitigates against long-term success is insufficient attention to institutionalizing and proceduralizing the reforms— failing to embed these initiatives seamlessly into the normal functioning of government institutions. Sometimes this is a failure of poor follow-up to the reforms, a lack of sufficient capacity-building efforts, or haste to declare success and run on the part of the reformers. It also points to the failure of the toolkit approach—the idea that one size fits all. We have learned that for anticorruption interventions to be effective and sustainable, they must be tailored to the country context. Lacking sensitivity to these issues, anticorruption efforts are prone to backsliding and recorruption.[14]

Are there *any* positive findings from the myriad anticorruption programs implemented over the past decade? Business Environment and Enterprise Performance Survey (BEEPS) data from 1999, 2002, and 2005 have been compared to assess change, at least from the perspective of the business communities in Europe and Central Asia.[15] Overall, firms in most of these transition countries report a trend of less corruption and less frequent and smaller bribes. Several sectors have shown significant improvement; these include tax, customs, and business licensing. Public procurement and the judiciary, on the other hand, are areas where there have been less attention and increased corruption trends. Success seems to be tied to external incentives—notably the goal of joining the European Union, increased political and economic competition, and the political will of particular leaders.

It may be that the assessments of anticorruption programs conducted to date expect too much too soon. Fighting corruption, after all, is a long-term activity. In New York City, for instance, it took almost 150 years of enforcement, reforms, and culture shift to dampen the effects of political patronage, cronyism, and corruption that typified the activities of Tammany Hall, which influenced not only municipal but national politics. How can we seriously expect countries transitioning from conflict or from major political-economic change to demonstrate almost immediate anticorruption results?

In its 2005 Anticorruption Strategy, USAID acknowledges that the anticorruption field needs to experience a major shift from past approaches—from addressing only the symptoms of corruption to attacking the underlying political and economic dynamics that catalyze corruption. The expectation is that this will yield more effective and long-lasting results that are resistant to backsliding. In addition, the USAID strategy concludes that anticorruption initiatives need to be embedded into sectoral programs to reduce corruption and strengthen governance, for example, in the education, health, political financing, and public finance areas. Two analytical compendiums picked up on this theme.[16]

As the anticorruption field has progressed over the years, both the research and the practitioner communities have developed in their thinking about how best to strategize and implement programs to reduce and control the phenomenon. In the "first wave" of anticorruption programming (approximately 1993 to 1999), the focus was on measuring and ranking countries in terms of their corruption levels and helping them strategize action plans to deal with the problem. It became clear that such token interventions were not sufficient. There was minimal feedback of the "shame factor" for low-ranking countries, and even if action plans were designed, implementation was not always robust.

A "second wave" of programs was designed and implemented (mostly during the 2000s) to produce institutional reforms and build public awareness programs. While there were some successes, the results were often disappointing. Some international and bilateral donors, for example, invested aggressively in providing systems to developing countries to promote public financial management reforms—to deter fraud and abuse in public procurements, tax administration, customs collection, and budget allocation. In some cases, these systems have had positive impacts, reducing the opportunities for corrupt transactions and thereby increasing the revenues and funds collected by the state. In other cases, once the donor assistance ended, the systems were literally unplugged, and the embedded corrupt stakeholders reverted to their previous ways. Even when institutional anticorruption reforms were effective and sustained, they tended to reflect corruption reductions in particular sectors or functions of government, and the incidences of corruption shifted to other sectors or domains keeping the overall levels constant. The influx of public education programs on corruption has had some impact, resulting in citizen watchdog activities and an increase in the registration and prosecution of grievances about corrupt transactions with government and nongovernmental complaint and legal offices, but these efforts tended to be very localized and without the scaling-up power to affect national policy or behavior.

Based on these first two waves of activity, a belief emerged among the research and practitioner communities that there needs to be a major push to base future anticorruption programming on a more sophisticated understanding of the underlying causes of corruption—so that programs do not just deal with the symptoms of corruption. In the new "third wave" of programs, there needs to be meaningful and deep assessments of the problem that drive strategic approaches and programs. Corruption detectives need to take the lead. Their assessments need to address a "whole of government" approach—that is, they need to look at all key sectors where there are corruption vulnerabilities—and strong accountability and control measures must be designed and implemented across all sectors as a multidimensional strategy and program.

Designing the Third Wave

Designing and implementing anticorruption reforms that will have the intended impact and will endure is a daunting task. Research and practice have shown that there are many issues and challenges that need to be considered.

Deconstructing corruption. Corruption can be approached in a holistic fashion, but practical experience has shown that more targeted initiatives produce results that have a greater impact. This requires the corruption problem to be deconstructed into its component parts. If analysts or practitioners assess corruption vulnerabilities on a sectoral or functional basis, by level of government, by type of corruption, or by gender impact, for example, they can devise specific targeted remedies that are likely to attack the underlying root causes of the problem rather than only the symptoms. Thus, it is reasonable to address corruption sectorally—where it happens—whether it be in the procurement of HIV/AIDS pharmaceuticals, in the flow down of central budget funds to local school districts, in the granting of permits for rights to extract oil and minerals, in the registration or inspection of businesses, or in the financing of political parties and election campaigns, for example.

Similarly, corruption that occurs at the central level has different parameters and constraints than corruption that occurs at the local level and must be dealt with differently. Administrative corruption operates differently from state capture or grand corruption, and the remedies also must be different. As well, corruption that affects women, youth, and men differentially needs to be addressed through distinct and tailored mechanisms to have a lasting impact.

Deconstructing corruption also requires understanding the sources of resistance to reforms. By focusing on targeted initiatives, anticorruption champions can map out where, when, and how reforms are likely to be fought by vested interests. By identifying the sources of opposition to reforms, anticorruption champions can better assess the strengths and capacity of opposing interests relative to their own and can thus prepare accordingly.

A clear challenge in dealing with corruption issues in their deconstructed form is prioritizing what's to be done. In most developing countries, corruption is such an omnipresent phenomenon that dealing with the problem comprehensively can quickly yield an incredibly large and costly menu of proposed activities. As a result, it is essential to provide a way for practitioners to develop a strategic outlook, to help them focus programs on a manageable and prioritized set of strategic problems from the multitude of potential paths that can be pursued. They need a set of strategically focused criteria to help prioritize activities—where the greatest deficiencies lie, where the greatest opportunities for success exist, what the host government's views on major priorities are, where there is internal resistance or obstacles to reform, and where the host government or other donors already have programs planned or under way that would be duplicative.

The logic of deconstructing corruption leads directly to the notion that anticorruption activities should be embedded in existing programs—often labeled as "mainstreaming"—to strengthen sectoral governance, transparency, and accountability, in addition to conducting head-on and crosscutting anticorruption programs. To accomplish this, anticorruption mainstreaming workshops need to be conducted for practitioners and followed up by one-on-one technical assistance.

Challenges of grand corruption and state capture. Problems of grand corruption and state capture are often put on the backburner by host country and donor anticorruption programs because they are too difficult to address: hard evidence of abuse or misconduct is not readily available, prosecuting high-level officials and economic vested interests is too sensitive or becomes a show trial to damage the political opposition, and political and election financing operations are not transparent. Dealing with administrative and petty corruption is often more achievable, and there may be local political will for it even in the most corrupt states. As a result, many anticorruption campaigns have resorted to attacking corruption by picking these lower-hanging fruit and avoiding the larger and more critical problems of grand corruption.

However, there are ways to overcome these challenges. First, it is important to establish strategic goals, assessing where the greatest corruption problems lie and prioritizing grand corruption problems along with the administrative corruption issues. This effort is also important because it may yield insights as to where champions and openings for reform are located and can thus provide a level of realism about the definition and prospects of achieving strategic goals. Second, rather than targeting particular individuals who are abusing the system (unless host country prosecutors have hard evidence in hand), anticorruption programs can target preventive reforms in the government sectors and functions that are most vulnerable to grand corruption or capture, for example, public procurement, tax administration, customs, and political party and election financing. Supply-side reform programs that embed strict accountability and transparency controls might be feasible and appear innocuous to vested interests. If not, demand-side programs that mobilize civil society, business, and the media into advocacy and watchdog units and develop greater public legal literacy can serve as external pressure points to force the hand of high-level officials toward reform.

The challenges of corruption in the political process fall clearly into the grand corruption category. They seek to subvert the democratic selection of officials, the creation of level playing fields for parties, and the rule of law. Political financing that occurs outside lawful regulations can range the gamut from vote buying in elections to funds accepted from criminal groups, the selling of appointments, abuse of state resources, use of funds for personal enrichment, and demands for contributions from public servants, kickbacks, and extortion.[17] Possible reforms that have been applied to reduce the opportunity for corruption in political financing include providing public funding and subsidies for election campaigns, requiring parties and candidates to keep strict accounting of their campaign financing and provide public reports, requiring big donors to submit tax identification so their funds can be properly traced, regulating expenditure caps, and creating enforceable sanctions for violators.[18]

Diplomacy and international/regional agreements. The global landscape is now replete with international and regional conventions and agreements that promote country compliance by strengthening legal frameworks against corruption and ensuring predictable enforcement. Many of these conventions include periodic peer reviews and evaluations that can produce the social pressure required to make sure countries comply with the agreements. Moreover, some international loans and grants come with conditions that require the establishment of anticorruption institutions and reforms.

These international agreements and global standards can sometimes be helpful to anticorruption champions because they can point to these accords as the drivers of change. By sharing the risks with international actors and asserting external pressures, domestic champions may grab more maneuvering room. To be sure, there is a risk of backlash from local actors against this international "interventionism," so this approach requires careful implementation. Nevertheless, some countries only pay lip service to anticorruption requirements. Under these circumstances, donor programs can be helpful in forcing countries to pursue meaningful reforms. This is also where multidonor leverage and diplomatic pressure exercised at a country level can sometimes be effective in steering corrupt governments toward effective reforms.

Conflict, postconflict, and strategic interests. Corruption is at the nexus of many traditional problems in the developing world—poverty, slowed economic growth, and reduced rule of law. But nowadays corruption is also viewed as an incubator of security-related problems—conflict; fragile, failing, or failed states; terrorism; drug trafficking; money laundering; human trafficking; and organized crime. If unchecked, corruption's relationship to these security-related issues can further destabilize a country's neighbors and the wider region it inhabits. If the illicit funds and relaxed enforcement that corruption offers can be squelched, the risks can be minimized. Much more research still needs to be conducted—on a country-by-country basis—to trace the linkages between corrupt networks and these security-related problems.[19]

Not only is corruption a major factor that can stimulate and support conflict—funding rebel groups and facilitating the transport of weapons across borders, for example—but it has also been shown to be a potential factor that destabilizes postconflict situations, providing the means for "spoilers" to wreck peace agreements.[20] When the corruption problem is seen through security lenses, the issue is certainly elevated to the state capture and grand corruption levels. Under these circumstances, it is critical to understand the political-economic dynamics of the country situation in order to attack the underlying root causes of the corruption problem, thereby, it is hoped, having an impact on reducing the security threats.

Innovative tools and best practices. First- and second-wave technical assistance in the anticorruption field has yielded several toolkits (from the World Bank, Transparency International, the United Nations, etc.) that list a wide variety of interventions. There are two major problems with most of these inventories: they do not distinguish between successful and unsuccessful approaches, and they do not provide criteria to prioritize initiatives so that a customized anticorruption strategy can be developed for particular countries or for particular sectors within countries. The challenge for analysts and practitioners today is to determine not only which interventions are most appropriate for given corruption problems but also which will have an impact on the underlying causes of corruption rather than merely on the symptoms.

To accomplish this, several models or approaches have been designed, principally the Drivers of Change model used by the United Kingdom's Department for International Development[21] and USAID's Corruption Assessment Handbook.[22] Both of these emphasize early country analysis of the political-economic dynamics that are at the root cause of corruption and, based on the findings, select the most critical government sectors and functions to address and identify the appropriate anticorruption tools and techniques.

Another challenge facing analysts and practitioners is the limited best practice knowledge that exists about effective remedies for corruption. Many approaches have been tried, but few undergo rigorous monitoring and evaluation for performance. Kaufmann's recent analysis cited earlier (2003) indicates that many current techniques are not effective, and instead greater emphasis should be placed on external accountability and control mechanisms that implement visible checks and balances by a variety of stakeholders. These techniques will provide the right incentives to officials to comply with legal rules and procedures because they know someone is watching.

In general, more systematic analysis is required to assess the effectiveness of specific interventions under particular conditions. One pilot attempt is the meta-analysis study conducted by Spector, Johnston and Dininio.[23] They found that we can learn useable lessons from past cases if they are subjected to systematic comparative analysis rather than our trying to glean anecdotal information from each. There should be more investment in practical research along these lines, and new projects should implement carefully designed monitoring and evaluation systems to assess performance.

Political will and anticorruption readiness. Corruption analysts often emphasize that it takes strong leadership with political will to initiate anticorruption programs that have teeth. While there is no doubt that political will is essential, there are many examples of leaders with good intentions who champion anticorruption reforms but whose accomplishments are quickly reversed after they leave the political scene.[24] So, donors and reformers need to seek out *more* than just political will or individual champions; these are necessary but not sufficient conditions for pushing forward with anticorruption activities. More attention should be paid to the concept of *anticorruption readiness,* which goes beyond political will. Readiness is a more objective and multidimensional phenomenon that focuses on the ability of a country and its leaders to act. It incorporates the demonstration of anticorruption commitment through past actions, the existence of human capacity and skills within government to accomplish new reforms, and the mobilization of external forces in civil society to continue to put pressure on government for accountability reforms.[25]

Gender considerations. Corruption disproportionately affects women, youth, and pensioners because they typically depend the most on basic levels of public services that are diminished substantially by the siphoning off of public funds in highly corrupt societies. At the same time, empirical research has shown that women are typically less likely to give bribes or condone bribe taking.[26] All anticorruption reform programs need to take gender-prone inequalities and gender-related victimization into account by developing specific activities that monitor the extent to which corruption affects gender issues and how public awareness, prevention, and enforcement tasks can be designed to reduce these impacts.

Sustainability and the risk of recorruption. How can practitioners avert the threat of backsliding that reverses anticorruption gains when champions leave the political scene or other changes occur? Sustainability of anticorruption reforms requires careful planning, including institutionalization and proceduralization of reforms, so they do not rely exclusively on the presence of particular individuals. Interventions that are multifaceted are also more likely to be sustainable; they are not dependent on only one change agent to succeed. One of the goals certainly has to be to find local owners for reforms, those who are willing and able to carry the weight of implementing change, rather than rely on external or donor resources or pressure. In addition, sustainability of anticorruption reforms requires dismantling internal incentives for corruption that can undermine institutionalization of reforms. Changing systems and procedures that reduce the scope and opportunities for corruption and that increase risks of detection and sanctions will go a long way in avoiding recorruption and fostering sustainability.

Finally, there is the potential threat that removing corruption in a country may cause the collapse of traditional and practical networks that have enabled the country to thrive and grow or merely to survive. Predictable (though corrupt) networks can be removed and yield harm to the host country rather than improve the situation if governance replacement mechanisms are not well considered and implemented at the same time corruption is dismantled. For example, some businesspeople in Ukraine at the time of the Orange Revolution (2004–2005) indicated that corruption reduction campaigns effectively destroyed corrupt networks that were the lifeline of the country's economy— they allowed the economy to operate, grow, and prosper. No one considered how to replace those corrupt mechanisms with better governance methods, causing the country's economy to decline rapidly. There is a lesson to be learned here: *Seek to do no harm by programming anticorruption interventions, but do not forget to reprogram the governance mechanisms that are being dismantled.*

Organization of This Book

This book is designed to support this third wave and all the donor organizations and government policymakers that are seeking to address corruption and need help in formulating how to do it. The ultimate objective of this book is to help the practitioner community navigate its way into this third wave of anticorruption programming and to support the research community that supports the practitioners and provides them with new detection techniques and approaches to reach their development goals.

This book brings together findings from the research literature along with best practices in the field and recent case studies on how to conduct indepth assessments of corruption in developing countries and, thereby, how to develop strategies that are likely to yield results. In chapter 2, we review the research on corruption and poverty—demonstrating the very significant impact of corrupt behaviors on what many believe to be the ultimate purpose of development assistance, that is, poverty alleviation. Some say that poverty in society causes corruption, and others say that corruption produces poverty. But there are few who refute the strong connection between these two phenomena and the devastating results.

Chapter 3 provides a review of the practical approaches available to measure and monitor corruption levels. The key questions that need to be asked to address each measurement approach are discussed, providing new perspectives on the corrupting influences that need to be in the crosshairs.

Chapter 4 provides an example of self-assessment. It describes the design and piloting of a rapid corruption self-assessment checklist tool for development practitioners in Africa that is meant to support field analysts in detecting positive features and deficiencies in current anticorruption programs. The tool can be applied by development programs to assess the extent to which countries have put in place the appropriate laws, institutions, and programs that are typically required to implement comprehensive anticorruption strategies. The results are displayed quantitatively and graphically in a radar web chart. The self-assessment tool analyzes the *state of readiness* of the host country and can help appropriately program for anticorruption activities. The tool can also be used to collect comparative data across countries to identify general patterns regionally. This chapter reports on a pilot test of the methodology that includes data collected from 16 USAID missions in Africa.

Chapter 5 offers a concise theoretical and practical description of an integrated diagnostic approach to detecting and assessing corruption, which constitutes a handbook for corruption assessment worldwide. Then, chapters 6 through 10 present case studies of corruption assessments, using this integrated assessment approach, that were conducted between 2005 and 2009 in Ukraine, Senegal, Honduras, and Timor Leste. These cases summarize much longer reports but home in on the key elements uncovered in the assessments: the drivers of corruption, the sectors most affected, and recommendations for action. Epilogues have been written for each case to offer a near-term perspective on how and if the assessment's findings impacted programs in the countries.

The final chapter addresses what we have learned from corruption assessments and what the new generation of assessment tools is likely to add. Overall, the book provides a blueprint for detecting and fighting corruption in developing countries based on research and practical experience and an improved way forward. Progress has been made since the anticorruption programs of the early 1990s. Documenting and disseminating the next wave of research and practice can promote more effective programs that will make a real difference.

Notes

1. James Lewis. 2005. "Earthquake Destruction: Corruption on the Fault Line?" in *Global Corruption Report 2005*. Berlin: Transparency International.

2. Robert Worth and James Glanz. 2006. "Oil Corruption Fuels Insurgency in Iraq." *New York Times*, February 5.

3. Management Systems International. 2010. *Promoting Citizen Engagement in Combating Corruption in Ukraine: Final Report*. Washington, DC: MSI.

4. U.S. Agency for International Development. 2005. *Anticorruption Strategy*. Washington, DC: USAID.

5. Samuel Huntington. 1968. *Political Order in Changing Societies*. New Haven, CT: Yale University Press.

6. World Bank. 2001. *Diagnostic Surveys of Corruption in Romania*. Washington, DC: World Bank, in association with Management Systems International.

7. Management Systems International. 2009. *Corruption Assessment Handbook*. Washington, DC: MSI; Derick Brinkerhoff and Benjamin Crosby. 2002. *Managing Policy Reform: Concepts and Tools for Decision-Makers in Developing and Transitioning Countries*. Bloomfield, CT: Kumarian Press.

8. Management Systems International. 2000. *Ukraine Anticorruption Support Project: Final Report*. Washington, DC: MSI.

9. Michael Johnston. 2005. *Syndromes of Corruption*. New York: Cambridge University Press.

10. Debbie Warrener. 2004. *The Drivers of Change Approach*. London: Overseas Development Institute.

11. Ben W. Heineman and Fritz Heimann. 2006. "The Long War Against Corruption." *Foreign Affairs* 8 (3): 75–86.

12. Daniel Kaufmann. March 11, 2003. "Rethinking Governance: Empirical Lessons Challenge Orthodoxy." http://papers.ssrn.com/so13/papers.cfm?abstract_id=386904.

13. Bertram I. Spector, Michael Johnston and Phyllis Dininio. 2005. "Learning Across Cases: Trends in Anticorruption Strategies." In Bertram I. Spector, editor, *Fighting Corruption in Developing Countries*. Bloomfield, CT: Kumarian Press.

14. Phyllis Dininio. 2005. "The Risks of Recorruption." In Bertram I. Spector, editor, *Fighting Corruption in Developing Countries*. Bloomfield, CT: Kumarian Press.

15. James Anderson and Cheryl Gray. 2006. *Anticorruption in Transition 3: Who Is Succeeding and Why?* Washington, DC: World Bank.

16. Bertram I. Spector, editor. 2005. *Fighting Corruption in Developing Countries*. Bloomfield, CT: Kumarian Press; J. Edgardo Campos and Sanjay Pradhan, editors. 2007. *The Many Faces of Corruption: Tracking Vulnerabilities at the Sector Level*. Washington, DC: World Bank.

17. Marcin Walecki. 2004. "Political Money and Corruption." In *Global Corruption Report 2004*. Berlin: Transparency International.

18. Marcus Mietzner. 2010. "Funding Pilkada: Illegal Campaign Financing in Indonesia's Local Elections." In Edward Aspinall and Gerry van Klinken, editors, *Illegality and the State in Indonesia*. Leiden: KITLV Press.

19. Bertram I. Spector. 2011. *Negotiating Peace and Confronting Corruption: Challenges for Postconflict Societies*. Washington, DC: US Institute of Peace Press.

20. P. Le Billon. 2005. "Overcoming Corruption in the Wake of Conflict." In *Global Corruption Report 2005*. Berlin: Transparency International; Emil Bolongaita. 2005. "Controlling Corruption in Post-Conflict Countries." Kroc Institute Occasional Paper #26:OP:2, University of Notre Dame.

21. Warrener 2004.

22. Management Systems International 2009.

23. Spector, Johnston, and Dininio 2005.

24. Robert E. Klitgaard, Ronald MacLean Abaroa, and H. Lindsey Parris. 2000. *Corrupt Cities: A Practical Guide to Cure and Prevention*. Oakland, CA: ICS Press.

25. Management Systems International. 2005. *A Rapid Anticorruption Assessment Technique for USAID/Africa: Developing a Practical Checklist for USAID Missions in Africa*. Washington, DC: MSI.

26. Anand Swamy, Stephen Knack, Young Lee, and Omar Azfar. 2000. "Gender and Corruption." Center for Development Economics, Department of Economics, Williams College.

2

Corruption Hurts

How badly does corruption hurt? A substantial number of recent studies have examined the relationship between poverty and corruption to clarify the consequences of corruption on the economic well-being of ordinary citizens and entire societies. An understanding of this complex relationship can inform better planning and programming for corruption reduction, as well as poverty reduction strategies.[1]

Corruption in the public sector is often viewed as exacerbating conditions of poverty (low income, poor health and educational status, and vulnerability to economic shocks, for instance) in countries already struggling with the strains of economic growth and democratic transition. Alternatively, countries experiencing chronic poverty are seen as natural breeding grounds for systemic corruption because of social and income inequalities and perverse economic incentives.

The development literature is rich with theoretical insights on these relationships, many of them founded on practical experience and careful observation. The World Bank's *World Development Report 2000/2001: Attacking Poverty* summarized recent thinking on the corruption-poverty linkage as follows:

> The burden of petty corruption falls disproportionately on poor people. . . . For those without money and connections, petty corruption in public health or police services can have debilitating consequences. Corruption affects the lives of poor people through many other channels as well. It biases government spending away from socially valuable goods, such as education. It diverts public resources from infrastructure investments that could benefit poor people, such as health clinics, and tends to increase public spending on capital-intensive investments that offer more opportunities

for kickbacks, such as defense contracts. It lowers the quality of infrastructure, since kickbacks are more lucrative on equipment purchases. Corruption also undermines public service delivery.[2]

Much of the literature dates from the mid-1990s when major international donors began to focus attention on corruption issues and researchers initiated cross-country measurement of the corruption phenomenon.[3]

The research literature reviewed in this chapter demonstrates that corruption *does* exacerbate and promote poverty, but this relationship is complex and moderated by key economic and governance factors. On the basis of these findings, anticorruption programs that are crafted to address issues of economic growth, income distribution, governance capacity, government services in health and education, and public trust in government are likely to not only reduce corruption but reduce poverty as well.

Defining Poverty and Corruption

Poverty is a complex phenomenon. It is usually defined in relation to *income*, often measured in terms of per capita gross domestic product (GDP). Extreme poverty is often defined as an income of less than $1 per person per day in terms of purchasing power parity (PPP).[4] Some researchers define poverty as the lowest income quintile in a referenced population. But critics argue that measuring poverty in terms of GDP or PPP does not fully capture the phenomenon of poverty. A broader definition treats poverty in a multidimensional way, including low income, low levels of education and health, vulnerability (to health or income loss, natural disaster, crime and violence, and education curtailment), and voicelessness and powerlessness (feeling discrimination, lacking income-earning possibilities, being mistreated by state institutions, and lacking status under the law).[5] Many other indicators such as caloric intake and female literacy are also used. Measuring poverty in terms of income level may seem relatively straightforward, but the multidimensional approach is more complex and involves factors that are difficult to quantify. To manage this complexity, researchers have developed indices, such as the UN Development Programme (UNDP) Human Poverty Index, which conceives of poverty in terms of longevity, knowledge, and economic provisioning.

Public sector corruption is commonly defined as *the misuse of public office for private gain*. The US Agency for International Development's (USAID) *A Handbook on Fighting Corruption* describes the various ways that corruption can manifest itself:

It encompasses unilateral abuses by government officials such as embezzlement and nepotism, as well as abuses linking public and private actors such as bribery, extortion, influence peddling and fraud. Corruption arises in both political and bureaucratic offices and can be petty or grand, organized or disorganized.[6]

Corruption is inherently a secretive transaction and, thus, difficult to observe and measure. Several organizations—including the World Bank and Transparency International—have attempted to develop corruption indicators; all of them depend on aggregate surveys of citizens, businesses, or experts and therefore base their results on *perceptions* of the problem as opposed to more objective data. While these measurement approaches have acknowledged reliability and validity problems, they are the best that we have for the time being.[7] In general, these are the indices employed in the corruption-poverty research. "Second-generation" governance indicators currently under development may resolve some of the measurement and methodological issues.[8]

Examining the Relationship Between Corruption and Poverty

Few studies examine or establish a *direct* relationship between corruption and poverty.[9] Corruption, by itself, does not produce poverty. Rather, *corruption has direct consequences on economic and governance factors, intermediaries that in turn produce poverty.* Thus, the relationship examined by researchers is an *indirect* one.

Two models emerge from the research literature. The economic model postulates that corruption affects poverty by first impacting economic growth factors, which, in turn, impact poverty levels (see figure 2.1). In other words, increased corruption reduces economic investment, distorts markets, hinders competition, creates inefficiencies by increasing the costs of doing business,

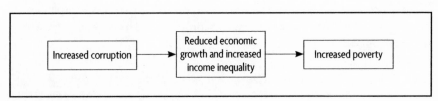

Figure 2.1 The economic model.

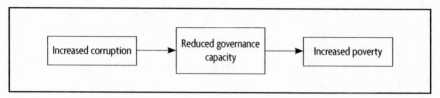

Figure 2.2 The governance model.

and increases income inequalities. By undermining these key economic factors, poverty is exacerbated.

The governance model asserts that corruption affects poverty by first influencing governance factors, which, in turn, impact poverty levels (see figure 2.2). So, for example, corruption erodes the institutional capacity of government to deliver quality public services, diverts public investment away from major public needs into capital projects (where bribes can be sought), lowers compliance with safety and health regulations, and increases budgetary pressures on government. Through these serious challenges to governance practices and outcomes, poverty is affected.

Economic Model

The literature shows an inverse correlation between aggregate economic growth and corruption; in general, countries with higher corruption experience less economic growth. Many of the studies reviewed address the channels through which corruption affects economic growth, for instance, through impacting investment and entrepreneurship, distorting markets, and undermining productivity. Furthermore, there is empirical evidence that corruption aggravates income inequality and is associated with slower economic growth. Finally, studies present evidence that as the rate of economic growth increases, the number of people above the poverty line tends to rise as well.

Corruption Impedes Economic Growth

The relationship between corruption and economic growth is complex. Economic theory supports the notion that corruption hinders economic growth in the following ways:[10]

- *Corruption discourages foreign and domestic investment.* Rent taking increases costs and creates uncertainty, reducing incentives for both foreign and domestic investors.

- *Corruption taxes entrepreneurship.* Entrepreneurs and innovators require licenses and permits, and paying bribes for these goods cuts into profit margins.
- *Corruption lowers the quality of public infrastructure.* Public resources are diverted to private uses, standards are waived, and funds for operations and maintenance are diverted in favor of more rent-seeking activity.
- *Corruption decreases tax revenue.* Firms and activities are driven into the informal or gray sector by excessive rent taking, and taxes are reduced in exchange for payoffs to tax officials.
- *Corruption diverts talent into rent seeking.* Officials who otherwise would be engaged in productive activity become preoccupied with rent taking, in which increasing returns encourage more rent taking.
- *Corruption distorts the composition of public expenditure.* Rent seekers will pursue those projects for which rent seeking is easiest and best disguised, diverting funding from other sectors such as education and health.

These theoretical propositions are supported by a number of empirical studies. They demonstrate that high levels of corruption are associated with low levels of investment and low levels of aggregate economic growth.[11] For example, the results of several World Bank corruption surveys illustrate this inverse relationship between corruption and economic growth.[12]

- *Corruption discourages domestic investment.* In Bulgaria, about one in four businesses in the entrepreneur sample had planned to expand its business (mostly through acquiring new equipment) but failed to do so, and corruption was an important factor in this change of plans. The Latvia study surveyed enterprises that had dropped planned investments. It found that the high cost of complying with regulations and the uncertainty surrounding them, including uncertainty regarding unofficial payments, were important factors for 28% of businesses forgoing new investments.
- *Corruption hurts entrepreneurship, especially among small businesses.* Several studies reported that small businesses tend to pay the most bribes as a percentage of total revenue (especially in Bosnia, Ghana, and Slovakia). In Poland, businesses have to deal

with a large number of economic activities that are licensed, making them more prone to extortion.

• *Corruption decreases revenue from taxes and fees.* In Bangladesh, more than 30% of urban household respondents reduced electric and/or water bills by bribing the meter reader. In several studies, respondents were so frustrated that they indicated a willingness to pay more taxes if corruption could be controlled (Cambodia, Indonesia, and Romania).

In a cross-national analysis of corruption and growth for the International Monetary Fund, four hypotheses designed to explain four channels through which corruption reduces growth were tested.[13] Through regression analysis, results established that higher levels of corruption were associated with (1) increasing public sector investment (but decreased productivity), (2) reduced government revenues (reducing resources for productive expenditures), (3) lower expenditures on operations and maintenance (where other studies show that high government consumption is robustly associated with lower economic growth),[14] and (4) reduced quality of public infrastructure (as shown by indicators for road conditions, power and water losses, telecom faults, and proportion of railway diesels in use). All of these findings are consistent with the observation that corruption is inversely correlated with growth in gross national product (GNP).

A seminal study by Mauro used a composite of two corruption indices and multiple regression analyses with a sample of 106 countries to show that high levels of corruption are associated with lower levels of investment as a share of GDP and with lower GDP growth per capita.[15] Extrapolation of these results by the researcher suggested that if a country were to improve its corruption index from a score of 6 to 8 on a 10-point scale, it would increase the investment rate more than 4%, and annual per capita GDP growth would increase by nearly one-half percent.

A study by Lambsdorff casts additional light on how corruption affects investment, specifically, the relationship of investment to GDP.[16] The study categorized investment into domestic savings and net capital inflows. Regression results provided evidence that corruption negatively affects capital accumulation by deterring capital imports. To explore causation, Lambsdorff decomposed the corruption index into several subindicators that look at corruption through the lens of bureaucratic quality, civil liberties, government stability, and law and order. Only the law and order subindicator turned out to be important for attracting capital flows.

Another World Bank study suggests that higher levels of corruption reduce growth through decreased investment and output.[17] This comprehensive study looked at 22 transition countries and examined two forms of corruption—state capture and administrative corruption—and their impact on selected economic and social indicators. Data for the study were derived from the Business Environment and Enterprise Performance Survey (BEEPS).

Corruption Exacerbates Income Inequality

Several studies have demonstrated a relationship between corruption and income inequality. The theoretical foundations for this relationship are derived from rent theory and draw on the ideas of Rose-Ackerman, Krueger, and Gupta, Davoodi, and Alonso-Terme, among others.[18] Propositions include the following:

- Corruption may create permanent distortions from which some groups or individuals can benefit more than others.
- The distributional consequences of corruption are likely to be more severe the more persistent the corruption.
- The impact of corruption on income distribution is in part a function of government involvement in allocating and financing scarce goods and services.

A World Bank study of poverty following the transition to a market economy in Eastern Europe and Central Asia (ECA) produced important findings concerning income distribution and corruption.[19] The study analyzed data on firms' perceptions of corruption and notes that more firms in ECA report that corruption is a problem than do firms in most other geographic regions.[20] The authors analyzed whether there "is any apparent link, within ECA, between corruption and measures of income inequality."[21] When Gini coefficients for income per capita (measures of income inequality) were graphed against the Transparency International Corruption Perceptions Index (CPI), *lower levels of corruption were seen to be statistically associated with lower levels of income inequality* (simple correlation was +.72). Similar results were obtained using different measures of corruption. The authors add that closer examination of the links between corruption and inequality shows that the costs of corruption fall particularly heavily on smaller firms.[22]

This report also examined the relationship between a particular type of corruption, *state capture*, and income inequality. State capture describes the situation where businesses have undue influence over the decisions of public officials. The report notes that *differences in income inequality in the ECA countries are greatest in those countries where the transition has been least success-ful and where state capture is at its highest.* In these countries, state capture has allowed large economic interests to distort the legal framework and the policy-making process in a way that defeats the development of a market economy.[23] The report explores the relationship between state capture and income inequal-ity through regressions of the Gini coefficient on measures of state capture and other variables and finds that *a higher degree of state capture is correlated with higher inequality.* The relationship holds even when controlling for political freedoms, location, and years under state planning.[24]

A cross-national regression analysis of up to 56 countries was conducted to examine the ways that corruption could negatively impact income distribu-tion and poverty.[25] The study looked at the following relationships:

- *Growth.* Income inequality has been shown to be harmful to growth, so if corruption increases income inequality, it will also reduce growth and thereby exacerbate poverty.
- *Bias in tax systems.* Evasion, poor administration, and exemp-tions favoring the well-connected can reduce the tax base and progressivity of the tax system, increasing income inequality.
- *Poor targeting of social programs.* Extending benefits to well-to-do income groups or siphoning from poverty alleviation programs will diminish their impact on poverty and inequality (and will tend to act as a regressive tax on the poor, enhancing income inequality).

The Gupta et al. study examined these propositions through an inequal-ity model using a Gini coefficient to measure inequality. The model specified the personal distribution of income in terms of factor endowments, distribu-tion of factors of production, and government spending on social programs. The model used several indices of corruption. Statistically significant results include the following:

- Higher corruption is associated with higher income inequality such that a worsening of a country's corruption index by 2.5 points on a scale of 10 corresponds to an increase in the Gini co-efficient (worsening inequality) of about 4 points. Tests showed the same results for an average decrease in secondary schooling by 2.3 years, as an example of the significance of corruption.

- Even controlling for stage of economic development, corruption appears to be harmful to income inequality. Moreover, a test of directionality suggests that it is corruption that increases inequality and not the reverse.[26]
- Corruption tends to increase the inequality of factor ownership.
- Corruption increases income inequality by reducing progressivity of the tax system; that is, the impact of corruption on income inequality was shown to be higher after taxes.

In another study of 35 countries (mostly OECD [Organisation for Economic Co-operation and Development] countries), it was hypothesized that corruption supports, stabilizes, and deepens inequality.[27] Measures of corruption (Transparency International's CPI and Bribery Propensity Index) were tested against measures of income distribution (as well as measures of power distance between elites and other ranks and general trust). Results showed that *societies with high income inequality have high levels of corruption, while those with high levels of secondary education and a high proportion of women in government positions have decreasing levels of corruption.* The relation between measures of corruption and the Gini index of income inequality was nonlinear, indicating that after countries attain a specific level of income equality, corruption tends to decrease exponentially.

How does corruption exacerbate income inequality? Evidence from diagnostic surveys of corruption in several countries suggests that corruption aggravates income inequality because lower-income households pay a higher proportion of their income in bribes.

In conclusion, the literature establishes clearly that corruption impedes economic growth and augments income inequalities. But how does reduced economic growth, in turn, increase poverty?

Reduced Economic Growth Rates Increase Poverty

There is evidence that the absence of economic growth (or negative growth) increases poverty. The burden of rapid economic retrenchment, such as seen in Thailand and Indonesia in the late 1990s, hurts the poor most heavily.[28] Similarly, in the transition countries of the former Soviet Union (FSU), the changeover to a market system was associated with a sharp initial drop in output and significantly higher levels of poverty. The expansion of poverty was initiated by the collapse of GDP, which fell by 50% in the FSU countries and 15% in Central and Eastern Europe (CEE). Poverty was found to be highly correlated with administrative corruption, and corruption was empirically associated with lower economic growth rates.[29]

Using a poverty model, another study conducted a cross-national analysis of up to 56 countries to examine the relationship between growth and poverty.[30] This poverty model used the income growth of the bottom quintile as the dependent variable regressed against growth in GNP, natural resources, initial income of the lower quintile, initial secondary schooling, education inequality, initial distribution of assets (Gini for land), social spending, and growth in corruption. The authors found that higher growth is associated with poverty alleviation.

The World Bank Development Research Group studied a sample of 80 countries over four decades and showed that income of the lowest 20% of the population rises one for one with increases in per capita GDP.[31] Moreover, using tests for directionality, they concluded that a 1% increase in GDP actually causes a 1% increase in the incomes of the poor.[32]

A comprehensive study of the so-called Asian Tigers provides a good example of rapid economic growth (during the 1980s and 1990s) leading to a substantial decrease in those living below a poverty line of $1.25 per day.[33] Furthermore, in those countries with a more equitable distribution of income at the outset, the decrease in poverty tended to be more robust. However, even in this special case of multiple country rapid growth in a particular region, income distribution remained more or less constant over the period of growth. Similarly, other researchers who examined 65 developing countries between 1981 and 1999 found that the number of people below the poverty line of $1 per day was reduced in countries with positive economic growth. However, they concluded, "Measures of inequality show no tendency to get either better or worse with economic growth."[34]

In conclusion, these studies show conclusively that income rises with economic growth and vice versa. It should be noted that economic growth does not necessarily lead to *more equal* income distribution; an increase in income may benefit the better off rather than bring the poor out of poverty. Income distribution seems to be an important moderating factor in the relationship between economic growth and poverty reduction.

Governance Model

The governance model postulates that increased corruption reduces governance capacity, which, in turn, increases poverty conditions. Governance has been defined as the traditions and institutions by which authority in a country is exercised. This includes (1) the process by which governments are selected, monitored and replaced, (2) the capacity of the government to effectively formulate and implement sound policies, and (3) the respect of citizens and the state for the institutions that govern economic and social interactions among them.[35]

Corruption disrupts governance practices, destabilizes governance institutions, reduces the provision of services by government, reduces respect for the rule of law, and reduces public trust in government and its institutions. Impaired governance, in turn, reduces social capital and public trust in governance institutions; this reduces the public funds available to support effective economic growth programs and reduces the capability of government to help its citizens and the poor in particular.

Corruption Degrades Governance

Johnston suggests that serious corruption threatens democracy and governance by weakening political institutions and mass participation and by delaying and distorting the economic development needed to sustain democracy.[36] In a study of 83 countries, he compares Transparency International's CPI with an index of political competitiveness and finds that well-institutionalized and decisive political competition is correlated with lower levels of corruption.[37] These results were confirmed, even when controlling for GDP and examining the relationship over time.

Diagnostic surveys of corruption in Bosnia-Herzegovina, Ghana, Honduras, Indonesia, and Latvia report that government institutions with the highest levels of corruption tend to provide lower-quality services. The converse is also true: in Romania, the survey shows that state sector entities with better systems of public administration tend to have lower levels of corruption.

The literature shows that corruption impacts the quality of government services and infrastructure and that through these channels it has an impact on the poor. This is particularly the case in the health and education sectors. Enhanced education and health care services and population longevity are usually associated with higher economic growth. But under conditions of extensive corruption, when public services, such as health and basic education expenditures that especially benefit the poor, are given lower priority in favor of capital intensive programs that offer more opportunities for high-level rent taking, lower income groups lose services on which they depend. As government revenues decline through leakage brought on by corruption, public funds for poverty programs and programs to stimulate growth also become more scarce.

Other researchers used regression analysis across a large sample of countries to assess an aggregate measure of education outcome and health status in a model that includes several corruption indices, per capita income, public spending on health care and education, and average years of education completed. The results supported the proposition that better health care and education outcomes are positively correlated with lower corruption. In particular, corruption is consistently correlated with higher school dropout rates,[38] and corruption is significantly correlated with higher levels of infant mortality and lower birth weights of babies.

Another study looked at the relationship between corruption and the composition of government spending.[39] It found evidence that corrupt governments may display predatory behavior in deciding how to distribute government expenditures. Specifically, this data showed corruption negatively related to education and health expenditures. An extrapolation from these findings shows an increase in the 10-point corruption score, from 6 to 8, would yield an increase in education spending by one-half of 1% of GDP.

Yet other researchers have found that corruption can lead to reduced social spending on health and education. Countries with higher corruption tend to have lower levels of social spending,[40] regardless of level of development. Corruption lowers tax revenues, increases government operating costs, increases government spending for wages, reduces spending on operations and maintenance, and often biases government toward spending on higher education and tertiary health care (rather than basic education and primary health care).

Impaired Governance Increases Poverty

Pioneering research on the relationship between corruption, governance, and poverty has been conducted at the World Bank by the team of Kaufmann, Kraay, and Zoido-Lobaton. Their studies suggest an association between good governance (with control of corruption as an important component) and poverty alleviation.

In a 1999 study, they analyzed the effect of governance on per capita income in 173 countries, treating "control of corruption" as one of the components of good governance. Using a database of over 300 indicators of governance taken from a wide variety of cross-country studies for the years 1997–1998, the team constructed aggregate indicators corresponding to six governance concepts. Analysis showed a strong positive causal relationship running from improved governance to better development outcomes as measured by per capita income.[41] A one standard deviation improvement in governance raised per capita incomes 2.5 to 4 times. Analysis of updated indicators for 2000–2001 did not change these conclusions.[42]

In a 2002 study, they used updated governance indicators to gain a more nuanced understanding of the role of good governance in the relationship between corruption and growth in per capita incomes.[43] Using governance data for 2000–2001, the authors establish empirically that for Latin American and Caribbean countries (1) better governance tends to yield higher per capita incomes, but (2) higher per capita incomes tend to produce reduced governance capacity. The authors attribute this second finding to state capture. In short, the authors suggest that corruption (in the form of state capture) may interfere with the expected relationship between economic growth (higher per capita incomes) and better governance. The authors note that an empirical in-depth examination of the phenomenon of state capture in the Latin American and Caribbean (LAC) region is part of the upcoming research agenda.[44]

The effect of governance on corruption and poverty is illuminated by another World Bank study.[45] The deterioration in governance discussed in this study was accompanied by an increase in both corruption and poverty. Thus, as seen earlier, increases in corruption tend to deteriorate governance practices, but the reverse holds true as well—reduction in governance capacity increases the opportunities for corruption.

Reduced Public Trust in Government
Increases Vulnerability of the Poor

Corruption that reduces governance capacity also may inflict critical collateral damage: reduced public trust in government institutions. As trust—an important element of social capital—declines, research has shown that vulnerability of the poor increases as their economic productivity is affected. The concept of social capital refers to social structures that enable people to work collectively for the good of the group.[46] One of the most important and widely discussed elements of social capital is trust, both interpersonal trust and trust in institutions of government.[47]

Recent research on social capital suggests that there is a relationship between corruption, trust, and poverty. The proposition is that corruption destroys people's trust in government and other institutions. This effect is most salient for the lowest income groups, and low social capital affects people's willingness and ability to engage in productive activity. Empirical studies point to an association between low social capital and poverty, although the relationship is difficult to test and difficult to disentangle empirically from affluence and democracy.

One of the effects of widespread corruption in government services is that it appears to contribute to disaffection and distrust, and this appears to impact particularly heavily on the poor.[48] This is not surprising, because low-income people are the ones who are most likely to be dependent on government services for assistance with basic needs, such as education and health care, and least likely to be able to pay bribes to cut through complex and unresponsive bureaucracies. Lack of trust has economic consequences: when people perceive that the social system is untrustworthy and inequitable, this can affect incentives to engage in productive activities.[49]

The relationship between social capital and economic performance in 29 market economies was tested using indicators from the World Values Surveys (WVS) on interpersonal trust.[50] The researchers added the WVS trust measure to investment and growth regressions and found that *trust correlated highly with economic growth*. Each 12-percentage-point rise in trust was associated with an increase in annual income growth of about 1 percentage point. They also found that *the impact of trust on growth is significantly higher for poorer countries*, suggesting that interpersonal trust is more essential where legal systems and financial markets are less well developed.

In a later study, it was found that trust is higher in nations with stronger formal institutions for enforcing contracts and reducing corruption and in nations with less polarized populations (as measured by income or land inequality, ethnic heterogeneity, and a subjective measure of the intensity of economic discrimination).[51] These researchers also showed that formal institutions and polarization appear to influence growth rates in part through their impacts on trust. For example, income inequality, land inequality, discrimination, and corruption are associated with significantly lower growth rates, but the association of these variables with growth dramatically weakens when trust is controlled for.

In another study, researchers also looked at the effect of social capital on income inequality.[52] They regressed various indicators of social capital and trust against income data by quintile and found that higher scores on property rights measures were associated with declines in income inequality. Using the WVS trust indicator, they also found that inequality declined in higher trust societies. For each 8- or 9-point increase in the percent, trusting was associated with a 1-point decline in Gini. This partial correlation was only marginally significant, however. The researchers conclude that social capital reduces poverty rates and improves—or at a minimum does not exacerbate—income inequality.

Conclusion

Overall, the literature reviewed in this chapter demonstrates that corruption does exacerbate and promote poverty, but this pattern is complex and moderated by economic and governance factors. Table 2.1 summarizes the major findings.

If carefully crafted, anticorruption programs might yield important poverty reduction results. The literature suggests that programs that succeed in

Table 2.1
Major Propositions Linking Corruption and Poverty

- Economic growth is associated with poverty reduction.
- The burden of rapid retrenchment falls most heavily on the poor. Corruption is associated with low economic growth.
- Corruption reduces domestic investment and foreign direct investment.
- Corruption increases government expenditures.
- Corruption reduces public sector productivity.
- Corruption distorts the composition of government expenditure, away from services directly beneficial to the poor, and the growth process, for example, education, health, and operation and maintenance.
- Better health and education indicators are positively associated with lower corruption.
- Corruption reduces government revenues.
- Corruption lowers the quality of public infrastructure.
- Corruption lowers spending on social sectors.
- Corruption increases income inequality.
- Corruption increases inequality of factor ownership.
- Inequality slows growth.
- Corruption decreases progressivity of the tax system.
- Corruption acts as a regressive tax.
- Low-income households pay more in bribes as a percentage of income.
- Better governance, including lower graft levels, affects economic growth dramatically. Better governance is associated with lower corruption and lower poverty levels. High state capture makes it difficult to reduce inequality, even with growth.
- Extensive, organized, well-institutionalized, and decisive political competition is associated with lower corruption.
- Trust is a component of social capital. Higher social capital is associated with lower poverty. Corruption undermines trust (in government and other institutions) and thereby undermines social capital.

reducing corruption will contribute to poverty alleviation especially if they also achieve the following:

- Increase economic growth
- Create more equitable income distribution
- Strengthen governance institutions and capacity
- Improve government services, especially in health and education
- Increase public trust in government

There are many unanswered questions in the research, particularly regarding the manner in which these factors manifest themselves in different countries. More attention needs to be given to linking theory to empirical endeavors and to generating practical policy insights based on this research. Finally, much can be learned from the experience of countries and donor organizations that initiate anticorruption and antipoverty programs. Compiling and analyzing such experience would provide valuable insights for future planning.

Bibliography of Country Surveys

Bangladesh: Manzoor Hasan. Undated. *Corruption in Bangladesh Surveys: An Overview.*

Bolivia: World Bank. April 18, 2000. *Governance Modes and Institutional Effectiveness in the Bolivian Public Sector: Evidence From the Public Officials' Survey.* Draft.

Bosnia-Herzegovina: World Bank. 2001. *Bosnia and Herzegovina: Diagnostic Surveys of Corruption.*

Bulgaria: Vitosha Research. 2002. *Corruption in Small and Medium-Sized Enterprises.* Regional Networking Project, Freedom House.

Cambodia: World Bank. May 2000. *Cambodia Governance and Corruption Diagnostic: Evidence From Citizen, Enterprise and Public Official Surveys.*

Colombia: World Bank. Undated. *Corrupcion, Desempeno Institucional, y Gobernabilidad: Desarrollando Una Estrategia Anti-Corrupcion Para Colombia.* Executive Summary, Second Draft.

Ghana: Center for Democracy and Development, Ghana. August 2000. *The Ghana Governance and Corruption Survey: Evidence From Households, Enterprises and Public Officials.* Commissioned by the World Bank.

Honduras: World Bank Institute. January 9, 2002. *Governance and Anticorruption in Honduras: An Input for Action Planning.* Draft.

Indonesia: Partnership for Governance Reform in Indonesia. February 2002. *A Diagnostic Study of Corruption in Indonesia: Final Report.*

Latvia: James Anderson. 1998. *Report: Corruption in Latvia: Survey Evidence.*

Poland: World Bank, Warsaw Office. October 11, 1999. *Corruption in Poland: Review of Priority Areas and Proposals for Action.*

Romania: World Bank and MSI. 2001. *Diagnostic Surveys of Corruption in Romania.*

Slovakia: World Bank and USAID. 2000. *Corruption in Slovakia: Results of Diagnostic Surveys.*
Uganda: CIETinternational. August 1998. *Uganda National Integrity Survey: Final Report.* Submitted to the Inspectorate of Government, Kampala, Uganda.

Notes

1. This chapter is adapted from a report written by Bertram Spector, Eric Chetwynd, and Frances Chetwynd for Management Systems International under a USAID contract.

2. World Bank. 2001b. *World Development Report 2000/2001: Attacking Poverty.* New York: Oxford University Press, 201.

3. Many studies address the issue indirectly; few address it directly.

4. For instance, the UN Millennium Development goal (baseline 1990) of reducing by one-half by the year 2015 the number of persons who fall under an income-determined extreme poverty line of less than $1.00 per day per person (UNDP 2002).

5. World Bank 2001b.

6. US Agency for International Development. 1999. *A Handbook on Fighting Corruption.* Technical Publication Series, Center for Democracy and Governance. Washington, DC: USAID, 5.

7. Management Systems International. 2002b. *Handbook on Using Existing Corruption Indices.* Washington, DC: MSI; Michael Johnston. 2000b. "The New Corruption Rankings: Implications for Analysis and Reform." Paper presented at the International Political Science Association, World Congress, Quebec City, Canada; Michael Johnston and Sahr Kpundeh. January 2002. "The Measurement Problem: A Focus on Governance." Unpublished.

8. See Stephen Knack. 2002b. "Social Capital, Growth and Poverty: A Survey of Cross-Country Evidence." In Christiaan Grootaert and Thierry van Bastelaer, editors, *The Role of Social Capital in Development: An Empirical Assessment.* Cambridge, UK: Cambridge University Press, 18–19. Knack suggests that second-generation governance indicators should have greater specificity in measuring performance, have increased transparency and replicability in their construction, and give greater attention to measuring governmental processes or institutions. The World Bank is currently working with OECD and the Department for International Development on new indicators; see http://www.bellanet.org.

9. One group of researchers, Gupta et al. (1998), found a statistically significant positive association directly between corruption and poverty. Tests for directionality showed that it appears to be corruption that increases poverty. Sanjeev Gupta, Hamid Davoodi, and Rosa Alonso-Terme. 1998. "Does Corruption Affect Income Equality and Poverty?" IMF Working Paper 98/76.

10. For a summary discussion of these points, see Paulo Mauro. 2002. "The Effects of Corruption on Growth and Public Expenditure." In Arnold J. Heidenheimer and Michael Johnston, editors, *Political Corruption: Concepts and Contexts*, 3rd ed. New Brunswick, NJ: Transaction. For further discussion of the theoretical reasoning, see Arnold J. Heidenheimer and Michael Johnston, editors. 2002. *Political Corruption: Concepts and Contexts*, 3rd ed. New Brunswick, NJ: Transaction, specifically chapter 19, "Corruption and Development: A Review of the Issues," pp. 329–38 (Pranab Bardhan); chapter 20, "The Effects of Corruption on Growth

and Public Expenditure," pp. 339–52 (Paolo Mauro); chapter 21, "When Is Corruption Harmful?" pp. 353–71 (Susan-Rose Ackerman).

11. See Susan Rose-Ackerman. 1999. *Corruption and Government: Causes, Consequences and Reform.* Cambridge, UK: Cambridge University Press, 3–4. (Cross-country empirical studies confirm the negative impact of corruption on economic growth.) See also Heidenheimer and Johnston, 2002, "Introduction to Part VI, Corruption and Economic Growth," 303.

12. For clarity, abbreviated references to the diagnostic studies are by country name rather than by name of author. References to the diagnostic studies are grouped at the end of the chapter.

13. Vito Tanzi and Hamid Davoodi. 1997. "Corruption, Public Investment, and Growth." IMF Working Paper 97/139.

14. Robert J. Barro. 1996. "Determinants of Economic Growth: A Cross-Country Empirical Study." National Bureau of Economic Research Working Paper 5698.

15. Mauro 2002.

16. Johann Graf Lambsdorff. 2003. "How Corruption Affects Persistent Capital Flows." *Economics of Governance* 4 (3): 229–44.

17. World Bank. 2000a. *Anticorruption in Transition: A Contribution to the Policy Debate.* Washington, DC: World Bank.

18. See Susan Rose-Ackerman. 1978. *Corruption: A Study in Political Economy.* New York: Academic Press; Anne O. Krueger. 1974. "The Political Economy of the Rent-Seeking Society." *American Economic Review* 64:291–303; and Gupta et al. 1998.

19. World Bank. 2000c. *Making Transition Work for Everyone: Poverty and Inequality in Europe and Central Asia.* Washington, DC: World Bank.

20. Data are taken from the World Bank's BEEPS and show that 70% of firms in the Commonwealth of Independent States (CIS) report that corruption is a problem, compared to 50% in Central and Eastern Europe (CEE), 40% in Latin America, and 15% in OECD (World Bank 2000c, 168–69).

21. World Bank 2000c, 169.

22. See World Bank (2000c, 170), citing European Bank for Reconstruction and Development (EBRD), *Transition Report* (1999).

23. See generally World Bank (2000c, 139–70), chapter 4, "A Look at Income Inequality." The transition economies have been particularly vulnerable to state capture because of the socialist legacy of fused economic and political power.

24. World Bank 2000c, 172.

25. Gupta et al. 1998.

26. In a review of empirical studies, Lambsdorff (1999) cites other studies that agree with Gupta on this relationship. Lambsdorff questions whether inequality may also contribute to corruption. We have not found direct empirical support for reverse causality, though there is some indirect support in Kaufmann and Kraay (2002), discussed later. Johann Graf Lambsdorff. 1999. "Corruption in Empirical Research: A Review." Transparency International Working Paper; Daniel Kaufmann and Aart Kraay. 2002. "Growth Without Governance." *Economia* 3.1, Fall.

27. Susan Karstedt. 2000. "The Culture of Inequality and Corruption: A Cross-National Study of Corruption." Paper presented at the ASC Conference, Department of Criminology, Keele University, San Francisco.

28. M. G. Quibria. 2002. "Growth and Poverty: Lessons From the East Asian Miracle Revisited." Asia Development Bank Research Paper 33.

29. World Bank 2000a.

30. Gupta et al. 1998.

31. David Dollar and Aart Kraay. 2002. "Growth Is Good for the Poor." *Journal of Economic Growth* 7 (3): 195–225.

32. See Dollar and Kraay (2002). The question of the direction of causality is debated in several of the sources reviewed for this report. There is some empirical evidence of causality running from corruption to poverty (Dollar and Kraay 2002; Gupta et al. 1998). Although intuitively it seems that there might also be reverse causality (i.e., running from poverty to corruption), we have not found empirical studies supporting this point. There is some evidence, however, of reverse causality running from per capita incomes to governance. See Kaufmann and Kraay (2002), discussed later.

33. Quibria (2002) suggests that a factor in this growth was the containment of corruption to the centralized type, which he considers less costly to growth than more generalized or chaotic corruption.

34. See William Easterly. 2001. *The Elusive Quest for Growth: Economists' Adventures and Misadventures in the Tropics.* Cambridge, MA: MIT Press, 13–14. In severe economic retraction, the poor suffer appreciably greater loss in income than the population's average. Easterly quotes from Martin Ravillion and Shaohua Chen. May 1997. "Distribution and Poverty in Developing and Transition Economies." *World Bank Economic Review,* no. 11.

35. Daniel Kaufmann, Aart Kraay, and Pablo Zoido-Lobaton. 1999. "Governance Matters." World Bank Policy Research Working Paper No. 2196, 1.

36. Michael Johnston. 2005. *Syndromes of Corruption.* New York: Cambridge University Press.

37. Johnston 2000b.

38. There was a problem of multicolinearity between corruption and public spending, which for all practical purposes invalidated the other education indicators. Sanjeev Gupta, Hamid Davoodi, and Erwin Tiongson. 2000. "Corruption and the Provision of Health Care and Education Services." IMF Working Paper 00/11, 17.

39. Mauro 2002.

40. Gupta et al. 1998.

41. See Kaufmann et al. (1999, 15). Although the relationship held for most of the aggregate indicators, the test of the relationship between the aggregate indicator for corruption and the increase in per capita income did not hold up. Specification tests reported the p value associated with the null hypothesis that the instruments affect income only through their effects on governance. For five out of the six aggregate indicators, the null hypothesis was not rejected, which was evidence in favor of the identifying assumptions. Corruption was the aggregate indicator for which the null hypothesis was rejected. This suggested that the aggregate indicator was not an adequate independent measure of corruption. "This is not to say that graft is unimportant

for economic outcomes. Rather, in this set of countries, we have found it difficult to find exogenous variations in the causes of graft which make it possible to identify the effects of graft on per capita incomes" (p. 16, n. 15).

42. See Daniel Kaufmann, Aart Kraay, and Pablo Zoido-Lobaton. 2002. "Governance Matters II: Updated Indicators for 2000/01." World Bank Policy Research Working Paper No. 2772. In an April 2002 presentation at the US Department of State, Dr. Kaufmann summarized this work on governance and the demonstrated link to better development outcomes such as higher per capita income, lower infant mortality, and higher literacy. He expects that donors will pay much more attention to governance and that the link between good governance and poverty alleviation is now a mainstream concept (Daniel Kaufmann. April 19, 2002. "Governance Empirics." Paper presented at State Department, Slide 44). New data will be released shortly and will be available at http://info.worldbank.org/beeps.kkz/.

43. See Kaufmann and Kraay (2002). In a forthcoming study that draws on a survey of public officials in Bolivia, Kaufmann, Mehrez, and Gurgur conclude (using a theoretical model for econometric analysis) that external voice and transparency have a larger effect on corruption (and quality of service) than conventional public sector management variables (such as civil servant wages, internal enforcement of rules, etc.).

44. This study would be similar to the BEEPS, developed jointly by the World Bank and the EBRD, which generated comparative measurements on corruption and state capture in the transition economies of the CIS and CEE. See http://info.worldbank.org/governance/beeps/.

45. World Bank 2000a.

46. For a discussion of various definitions of social capital and their evolution, see Tine Rossing Feldman and Susan Assaf. 1999. "Social Capital: Conceptual Frameworks and Empirical Evidence: An Annotated Bibliography." World Bank Social Capital Initiative, Working Paper No. 5.

47. See Susan Rose-Ackerman. 2001. "Trust, Honesty and Corruption: Reflections on the State Building Process." *European Journal of Sociology* 42:27–71. Rose-Ackerman discusses the complex nature of the relationship between trust, the functioning of the state, and the functioning of the market. The study stresses the mutual interaction between trust and democracy and the impact of corruption.

48. See Rose-Ackerman (2001, 26), noting that this is especially the case in the FSU.

49. See Edgardo Buscaglia. 2000. "Judicial Corruption in Developing Countries: Its Causes and Economic Consequences." Hoover Institution, Essays in Public Policy, discussing corruption and its long-term impact on efficiency and equity, especially corruption in the judiciary.

50. Stephen Knack and Philip Keefer. 1997. "Does Social Capital Have an Economic Payoff? A Cross-Country Investigation." *Quarterly Journal of Economics* 112:1251–88.

51. Paul Zak and Stephen Knack. 1998. "Trust and Growth." IRIS Center Working Paper No. 219.

52. Stephen Knack. 1999. "Governance and Employment." ILO Employment and Training Papers 45.

3

Assessing Corruption

Country diagnostic assessments that guide programming to reduce corruption are important tools for corruption detectives. To develop a coherent response, it is important to understand how and why corruption manifests itself in a country's public institutions, what has already been done to address it, and what kind of opportunities and constraints present themselves for pursuing reform. Corruption takes different forms in every country and, so, calls for a tailored approach to fighting it. Assessments help identify the nature and origins of corruption abuses, priorities, and unique configurations for substantive reforms.

In addition to their usefulness for programming, assessments can also be important tools for monitoring the progress of reforms. They provide a framework for identifying trends, successes, and setbacks. In particular, they provide information on government responses to the problem.

In conducting assessments, corruption detectives can draw from many sources of information. Governments, think tanks, public policy research agencies, nongovernmental groups, and international donor organizations that are involved in the fight against corruption now undertake country diagnostic assessments on a regular basis. While these assessments may not cover all areas of relevance, they often contain information that is helpful for corruption detection and program design.

Country diagnostic assessments come in different forms, each offering unique information about different aspects of corruption: country rankings, changes in corruption levels, identification of corruption problems, public attitudes toward corruption, laws related to corruption, the functioning of government institutions, anticorruption initiatives, and the politics of reform. Each element, on its own, provides useful but limited information. Together, they yield a comprehensive picture that offers a meaningful basis for corruption detection and the design of tailored anticorruption strategies and action.

For each of these essential elements of a corruption assessment, there are key questions that need to be answered and information sources that can be tapped. While much information is readily available from government reports, scholarly analyses, the media, and the work of other organizations, additional information may need to be collected through interviews and focus groups with key stakeholders, legal analyses, and public opinion surveys.

1. *Corruption rankings* provide an overall indication of the severity of the problem in a country and a comparison to other countries in the region and worldwide. Although a low ranking may indicate that anticorruption reform is a priority, it may also suggest the difficulty of making progress in such a context. Countries with middling levels of corruption typically offer more opportunities for fighting corruption. The ranking, by itself, is of limited value in explaining the problem or devising a way forward. It does not identify the particular sectors, institutions, or practices that are vulnerable to corruption and in need of reform. The following principal questions need to be asked:

a. How do major international corruption-ranking organizations rate this country?
b. What stakeholders were questioned and methods employed to develop the ranking?

Refer to Transparency International's Corruption Perceptions Index (CPI), the World Bank Institute's Governance Indicators, the Global Integrity Report, and Freedom House rankings (see annex A for links to these indicators).

2. *Changes in corruption levels* indicate the country's trajectory. If corruption levels are improving, the initiatives under way merit further support, and an expansion of those efforts may be warranted. Alternatively, if corruption levels are deteriorating, the initiatives may require adjustment to reverse this trend. The major questions asked by corruption detectives are as follows:

a. How has the level of corruption changed over the preceding year or years?
b. What is the cause of any changes?

Refer to Freedom House rankings, Transparency International's CPI, and business surveys (e.g., the Opacity Index, the Global Competitiveness Report, and the Business Environment and Enterprise Performance Survey [BEEPS]) for numeric changes. Within Europe, refer to Group of States Against Corruption (GRECO) evaluations and surveys for quantitative assessments of changes in corruption levels.

3. Identifying *the underlying nature of the corruption problem* is the most challenging aspect of a diagnostic assessment. To diagnose the problem, assessments need to consider the locus, severity, types, and sources of corruption. This information is necessary to identify priorities and suggest a unique configuration of substantive reforms. Key questions to ask include the following:

    a. What government institutions or services are most vulnerable to corruption (e.g., procurement, customs, police, courts, campaign financing, voting, the formulation of laws and policies, licenses, university entrance, hospital admission, or telephone installation)?

    b. What kinds of corruption are present (e.g., bribes, theft, patronage, or state capture)?

    c. Who benefits and who is hurt by this? Do benefits and costs differ among high-, mid-, and low-level officials or across different agencies and branches of government? Where and how does the private sector initiate or tolerate corruption, and where is the private sector a victim of corruption? Do some citizens gain timely and effective service, while others face excessive delays and interruption in public services? Does the public complain that corruption imposes a real barrier to their access to public services?

    d. What are the proximate costs? Is the scale petty or grand? Does the corruption entail a fixed fee or a percentage of the transaction (e.g., in procurement contracts)? Are public revenues reduced? Are public resources wasted?

    e. What are the possible causes, remedies, and obstacles to reform?

Refer to Freedom House's Nations in Transit, GRECO evaluations, and country surveys.

4. *Public attitudes toward corruption* are another important aspect of a country diagnostic assessment. They reveal whether the public are tolerant of the situation and are willing to support change at the ballot box, on a corruption hotline, or in their dealings with public officials. If tolerance is the norm, anticorruption efforts need to increase public awareness about the costs of corruption through such avenues as legal education campaigns and investigative journalism. Key questions to ask include the following:

a. Is the public tolerant of corruption? Is the public aware of the threat that corruption represents for society?
b. Are there organizations involved in educating public officials and the public about their rights and responsibilities?
c. Is investigative journalism well developed? Does the public have a choice of independent media?
d. Do social scientists publish research on corruption?
e. Does the business community advocate corporate responsibility, including codes of conduct, modern accounting standards, internal controls, and integrity pacts?

Refer to surveys, Freedom House reports, and GRECO evaluations.

5. An *inventory of laws* related to corruption is a necessary element of a diagnostic assessment. This inventory needs to describe not just the laws on the books but how they are implemented as well. Reviews of the criminal and civil procedure codes, public procurement regulations, campaign financing laws, administrative codes of conduct, financial disclosure rules, access to information, and relevant international conventions must be conducted. These reviews need to point to notable strengths and weaknesses, including gaps, in the legislative framework. Key questions to ask include the following:

a. Are there effective laws against bribery, embezzlement, and other abuses of public office?
b. Is there an effective law on party financing, which limits the extent to which special interests can contribute to parties?
c. Is there an effective law on conflict of interest, which restricts the ability of politicians and bureaucrats to participate in and accept compensation for activities that are contrary to the public interest?
d. Is there an effective law on financial disclosure for senior public officials that allows for public scrutiny of their accumulation of wealth?
e. Is there effective freedom of information and sunshine legislation that allow public access to government documents and meetings? Do libel and slander laws protect journalists' rights?
f. Is there an effective law against money laundering?
g. Is the country a signatory to key international conventions related to anticorruption?
h. Are the country's corruption laws consistent?

i. Are these laws implemented effectively?
j. Is the punishment for violation of these laws adequate?
k. Has the government enforced corruption laws, free of political control and influence?

Refer to regional anticorruption regime reports. For additional information, refer to Freedom House reports.

6. A *review of government institutions* is another key aspect of the assessment. Such a review examines the functioning of government institutions to identify where there is insufficient accountability and obstacles that promote corruption and opportunities and incentives to reduce these abuses. On the one hand, it examines the institutions involved in the prevention, detection, and prosecution of corruption. On the other hand, it looks at the role of government in the economy, conditions in the civil service, and accountability systems more broadly in the public sector. Key questions to ask include the following:

a. What specialized institutions are involved in the fight against corruption? For example, does the country have (1) an independent auditor general's office or equivalent organization that regularly audits government accounts, (2) an inspector general's office that regularly monitors government contracting and procurement practices, (3) an office of government ethics that promotes a code of conduct and verifies wealth reports submitted by officials, and (4) an anticorruption agency with a mandate to investigate complaints about corruption, prosecute cases, implement preventive actions, and promote public education?
b. To whom do these institutions report? Is there any oversight of these institutions?
c. Is there adequate coordination between the various institutions involved in fighting corruption, including specialized units within the police, the prosecution service, the judiciary, and intelligence services?
d. Do these institutions and units have adequate resources to carry out their work? Do they enjoy the necessary independence to perform their functions in order to avoid pressure from superiors or political powers?
e. Do civil servants earn a living wage? Do civil servants have job security?

f. Is there meritocracy in hiring, compensating, and promoting civil servants?
g. Do public officials have limited discretion in carrying out their functions, particularly in the area of regulation?
h. Do taxes and regulations pose an excessive burden on businesses and households? Are they overly complex, costly, or incoherent?
i. Is the management and privatization of state-owned enterprises characterized by transparency and competition?
j. Are there effective systems for managing public expenditures, including budgetary planning, execution, procurement, and audit?
k. Are there effective systems for demanding vertical accountability of public officials? For example, are public officials elected in free and fair contests? Is there an ombudsman, a citizens' hotline, or a citizen oversight board? Are there safeguards for whistleblowers and a witness protection program?
l. Is the legislature able to provide a check against corruption in the other branches of government?
m. How are political campaigns financed?

Refer to GRECO evaluations, surveys, and Freedom House reports.

7. Diagnostic assessments also need to examine ongoing *anticorruption programs* that a country has already initiated. Such an examination looks at the efforts of both government and civil society to fight corruption. It considers whether a national strategy exists and the extent to which it includes prevention, public education, and enforcement. The major questions asked here include the following:

a. Is there a strategy or policy for fighting corruption? What are its principal components? Does the anticorruption program include public education, prosecution of corrupt officials, and institutional reforms to prevent corruption?
b. What major anticorruption initiatives have been implemented? What, if anything, have they accomplished? What obstacles have they encountered?

Refer to GRECO and Freedom House reports.

8. Finally, the assessment needs to consider *the politics of reform*. A careful look at the political forces arrayed in support of and against the corrupt

system is necessary for crafting a strategic response to the problem and identifying possible entrées for assistance. Such an examination entails looking at the regime in place (e.g., consolidating democracy, late nation-builder, retreating democracy, consolidating authoritarian, or reintegrating state), the unity and capacity of the government (including a look at factions, constituent bases, and patron-client networks), and the people and groups who control specific institutions (e.g., is the justice minister a relative of the president or from a rival faction of the governing party?). It also entails looking for any openings for reform, such as an economic crisis, a scandal causing pressure for change, or a champion of reform or external pressure (such as from the International Monetary Fund or World Bank). Corruption detectives may need to hold meetings or focus groups with key stakeholders or gather this kind of information from government reports, scholarly analyses, and the media. Key questions to ask include the following:

a. Is the government's political survival dependent on effective measures to fight corruption? Has the country experienced a recent political or economic crisis linked to corruption? Was a promise to fight corruption a key element in the party platform of the government?

b. How would the government's constituent base and any patron-client networks be affected by inroads against corruption? Is the government unified or composed of competing factions?

c. Are there credible leaders in government who can champion implementation of anticorruption reforms? Are the key champions of anticorruption likely to remain in government for at least one year?

d. Is the debate within government on corruption open and transparent? Is the government willing to commission independent studies of corruption and disseminate the results? Is the government open to NGO monitoring of anticorruption reforms?

e. What groups benefit from corruption? How powerful are they? Do they control specific institutions? Can they be co-opted or contained?

f. Is there a broad coalition of support for an anticorruption program? Are NGOs, research organizations, business and professional groups, political parties, or citizens groups actively involved in this effort?

g. Finally, what kind of regime is governing the country? For example, is the regime a consolidating democracy, late nation-builder, retreating democracy, consolidating authoritarian, or reintegrating state?

The following chapter presents a pilot test of a self-assessment technique that was conducted in Africa that incorporates many of these elements. Chapter 5 offers a widely accepted integrated approach to assessing corruption.

4

Self-Assessment

A self-assessment corruption checklist was designed to collect information that would help development assistance programs, host governments, and international and bilateral donors develop a clear picture of the current status of corruption in a country and of efforts to combat corruption. Specifically, the tool seeks to capture whether countries have adopted and implemented the prerequisites—the laws, institutions, and programs—that are generally considered necessary components of a comprehensive anticorruption strategy. In selecting the questions to include in the checklist, we relied heavily on recommendations contained in Transparency International's *Source Book.*[1]

Several existing indices, for example, Transparency International's Corruption Perception Index (CPI) and the World Bank's Governance Indicators, attempt to measure levels of national corruption. Because corruption is difficult to measure objectively, these indicators typically monitor the *perceptions* of governmental abuse from the perspectives of surveyed stakeholders. The approach selected for this self-assessment approach focuses, alternatively, on phenomena that are more easily measurable and on which objective data can be gathered—for example, the extent to which countries have adopted and implemented appropriate *reform initiatives* to combat corruption. The value added of this technique is that it pinpoints where countries are trying to implement corruption control mechanisms and with what effect. It highlights those areas where successes have been achieved and those areas where more reforms are required. Based on these results, it is possible to identify key areas of corruption vulnerability and options for anticorruption programming.

The checklist is divided into five broad categories. Table 4.1 lists the specific areas that are included in each component.

Across the five categories, the checklist assessment tool includes 119 questions on 31 specific areas (see annex B). The checklist seeks information about the breadth and depth of anticorruption programs—in words and in

Table 4.1
Checklist Components

Part 1: Legal Environment • Criminal code • Conflict of interest • Public hiring/appointments • Freedom of information • Sunshine law • Asset disclosure • Codes of conduct • Whistleblower protection • International conventions	**Part 4: Budget and Public Expenditure Process** • Financial management system • Audits • Parliamentary oversight of budget • Procurement
Part 2: Enforcement and Prosecution • Enforcement • Judiciary • Money laundering • Asset recovery • Witness protection • Police	**Part 5: Civil Society, Media, and Business** • Civil society • Media • Corruption surveys • Public awareness campaigns • Business • International dimensions
Part 3: Government Oversight Institutions • Anticorruption agency • Ombudsman (public complaints unit) • National strategy • Parliament • Municipal/regional level • Corruption in public services	

action. The questions are divided between those that ask for factual information (e.g., Does a certain law exist?) and those that ask for expert judgment (e.g., Is the law being effectively enforced?). The tool focuses primarily on public sector corruption—the misuse of public resources for private gain. By and large, we left aside private sector corruption issues, although we did include questions on local and multinational corporations. Corruption in the electoral process was not added but could be in the future.

Pilot Study Methodology

The checklist was transmitted by e-mail between June and August 2004 to representatives in US Agency for International Development (USAID) missions and US embassies in Africa, African governments, host country institutions, international NGOs, host country NGOs, and local academics in each country. Completed surveys were received from 35 respondents in 20 countries. Sixteen respondents (1 each from 16 countries) were US government (USG) officials in either US embassies or USAID missions. This small, but targeted, sample served as the basis for the analysis that follows. As a pilot test of a new assessment methodology, focusing on this limited sample enables us to

- analyze the extent to which international development personnel in the field have the information to answer the questions in the checklist,
- evaluate the degree to which international development personnel respond differently from host country respondents, and
- obtain feedback from respondents on the ease or difficulty of using the checklist and drawing implications for programming from it.

In most cases, individuals responded to the checklist tool as individuals. In a few cases, we were told that a team of people was gathered together to answer the questions—each drawing on his or her areas of specialization and knowledge. In general, feedback from USG respondents was very positive; several respondents indicated that the very act of completing the checklist helped them consider anticorruption programming anew by integrating the various dimensions of anticorruption activities and demonstrating the areas of accomplishment and deficiency in controlling corruption. Several respondents indicated that some of the yes-no questions were too constraining; the answers they wanted to provide were somewhere in between.

For each country, a score was calculated for each of the five areas of the checklist (legal environment, enforcement and prosecution, government oversight institutions, budget and public expenditure process, and civil society, media, and business). The score for each component is a simple average of all questions within that section. The scale runs from 1 to 5, where a score of 5 indicates that a country has implemented all reform programs, and a score of 1 indicates that none of the reform programs are implemented. An overall country score was also calculated by averaging these five component scores.

Africa-wide Results

Table 4.2 presents the country and component scores for the sample. The countries are ordered in relation to their overall country score, from highest to lowest. There is wide variance in aggregate scores across the sample of countries. At the top end of the spectrum, South Africa received a rating of 4.13. At the bottom end of the spectrum, Liberia received a score of 2.15.

Is this the ranking of countries that we would anticipate in terms of country attempts and successes at fighting corruption? It is encouraging to find that South Africa received the highest ranking. But it is suspected that Cameroon and Nigeria received overly optimistic scores; they rank much lower in other surveys (TI CPI and World Bank Control of Corruption indicators). On the other hand, Madagascar and Burkina Faso are probably underrated in the scoring, as they rank considerably higher in these other surveys.

Correlation With Other Indicators

In principle, we might expect that the country scores from the checklist tool would correlate with the major indicators of perceived levels of corruption, in particular, the TI CPI and the World Bank Control of Corruption indicator. However, the correlations are neither strong nor statistically significant. Overall country scores have only modest correlations with the TI CPI ($r = .336$, not significant) and with the Control of Corruption indicator ($r = .280$, not significant). An obvious explanation is that these indicators do not measure the same thing. Whereas our checklist is a composite measure of the extent to which reforms have been put in place based on the judgment of experts, the CPI and the Control of Corruption indicator are both measures of the perceived incidence of corruption based largely on citizen public opinion polls.

However, we do find that the anticorruption scores from the checklist tool correlate strongly and in the expected direction with several aggregate indices of human development and political rights—more positive measures of reform programs. For example, the overall anticorruption score correlates significantly ($r = .586$, $p < .02$) with the UN Development Programme's Human Development Index (HDI for 2002); this suggests that the extent of anticorruption reforms in a country covaries with the quality of social and economic development.

The HDI is also correlated with two of the components of the overall anticorruption score—Legal Environment ($r = .524$, $p < .045$) and Government Oversight Institutions ($r = .521$, $p < .046$). In addition, the Civil Society, Media, and Business participation component of the anticorruption score

Table 4.2

Checklist Country Ratings Compared With Transparency International and World Bank Indicators

	Overall Country Score	1. Legal Environment	2. Enforcement and Prosecution	3. Government Oversight Institutions	4. Budget and Public Expenditure Process	5. Civil Society, Media, and Business	TI Corruption Perception Index (2004)	World Bank Control of Corruption (2002)
South Africa	4.13	3.96	4.42	3.63	4.52	4.11	4.6	67.5
Mali	3.94	4.13	4.23	3.28	4.14	3.93	3.2	46.4
Benin	3.80	3.80	3.41	3.72	3.71	4.37	3.2	34.0
Cameroon	3.62	3.24	3.80	3.81	3.75	3.53	2.1	8.8
Nigeria	3.55	3.55	3.83	3.58	3.05	3.75	1.6	3.1
Senegal	3.50	3.73	3.53	3.04	3.13	4.06	3.0	53.1
Rwanda	3.43	3.65	3.80	2.63	3.67	3.43		35.1
Kenya	3.29	3.25	3.25	2.55	3.18	4.23	2.1	11.3
Zambia	3.22	2.75	3.67	3.17	3.17	3.37		17.0
Uganda	3.09	3.29	2.47	3.38	3.35	2.95	2.6	19.1
Madagascar	2.94	3.22	2.50	3.14	2.63	3.21	3.1	61.9
Burkina Faso	2.63	2.73	1.45	2.22	3.83	2.89		57.7
Tanzania	2.59	2.11	2.26	2.62	3.22	2.74	2.8	15.5
Mozambique	2.53	2.14	2.50	2.78	2.27	2.95	2.8	14.9
Sierra Leone	2.50	1.87	2.41	2.86	2.27	3.11		25.8
Liberia	2.15	1.56	1.83	1.17	2.95	3.24		16.5

Note. Checklist ratings for US government respondents only.

correlates strongly with the Freedom House Political Rights score ($r = -.596$, $p < .015$).

USG Responses Compared With Host Country Responses

Are the USG respondents knowledgeable and accurate informants on these issues of anticorruption activities in their resident countries? To test for bias across respondent groups, we compared the scores of USG respondents with those of host country respondents (from civil society and business organizations). For the five countries from which we received completed checklists from both USG and local respondents, USG respondents in four countries (all but Burkina Faso) were significantly more optimistic about the implementation of anticorruption controls, institutions, and procedures than the local groups (see figure 4.1). This finding suggests a potentially systematic bias by USG officials to be too optimistic or by local respondents to be too pessimistic. It also suggests that corrections for the future might be implemented by formulating joint USG–host country teams to answer the checklist questions.

Detailed Discussion

The following results from the 16 countries reflect information current in 2004.

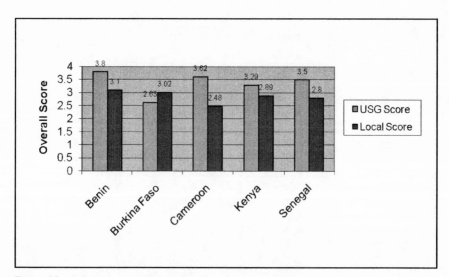

Figure 4.1 US government and local respondent scores compared.

Component 1: Legal Environment

This component measures whether the appropriate laws have been put in place and whether these laws are being enforced in practice. The major finding from this section is that, by and large, the countries in the sample have put the requisite laws in place, but enforcement is lagging. Table 4.3 shows "Laws in Place" and "Implementation" scores for each country. The average score for Laws in Place is 3.56, yet the average for Implementation is only 2.40, indicating that across the sample there is a major implementation gap in the area of legal reform.

For example, most countries have laws in place that require public hiring to be based on merit rather than on nepotism, connections, and bribery. However, public hiring decisions are actually based on merit only some of the

Table 4.3
Results for Legal Environment

	Laws in Place	Implementation	Overall Legal Environment Score
Benin	5.00	2.69	3.80
Burkina Faso	3.29	1.75	2.73
Cameroon	4.00	2.22	3.24
Kenya	3.46	2.86	3.25
Liberia	1.57	1.50	1.56
Madagascar	3.86	2.22	3.22
Mali	5.00	3.18	4.13
Mozambique	2.43	1.63	2.14
Nigeria	3.86	3.00	3.55
Rwanda	4.00	3.13	3.65
Senegal	4.38	2.78	3.73
Sierra Leone	1.73	2.25	1.87
South Africa	5.00	2.85	3.96
Tanzania	2.71	1.46	2.11
Uganda	3.67	2.78	3.29
Zambia	3.00	2.17	2.75
Average	3.56	2.40	3.06

time, and senior-level appointments are often given to supporters and friends rather than to qualified persons. Similarly, in the area of asset disclosure, most countries have laws in place that require government officials to disclose their assets. Yet, this information is rarely made available to the public. As a third example, all countries, except Liberia and Mozambique, have national laws in place that define conflict of interest for public officials. However, within government agencies conflict of interest policies are not widely understood. This pattern holds true for the entire range of legal questions included in the checklist. As such, we conclude that for the sample as a whole, the challenge for the future in the area of legal reform will be to move beyond enacting laws to a new focus on strengthening their implementation.

Criminal Code (Question 1)
Most countries (14 of 16) have put in place national laws that explicitly define corruption as an illegal behavior. Typically, these laws specify the actions considered as corrupt and indicate punishments for cases of corruption.

Conflict of Interest and Asset Disclosure (Questions 2 and 6)
In these areas, most countries have the requisite laws in place, but their implementation remains spotty. Thirteen countries have enacted national laws that define conflict of interest for public officials. However, only 7 countries have put in place clear conflict of interest policies within government agencies, and in many instances these policies are not widely understood by the officials working in the agencies. Similarly, with asset disclosure, the majority of countries (12 of 16) require government officials to disclose their assets. In practice, though, officials fail to provide this information in some countries, and asset information is rarely made available for public scrutiny.

Public Hiring/Appointments (Question 3)
While most countries (12 of 16) have laws in place that require public hiring to be based on merit, in practice, hiring decisions are made on merit only some of the time. Furthermore, in most countries senior-level appointments are given to political supporters and friends of the top leaders rather than to qualified persons.

Public Access to Information (Questions 4 and 5)
Citizen access to public information is problematic. In less than half of the sample (7 of 16), freedom of information laws exist that allow citizens to access public documents related to government decision making. Even in those

countries where freedom of information laws exist, obtaining documents in practice is frequently not possible. Furthermore, only two countries have in place sunshine laws requiring that the meetings of public boards or commissions be open to the public.

Codes of Conduct Within Public Institutions (Question 7)
In many countries (9 of 16), public institutions are legally required to have codes of conduct in place, and many institutions have in fact adopted codes of conduct with legally binding sanctions for offenders. However, awareness of these codes among public employees remains uneven.

Whistleblower Protection (Question 8)
Efforts in this area are lacking. Only five countries have put in place laws to provide protection for people who report cases of corruption. Even among those countries, the laws in practice provide protection for whistleblowers only some of the time.

International Conventions (Question 9)
Nine countries have ratified the UN Convention Against Corruption and the African Union's Convention on Combating Corruption.

Component 2: Enforcement and Prosecution
Component 2 measures whether countries are investigating and prosecuting offenders. Generally, the scores on enforcement were relatively good, though judicial independence was highlighted as an area of concern.

Prosecution of Offenders (Question 10)
In all countries except Liberia and Burkina Faso, governments have undertaken corruption-related investigations, and corruption cases were brought before the judiciary in the past year. In the majority of these countries, prosecution did lead to conviction and the enforcement of sentences against those found to be guilty.

Judiciary (Questions 11 and 14)
Judicial independence is a problem across the sample. In the overwhelming majority of countries, the judiciary is not sufficiently independent of political influence to issue verdicts against members of the ruling party. In addition, legal protection for witnesses in corruption cases is provided in only five countries.

Money Laundering and Asset Recovery (Questions 12 and 13)
In this area the record is mixed. Nine countries out of 16 have put in place laws prohibiting money laundering (the process through which money derived from illegal activities is given the appearance of originating from a legitimate source). However, only 5 have created an investigative unit for money laundering, and only South Africa and Nigeria reported that investigations have led to convictions for offenses related to money laundering. The situation is similar for asset recovery. Only 5 countries have created an asset recovery unit, and the capacity of these units is generally seen as insufficient. Furthermore, only 4 countries—Benin, Nigeria, South Africa, and Zambia—reported any cases in which public assets have actually been recovered either domestically or from abroad.

The Police (Question 15)
The findings are encouraging. In all countries except Burkina Faso and Senegal, efforts are under way to monitor and curtail corruption within the police force. Furthermore, in 11 countries, police members have been reprimanded or dismissed for corruption in recent memory.

Component 3: Government Oversight Institutions
Component 3 looks at whether government institutions and agencies are able to provide the oversight needed to detect and combat public corruption. While oversight agencies and institutions do exist to detect and investigate corruption, generally the capacity and independence of these bodies are insufficient.

Anticorruption Commissions (Question 16)
In all countries except Liberia and Rwanda, the government has created an anticorruption agency or commission.[2] Generally these commissions have the power to investigate all branches of government, and their investigations do in practice lead to prosecution of offenders. However, commissions are only sufficiently independent to investigate members of the ruling party in 8 of the 16 countries. Furthermore, most commissions lack sufficient capacity to carry out their mission.

Ombudsman (Question 17)
Ten countries have an ombudsman to investigate claims of public corruption. However, like the national commissions, ombudsman's offices across the sample tend not to have sufficient capacity or independence to fulfill their mandate. On the positive side, nine countries have created hotlines or other mechanisms through which citizens are able to report cases of corruption.

National Strategy (Questions 18 and 20)

The findings related to national strategies are cause for concern. While the majority of countries (11 of 16) do have a national anticorruption strategy in place, the evidence suggests that government commitment to implementing these strategies may be limited. Seven have carried out assessments to understand the causes and consequences of corruption. Only 2 countries—Mali and South Africa—have taken "significant action" to implement their national strategies. Most governments have taken little or some action. In addition, only 6 countries have put in place mechanisms to monitor the implementation of the national strategy, and only 4 regularly report on progress. At the subnational level, only 1 country (South Africa) has put in place anticorruption strategies at the regional or municipal level. Taken together, these findings suggest that few governments have fully embraced the objective of substantively reducing corruption and put in place the requisite strategies and monitoring and reporting procedures to gauge progress.

Parliament (Question 19)

The findings related to the role of parliament suggest that the distribution of powers between the branches of government is problematic. While parliaments in some countries are engaged in efforts to combat corruption, they are generally not seen as an effective counterbalance to the executive branch. This suggests that the ability of parliaments to play an oversight and watchdog role vis-à-vis the executive branch is inadequate. Indeed, parliaments initiated investigations into corruption in only three countries within the past year (Benin, Nigeria, and Uganda).

Public Services (Question 21)

Within half of the countries (8 of 16), governments have put in place mechanisms to monitor the performance of public service agencies (health, education, etc.). In a larger number of countries (12 of 16), civil society groups monitor the performance of public services. However, in most countries citizens have inadequate avenues for seeking recourse in cases where public service fails.

Component 4: Budget and Public Expenditure Process

Component 4 assesses whether governments have put in place the necessary institutions and procedures to reduce discretionary use of public funds and detect misuse of funds. Across the sample, we found that procedures do exist to ensure that public revenues are used for the intended purposes. However, financial information is generally not available for public scrutiny, and some institutions—especially parliaments and supreme audit institutions—lack the capacity and/or independence to oversee the executive branch.

Financial Management Systems (Question 22)

All countries except two (Liberia and Sierra Leone) have put in place an integrated financial management system. Generally, these systems do provide information to legislative and parliamentary oversight committees. However, in most countries the quality of the data is seen as less than reliable. Furthermore, in most countries financial reports are not made available for public scrutiny in a routine manner.

Audits (Question 23)

The picture with audits looks similar. In most countries, periodic audits of public accounts are legally required. However, in some countries audits are not conducted with sufficient regularity, and recommendations are not implemented. Across the region, governments typically fail to make audit reports available for public scrutiny with sufficient regularity.

Furthermore, supreme audit institutions generally have low to medium capacity, and audit findings are subject to political interference at least some of the time in most countries.

Parliamentary Oversight of Budget (Question 24)

While parliaments in all countries have legally mandated oversight power for budgets and expenditures, in practice they ensure that public funds are actually used for the intended purposes only some of the time. Furthermore, in most countries parliaments rarely or never investigate executive fiscal practices.

Procurement (Question 25)

In all countries except Liberia, multiple bids are legally required for major procurements. In most countries, invitations to bid are routinely advertised to interested parties. In practice, however, procurement decisions are made in accordance with required procedures only some of the time, and procurement decision are made public with less regularity.

Component 5: Civil Society, Media, and Business

Component 5 assesses whether nongovernmental actors are able to play oversight and watchdog roles. The results in this section are generally more positive than in the preceding sections, suggesting that nongovernmental actors are mobilizing to combat corruption.

Civil Society (Question 26)
In most countries (15 of 16), civil society organizations exist that claim anticorruption as part of their mandate. Furthermore, in most countries civil society organizations have in fact initiated actions that have had an impact on government policy, even though governments across the region remain somewhat unreceptive to civil society oversight.

Media (Question 27)
In all countries, at least some of the major media outlets are privately owned. Across the sample, the media frequently reports on cases of corruption, and in most countries media reporting does in fact lead to government investigation of alleged cases of corruption some of the time. In some countries, the media is considered to be relatively free of political influence, but in others media independence continues to be a problem. Laws exist to protect the media's right to investigate cases of corruption in only six countries, and in eight countries laws exist that inhibit the media's ability to investigate corruption (e.g., libel laws).

Corruption Surveys (Question 28)
In all countries but three (Liberia, Mali, Rwanda), public opinion surveys of corruption have been carried out within the past three years, and in most of these countries, surveys have succeeded in elevating the issue of corruption in national debates.

Public Awareness Campaigns (Question 29)
In 11 countries anticorruption public awareness campaigns have been carried out in the past three years. Generally, these campaigns have succeeded in elevating the issue of corruption in national debates, although in some countries the impact of these campaigns was minimal.

Business (Questions 30 and 31)
In seven countries professional associations have been formed to promote ethical practices. However, business practices are monitored by independent watchdogs in only five countries. The record on multinational corporations is mixed. In some countries, they generally follow international ethical standards of good business conduct, but in others they do not. Generally, multinationals fail to meet acceptable standards for transparency and accountability.

Selected Country Profiles

This section presents country-specific anticorruption profiles based on the checklist responses for the worst, best, and mid-level rated countries, namely, Liberia (figure 4.2), South Africa (figure 4.3), and Zambia (figure 4.4), respectively. The profiles provide a quick window on the extent to which these countries have been successful or not in establishing the prerequisites for significant anticorruption programs as of the time the checklists were completed (2004). Strengths and weaknesses are highlighted in the discussion. On the basis of these profiles, corruption detectives can identify existing programs that might need strengthening and programmatic gaps that still need to be filled. The radar charts accompanying each country profile depict the extent to which anticorruption prerequisites are currently in place, component by component. The more area that is shaded in the chart, and the closer the shaded area is to the outer point in the chart, the more that anticorruption component is judged to be effective.

Liberia

1. *Legal Environment score = 1.56.* Few key anticorruption laws are in place. The criminal code does not explicitly define corruption as illegal. Conflict of interest laws are absent. While public hiring laws do exist, in practice these laws are generally disregarded. Hiring decisions are rarely made on merit, and senior-level appointments are typically given to political supporters and friends

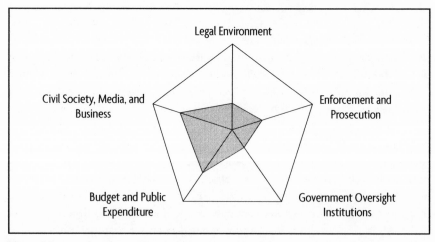

Figure 4.2 Anticorruption profile: Liberia.

of the top leaders rather than to qualified persons. Public access to information also remains insufficient, and citizens are frequently unable to obtain public records, even though freedom of information laws are in place. Sunshine laws, asset disclosure requirements, codes of conduct, and whistleblower protection are all absent.

2. *Enforcement and Prosecution score = 1.83.* There are few signs that any efforts are under way to enforce laws prohibiting corruption or to actually prosecute offenders. The government did not undertake any anticorruption investigations in the past year, and no cases have been brought before the judiciary. Money laundering and asset recovery units are both absent, as are legal protections for witnesses in corruption cases.

3. *Government Oversight Institutions score = 1.17.* By and large, oversight institutions within the government are lacking. As of 2004, the government did not have a national strategy to combat corruption, indicating that its political will may be weak. At the time this checklist was completed, the government had not created an anticorruption agency or hired an ombudsman. In public services (health, education, etc.), mechanisms to monitor service delivery agencies are absent.

4. *Budget and Public Expenditure Process score = 2.95.* Liberia does not have an integrated financial management system in place. However, periodic audits of public accounts are required, though in practice they are conducted only some of the time, and findings are never available for public scrutiny. Parliamentary oversight of the budget was noted as generally insufficient. On procurement, appropriate laws are not in place to require that the government collect multiple bids for major procurements. In practice, procurements are rarely made in accordance with required procedures, and procurement decisions are generally not made public.

5. *Civil Society, Media, and Business score = 3.24.* The one bright spot for Liberia is in the area of civil society and media. Civil society groups that claim anticorruption as part of their mandate do exist, and these organizations have had some impact on government policy. The media appears to be generally independent from the state, and the media frequently reports on corruption. Corruption surveys and public awareness campaigns have not been carried out.

South Africa

1. *Legal Environment score = 3.96.* The principal laws required to implement a comprehensive anticorruption strategy are in place in South Africa. In practice, results are generally good, but some deficiencies were noted. In the area of recruitment for civil service positions, hiring decisions are made on merit only

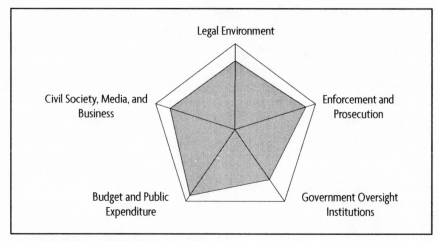

Figure 4.3 Anticorruption profile: South Africa.

some of the time, and senior-level appointments are typically given to political supporters and friends of the top leaders rather than to qualified persons. In the area of asset disclosure, information provided by government officials is rarely made available for public scrutiny.

   2. Enforcement and Prosecution score = 4.42. Corruption investigations did take place in the past year, and in some cases they resulted in fines or imprisonment. At the same time, the judiciary is not seen as being sufficiently independent to issue verdicts against members of the ruling party. In the areas of money laundering and asset recovery, South Africa is in an excellent position. Appropriate laws are in place, a money laundering investigation unit has been created, and money laundering investigations are in fact undertaken and have led to convictions. An asset recovery unit has been created, and there have been cases in which public assets have been recovered. However, this unit's capacity is seen as insufficient.

   3. Government Oversight Institutions score = 3.63. The government has established a national strategy to combat corruption and has taken significant action to implement the strategy. Furthermore, the government has put in place mechanisms to monitor progress and does routinely report on progress. These are all positive signs that indicate government commitment to fighting corruption.

   The government's anticorruption agency has appropriate powers to investigate cases of corruption, and in practice, investigations do lead to prosecution of offenders. This agency is generally seen as being independent of political influence, though its capacity is somewhat inadequate. Similarly, an ombudsman's office exists but lacks sufficient capacity and independence.

While parliament is somewhat engaged in the fight against corruption, distribution of powers remains problematic. The parliament lacks the ability to counterbalance the executive office and did not initiate investigations into corrupt practices in the past year. Finally, mechanisms exist within government to monitor the performance of public service agencies (health, education, etc.), but citizens have limited recourse in cases where service delivery fails.

4. *Budget and Public Expenditure Process score = 4.52.* South Africa has put in place appropriate rules and regulations for public financial management, parliamentary oversight of expenditures, and government procurement. The integrated financial management system generally provides reliable information to decision makers, and financial reports are generally available to the public. Audits of public accounts are carried out routinely, and reports are available for public scrutiny. However, it was noted that the supreme audit institution lacks capacity.

On procurement, the data are excellent. Appropriate laws are in place requiring that the government collect multiple bids for major procurements and notify potentially interested parties of invitations to bid. Procurement decisions are generally made public, and in practice, procurements are by and large conducted in accordance with required procedures.

5. *Civil Society, Media, and Business score = 4.11.* Civil society groups that claim anticorruption as part of their mandate do exist, and these organizations have had some impact on government policy. The media is independent from the state and frequently reports on corruption. In some cases, media reporting has led to government investigations. Corruption surveys have been carried out and have had some impact on elevating the issue of corruption in national debates. Public awareness campaigns have not been carried out.

Zambia

1. *Legal Environment score = 2.75.* Some of the key laws required as part of a comprehensive anticorruption strategy have been enacted in Zambia. Conflict of interest, asset disclosure, and whistleblower protection laws are in place. However, public hiring, freedom of information, and sunshine laws are absent. On the implementation side, findings are mixed. In the area of public hiring and appointments, hiring decisions are made on merit only some of the time, and senior-level appointments are frequently given to supporters and friends of the top leaders rather than to qualified persons. In the area of asset disclosure,

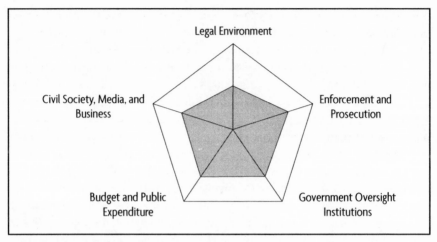

Figure 4.4 Anticorruption profile: Zambia.

government officials provide the required information only some of the time, and this information is not always available for public scrutiny

2. *Enforcement and Prosecution score = 3.67.* The data on enforcement and prosecution are positive. The government and judiciary carried out corruption investigations and brought cases to trial during the past year, and some cases led to convictions. However, the judiciary is not sufficiently independent of political influence to be able to issue verdicts against members of the ruling party.

A money laundering investigation unit has been created, and in practice, government agencies do carry out investigations related to the movement of money derived from criminal activity. An asset recovery unit has also been created. While its capacity is somewhat insufficient, there have been cases in which public assets were recovered.

3. *Government Oversight Institutions score = 3.17.* The government has established a national strategy to combat corruption but has taken limited action to implement the strategy. The government has not put in place mechanisms to monitor progress and does not routinely provide reports on its progress. These findings raise questions about the government's commitment to fighting corruption.

The government's anticorruption agency has appropriate powers to investigate cases of corruption, and in practice, investigations do lead to prosecution of offenders. While this agency lacks capacity, it is thought to be relatively independent from political influence. The parliament appears to be engaged in efforts to combat corruption but has limited ability to counterbalance the executive office. In practice, debates about corruption are common in the parliament, but there were not many investigations of corrupt practices in the past year.

Finally, mechanisms do exist within the government to monitor the performance of public service agencies, yet citizens have limited recourse in cases when service delivery fails.

4. *Budget and Public Expenditure Process score = 3.17.* Some steps have been taken to put in place appropriate rules and regulations for public financial management, parliamentary oversight of expenditures, and government procurement. Nonetheless, deficiencies were noted in the reliability of these systems and in the government's willingness to allow public scrutiny. Specifically, the integrated financial management system does not routinely provide reliable and timely information to public officials. Financial reports are rarely made available to the public. Audits are not conducted regularly, but reports are generally available to the public. The supreme audit institution is severely lacking in capacity.

Procurement practices are problematic. While appropriate laws are in place requiring that the government collect multiple bids for major procurements, in practice, procurements are rarely conducted in accordance with required laws. Procurement decisions are made available to public scrutiny only some of the time.

5. *Civil Society, Media, and Business score = 3.37.* Civil society groups that claim anticorruption as part of their mandate do exist, but these organizations have had limited impact on government policy. The media is generally free of political influence, and it frequently reports on corruption. Media reporting does lead to government investigations of alleged corruption at times. Corruption surveys and public awareness campaigns have been conducted but have had a limited impact in elevating the issue of corruption in national debates.

Practical Implications Concerning the Checklist Assessment Technique

The self-assessment checklist tool provides a detailed overview of a country's anticorruption program. Rather than focus on the extent of the corruption problem, the technique directs the attention of assessors to what is being accomplished to control the problem. Importantly, it is an easy-to-use and quick tool that highlights the important questions that corruption detectives should be asking to develop a broad diagnosis of the state of anticorruption activities in a country. Moreover, the conclusions drawn from using the technique lend themselves readily to programmatic options that donors and governments can incorporate in future plans.

This pilot test demonstrated that the questions asked by the checklist are answerable by knowledgeable USG democracy and governance officers in the field. Because of the multidimensional nature of the checklist, we found that a better way to complete it might be to organize a team of specialists within a field mission or embassy or to convene a joint team of USG–host country experts.

For the purposes of cross-country comparisons, we transformed the checklist responses in this pilot test into quantitative indicators. However, such quantification is not necessary for practical assessment purposes in the field.

This checklist tool might be thought of as a first, high-level assessment of the state of anticorruption programs in a country. If the technique identifies particularly weak or nonexistent institutions or systems that need further analysis, additional and more probing assessments may be commissioned to detail alternative paths for future reform programs.

Recommendations Concerning the Checklist Technique

On the basis of this pilot study, we have several recommendations on how to implement the checklist for corruption detectives.

1. *Revise and refine the checklist tool.* Carefully assess the questions against the results to determine if certain questions should be reworded or deleted and if additional questions should be included, taking local context into account. Also, review the response values offered for each question and whether open-ended questions should be added.

2. *Obtain a larger sample.* Find additional respondents to complete the checklist. In addition, secure one or two appropriate think tanks in each country to complete it. With these new respondents, test a variety of ways to get the checklist completed—by individual respondents, group efforts, facilitated group exercises, and joint international–local team efforts. Assess the pros and cons of each approach.

3. *Conduct a more detailed analysis across the region.* With a larger sample of countries, it will be possible to conduct a more definitive analysis of the state of anticorruption programs across the entire region. As well, analyses can be conducted to assess if there is potential or unwarranted optimism or pessimism from respondents.

4. *Develop a set of toolkits based on the results.* On the basis of a broad comparative analysis across regions, it is likely that particular deficiencies and weaknesses in existing anticorruption programs will emerge. These findings can be used to develop basic toolkits that address common problems faced on a country-by-country basis.

Policy Implications

In the broadest sense, reducing corruption requires limiting the discretionary power of government officials to use public resources for their private and political gain. In Africa, since independence, leaders have been relatively unencumbered in their discretionary power. The transition to more democratic political systems has placed some restrictions on leaders. They are now subject to popular elections in many countries. Society and the media also have more freedom to voice criticism of the government and to demand information. Opposition political parties now exist in many countries to challenge the practices of incumbent parties.

Yet, despite these positive changes, leaders still retain significant discretion over the distribution of public resources. The data from the checklist strongly indicate that the distribution of power within African governments remains skewed toward the executive branch. Parliaments and judiciaries are generally unable to challenge the authority of the executive or carry out investigations into abuses of power. In addition, the checklist found that institutions and agencies that have been created to play oversight roles frequently lack the capacity or independence to fully investigate and sanction corrupt officials.

Across our sample of countries, a majority have carried out what we call "stroke of the pen" reforms—that is, reforms that can be enacted by either legislation or decree. Typically, these reforms include putting in place new laws and creating new commissions and agencies. However, new laws are frequently not implemented, and new agencies often do not have the power or resources to fulfill their mandates in practice. This is often intentional. African leaders rely on the use of state resources—distribution of public funds, jobs, business licenses, scholarships for students, and so on—to build and maintain networks of political supporters. As such, incumbent leaders have little incentive to implement substantive reforms that would reduce their discretionary power.

The challenge for those seeking to promote reform, therefore, is to find ways to change the incentive structure that government officials face. This can be done in multiple ways and at multiple levels. First, the international donor community and international financial institutions can continue to demand that governments adopt principles of good governance and transparency as a condition for receiving aid. However, donors must push for substantive reforms, not just window dressing. Second, donors can continue to support the development of the institutions needed for democracy—free and fair elections, strong political parties, and so on. Democracy provides an opportunity for the population to sanction corrupt leaders and may push incumbent leaders to embrace reforms. Third, donors can continue to support societies in developing the capacity to monitor government and hold it accountable. Finally, donors can continue to provide strategic support for reforms within governments. However, donors should be realistic about the broader political framework in which these reforms are being enacted. Providing support for anticorruption agencies, for example, may not make sense in countries where the executive office is determined to limit the power of that agency. Careful assessments of the political landscape need to be conducted when designing strategies. Where political will is weak or absent, donors may be better off using funds to support civil society.

Programmatic Recommendations

The recommendations that follow are addressed to donors and reformers working at the country level in Africa and are derived from the substantive findings of this pilot study.

1. *Focus on political will.* Government will for reform appears to be inadequate in many countries. While most countries have national strategies to combat corruption, few have taken significant actions to implement these strategies. Even fewer have put in place monitoring mechanisms to measure progress made on national goals or procedures for routinely reporting on progress. While it may be difficult to directly increase the political will of government officials, donors need to be realistic about the possibilities for affecting change in countries where political will is weak or absent.

2. *Focus on building checks and balances and extending the distribution of power.* Distribution of power between the main branches of government remains problematic. Parliaments and judiciaries generally have limited power to hold the executive office accountable, sanction corrupt practices, or perform an oversight function. Donors should look for strategic opportunities to provide support to strengthen these institutions. Support may be particularly useful following a transition of government or where incumbents appear genuinely committed to reform.

3. *Build capacity of institutions and agencies.* The capacity of agencies, commissions, and institutions with a mandated role to combat corruption is generally insufficient. Donors should look for strategic opportunities to strengthen anticorruption agencies, ombudsman's offices, supreme audit agencies, and service delivery agencies. Donors should be careful to target support to countries that have demonstrated a commitment to building the capacity and independence of these agencies.

4. *Continue to work with civil society.* Civil society is actively engaged in the effort to reduce corruption. The vast majority of countries reported the presence of civil society organizations that have adopted corruption as part of their mission, and in a significant number of countries, civil society organizations have succeeded in impacting government policy. Donors can conduct needs assessments to determine whether civil society could benefit from additional support and provide support where needed. One area that may be worth investigating is to strengthen the capacity of civil society groups to collect and disseminate data on corruption and the government's anticorruption progress. In many cases, basic information is absent or incomplete.

5. *Continue to work with media.* The media is actively engaged in investigating and reporting on corruption. In most countries, the media is reasonably free from government control and frequently reports on cases of corruption. In several countries, media reporting has led to government investigations of corruption. Donors can conduct needs assessments to determine whether the media in various countries could benefit from additional support and provide support where needed.

6. *Maintain pressure for open budget and expenditure systems.* In many countries, the availability of government financial data is limited. Though most countries reported the use of an integrated financial management system, financial data and audit reports are frequently not made available to oversight agencies or the public. Pressure from donor agencies and international financial institutions may play a pivotal role in creating incentives for incumbent leaders to adopt more transparent practices.

7. *Support initiatives to strengthen public access to information and transparency.* Across the sample, citizens in many countries have difficulty obtaining various types of information from the government. Governments are shielded from public scrutiny by outdated laws and practices. In some countries, donors should push for legal reforms that will legalize the public's right to access government information. Donors can support governments in drafting and ratifying freedom of information laws, sunshine laws, financial disclosure laws, and audit laws. Donor support may be useful as well in helping citizens'

groups learn how to take advantage of such laws where they exist. For example, in countries where freedom of information laws are in place, civil society and media groups may be unaware of their rights or of the process for obtaining information.

8. *Support money laundering and asset recovery laws and agencies.* Few countries in the sample have put in place appropriate legislation regarding money laundering and/or asset recovery. And few have created appropriate investigative units for implementing such laws. Donors may be able to support the development of legislation and the creation of appropriate agencies.

9. *Support public service reform.* In some countries, mechanisms exist to monitor the performance of public service agencies (health, education, etc.). However, these mechanisms are absent in many other countries. Across the sample, citizens generally have little recourse in cases where service delivery fails. For the vast majority of African citizens, the primary point of contact with the government is the public service sector, and corruption in this sector affects people's lives in tangible ways. There is presently limited knowledge about how to reduce corruption in this sector. Donors should take stock of what has been tried and continue to develop best practices. One option might be to strengthen civil society organizations that monitor the service sector (through report card surveys and social audits, for example) so that reliable data about performance become available, and citizens have an organization to turn to for support and advocacy in cases of service failure.

10. *Provide training on implementation of anticorruption laws.* A key finding of this study in the area of Legal Environment was that in many countries, relevant laws are in place but are not being fully implemented. Donors could target this "implementation gap" by providing technical assistance to institutionalize laws and procedures and by offering training to government agencies and civil society groups to build capacity, improve awareness, and strengthen enforcement of existing laws.

Notes

1. Jeremy Horowitz assisted in conducting this research. See Jeremy Pope. 2000. *TI Source Book 2000—Confronting Corruption: The Elements of a National Integrity System.* Berlin: Transparency International.

2. Liberia established an anticorruption commission in 2008, and Rwanda created an Office of the Ombudsman to deal with anticorruption cases in 2003.

5

An Integrated Diagnostic Approach

The US Agency for International Development's (USAID) 2005 Anticorruption Strategy signaled a clear recognition that new approaches need to be taken by host country governments, their civil society and business communities, and international donor organizations to address corruption as a serious obstacle to development. Corruption is both the product and the cause of numerous governance failures, economic dysfunctions, and political shortcomings. More than a decade of programming experience demonstrates that effective programs to address corruption must take into account a wide range of these factors to avoid the trap of tackling the symptoms but leaving the underlying disease untreated. A first step toward implementing improved anticorruption programs that are likely to have real impacts is to provide corruption detectives a comprehensive approach to assess the problem—how corruption manifests itself in a particular country, the array of factors that drive it, and the effectiveness of existing laws, institutions, and control mechanisms meant to reduce a country's vulnerability to corruption.[1]

This chapter describes the principal elements of a corruption assessment approach developed for USAID by Management Systems International.[2] It provides policymakers and analysts with an integrated framework and set of practical tools to conduct tailored corruption assessments efficiently, while at a level sufficiently detailed to produce targeted and prioritized recommendations for programming. The framework is guided by international best practice, theory, and research, as well as the results of pilot assessments that tested earlier versions of the methodology. By offering a common approach by which the dynamics of corruption can be understood and assessed, anticorruption strategies can be improved and programs made more effective and appropriate to different country conditions.

The main objective of this assessment approach is to *ensure that assessments start by casting a wide analytical net* to capture the breadth of issues that affect corruption and anticorruption prospects in a country *and then provide a clearly justified, strategic rationale for their final programmatic recommendations.* This methodology provides step-by-step practical assistance to implement the approach and produce an assessment report that addresses a wide range of issues and generates recommendations for action. The guidance provides assessment teams with tools for diagnosing the underlying causes of corruption by analyzing both the state of laws and institutions and the political-economic dynamics of a country. By understanding country-specific drivers of corruption, assessment teams should be able to develop reasonable insights on government sectors and functions that are most vulnerable to corruption and the types of initiatives that can reverse or control these problems. The framework also provides a rationale for setting priorities, choosing some approaches, and rejecting others.

The approach does not offer automatic cookie-cutter conclusions. The assessment team will have to assimilate and analyze information from a variety of sources to reach conclusions and recommendations that are context specific. The framework facilitates this process by offering organizing concepts, information-gathering tools, and corruption categories that can help in diagnosing the targeted country, prioritizing key sectors and functions in need of remediation, and developing an overall strategic plan for anticorruption programming. Each assessment team may find that it will want to adapt, expand, or alter these approaches based on the needs of the final users and/or the specifics of the country being assessed.

The methodology is intended to assist a variety of users in carrying out assessments—from anticorruption specialists to country experts, from donor teams to host country government and nongovernmental teams. It is not intended to be a primer in all things anticorruption, but it is meant to give users enough information to be part of a team led by an anticorruption expert.

Underlying Principles

This corruption detection approach is premised on several principles that are essential to understanding and addressing corruption.

1. *All corruption is not the same.* Corruption may manifest itself in similar ways across countries and over time—bribery, extortion, embezzlement, influence peddling, nepotism, and so on— but the underlying causes can be different, and the areas that corruption attacks can vary across geographic region and over

time. The assessment framework is built to help governments, donors, and other interested parties identify different types of corruption (grand and administrative corruption, as well as state capture and predation) and the sectors and functions that are vulnerable to corruption in particular locales or points in time. By providing a better understanding of the nature of the problem and its root causes, this framework supports development of a comprehensive strategic outlook that can offer a customized approach to controlling corruption.

2. *All countries do not possess the same proclivity toward the same types of corruption.* Rather, on the basis of different patterns of development and political-economic dynamics, countries manifest differing corruption tendencies and vulnerabilities. The assessment methodology incorporates a new method to distinguish among countries along these dimensions that may help provide new perspectives on the types of programs that would be appropriate and effective in different settings.

3. *All countries are not at the same level of anticorruption readiness.* The political will and commitment of governmental and nongovernmental leaders define only one aspect of a country's readiness to deal effectively with the problem of corruption. The capacity to act effectively is the other element that determines a country's readiness level. Thus, there needs to be a basic framework of anticorruption laws, regulations, and institutions in place that serve as the prerequisites or preconditions for all initiatives. As well, government officials and civil society, mass media, and business leaders must have the training, resources, and capacity to act effectively and with meaningful resolve over the long haul if anticorruption initiatives are to be adequately implemented.

Traditionally, corruption has been assessed primarily as a problem of weaknesses in *legal and institutional arrangements*. But to avoid government and donor responses that treat only the symptoms of corruption, it is essential to take a strategic perspective that assesses underlying causes and the deeper *political-economic dynamics* that have influenced the evolution of corruption in a country. This framework offers a way to combine these two approaches and to help users move from a *general understanding* of corruption issues to *problem definition* and then to *programming* (see figure 5.1). In addition, the

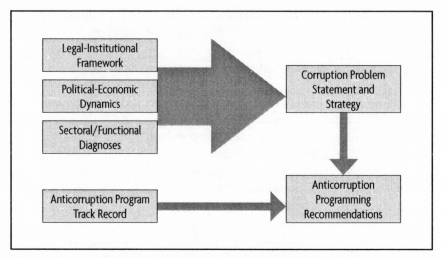

Figure 5.1 From understanding to problem definition to programming.

framework is applicable across development sectors, not simply in democracy and governance or economic-growth program areas.

The assessment methodology is driven by two overarching objectives:

1. *Develop a practical strategy by assessing the context and understanding the problem.* Valuable insight into the nature and underlying causes of the corruption problem in a country can be derived from a detailed understanding of the context within which corrupt practices and tolerances have developed in that country. Based on this contextual understanding and statement of the problem, a meaningful and implementable *anticorruption strategy* can be designed. To accomplish this requires a comprehensive assessment of the country's *legal-institutional framework* and analysis of the *political-economic dynamics* that have guided the country's development.

2. *Make recommendations by diagnosing sectors and assessing program track records.* Tailored and prioritized *programming recommendations* that specifically address a country's principal corruption problems can be derived from *in-depth diagnoses of key governmental sectors and functions* that target corruption vulnerabilities and opportunities for reform. Up-to-date information about *the track records of anticorruption programs elsewhere* can inform

the team about appropriate courses of action based on what has proven effective in similar contexts.

Understanding Corruption and Key Considerations for Programming

Over the past decade, international research and practice have demonstrated that there are several major characteristics of corruption that must be accounted for in any reform program. The brief summary below is intended not to be comprehensive in its treatment but to give users a sufficient overview for conducting assessments.

Corruption Is Multisectoral

Corruption is both a *governance* and an *economic problem*, and it is *manifested in all development and service delivery sectors.*[3] Its occurrence is facilitated by the absence or insufficiency of financial controls, performance monitoring for both personnel and programs, transparency, and mechanisms of accountability. Its consequences are often manifested in poor governance and economic distortions and stagnation. The crosscutting nature of corruption challenges governments and donors to integrate and mainstream anticorruption objectives and programming approaches into all of their initiatives across all sectors. While fighting corruption has traditionally been viewed as a "democracy and governance" task, it is also critical to address corruption vulnerabilities in each domain of a development portfolio. Often, *service delivery sectors (education, health, security, etc.) are where people encounter corruption most visibly or frequently* and where its impact can reduce the effectiveness of any number of other development initiatives.

Looking at the problem through a *governance lens* primarily focuses the analyst on determining if government institutions have the capacity and follow-through potential to deliver efficient, transparent, and accountable services within the law. Some of the key factors relate to adequacy of the legal and institutional framework, administrative complexity, capacity and professionalism of staff, and internal control and oversight mechanisms. A second important aspect of the governance equation is the role of the public in advocating, monitoring, and sanctioning. Key issues in this regard include access to information, freedom and capacity of civil society and the media, and the effectiveness of elections as sanctioning mechanisms. Essentially, corruption can be viewed as a governance problem *within each sector.* There may be some common approaches that can address corruption across sectors—related to budgeting and procurement, for example. But there are also sector-specific approaches that will be needed to deal with corruption vulnerabilities particular to certain sectors. Empirical analyses have shown that improvements in governance can have positive impacts on reducing corruption abuses, as can programs that directly attack corrupt practices.[4]

Looking at corruption through an *economic lens* puts the focus primarily on the extent of government intervention in the economy and its consequences on corrupt activities. Key factors from this perspective include overregulation, government control or rationing of resources, subsidies, procurement, revenue administration, and public expenditures, among many others.

Corruption Affects Multiple Levels of Government

Corruption can be found at all levels of government—from the *central to the regional to the local levels.* Preventive and control programs at the central level may have only limited reach and effectiveness down to the subnational levels of government. To be effective, initiatives are typically required from the top-down and from the bottom-up simultaneously. A strategic anticorruption assessment needs to access information at all levels to understand differences in the nature of the problem and in programming requirements. This is accomplished through probing diagnostic questions within key sectors and functions and special efforts to examine the phenomenon and impact of corruption at all levels.

Corruption Impacts Multiple Levels in Society

Administrative corruption is typically characterized as an everyday, low-level abuse of power that citizens and businesspeople encounter—for example, requests for small bribes or gifts, speed money, and influence peddling to turn a blind eye on circumvention of the rules or to get things done that should have been free or part of expected public service delivery.

Grand corruption involves higher-level officials and larger sums of money and typically includes, for example, kickbacks to win large public procurements, embezzlement of public funds, irregularities in political party and campaign financing, and political patronage and clientelism. Grand corruption can sometimes come in the extreme forms of

- *state capture*, where economic elites effectively dictate policies to suit their private interests, or
- *state predation*, where political power is used to extract financial benefits from a country's economic resources.

There is no clear line between administrative and grand corruption, and the two are often linked, but the distinction is nonetheless important for assessing problems and developing programmatic responses. If high-level corruption is endemic, for example, it may be much less likely that political leaders will be willing to implement meaningful reforms, even if those reforms are targeted only at lower-level officials. At the same time, administrative corruption in a particular ministry or agency may be addressed if the leadership of that agency is not entangled in webs of corrupt exchanges.

The assessment framework encourages the team to examine all levels of corruption and develop appropriate remedies. While a comprehensive program is not always possible to implement, international experience suggests that it is preferable to address all types of corruption—the high-level influence peddling, the low-level administrative corruption, the collusive state capture relationships, and the outright ravaging of the economy by political leaders. The logic of such an approach is that the combined impact of addressing all levels of corruption will increase the probability of detection and change corruption into a high-risk, high-cost activity and reduce popular tolerance for corrupt practices.

Countries With Similar Political-Economic Conditions May Have Similar Corruption Dynamics

Patterns of corruption and responses to legal and regulatory incentives differ across societies in ways that reflect deep and long-term development processes and political-economic conditions. By understanding the underlying factors that influence these patterns—that is, the way people pursue, use, and exchange wealth and power in particular societies—it may be possible to identify the kinds of corruption problems a country is likely to have and, thereby, better diagnose its basic difficulties and devise appropriate countermeasures, not just treat its symptoms. Thus, it is important to recognize that countries with similar political-economic conditions are likely to have similar, though not necessarily identical, corruption dynamics.

Corruption Is Strongly Influenced by Situational Factors

The types and levels of corruption in a society are largely affected by both situational opportunities and obstacles. The major factors at play include the following.

Actors and political will. There will be little hope for meaningful and sustainable change if critical stakeholders are not present and committed to reform. Important actors can be in government, civil society, business, and the media. Anticorruption programs can be initiated in whichever development sector is ready for change and willing to take a stand. Champions for change and ethical leadership may exist or can be nurtured. If there are none, it still may be possible to mobilize civil society groups, the media, or business leaders to advocate for reforms and exert external pressure on government.

There can also be political will *against* reform—vested interests who want to maintain the system of corruption in place as is. It is important to identify who these interests are and understand their incentives and their power. With accurate assessment of these forces, it may be possible to propose ways of diminishing or bypassing these opponents of good governance. Overall, this framework evaluates stakeholders—both pro and con—in the context of the priority sectors and functions that are diagnosed.

Institutional capacity. There may be motivation but little capacity and experience to fight corruption effectively. Training, technical assistance, and financial support can be used to strengthen the capacity of governmental and nongovernmental groups in the areas of advocacy, oversight, ethics, investigation, prosecution, awareness building, prevention, transparency, and accountability. No country needs to invent such programs from scratch; there is a wealth of international experience and a growing body of best practices that can be shared. Institutional capacity is analyzed during the sectoral-functional diagnostic phase of the assessment.

Culture and tradition. In many countries, the use of public office for private gain is viewed as a matter of their traditional and cultural heritage. It is often difficult to toss off approaches to the use of wealth, power, and influence that have become accepted and commonplace. Often, these practices can exist side by side with legal structures that prohibit them. While difficult, it is possible to reverse such cultural and traditional tendencies. Popular champions of reform and more modern institutions can emerge to promote rule of law, accountability, and transparency and exercise power responsibly. For example, if government can institute reforms to provide quality public services effectively and efficiently, without extorting bribes or unofficial payments from citizens, it can go a long way toward transforming traditional and cultural approaches that rely on corrupt transactions or kinship ties.

Prerequisites. It is important to determine if certain preconditions for anticorruption programs exist or if they need to be implanted early in a comprehensive strategy. These prerequisites or essential building blocks include

- the basic legal framework needed to fight corruption (such as an effective criminal and civil code, conflict of interest laws, meritocratic

hiring rules, freedom of information laws, sunshine laws, asset disclosure rules, codes of conduct, and whistleblower protection),
- effective law enforcement and prosecution,
- adequate government oversight institutions,
- accountable and transparent public finance processes, and
- active nongovernmental advocacy and oversight of government operations.

While anticorruption programs can proceed and sometimes thrive in the absence of some of these elements, fighting corruption is made more difficult if they are missing or not fully implemented. The assessment approach, through its legal-institutional analysis, will identify not only the existence of these laws and institutions but also how adequate they are and how well they are implemented. Inconsistencies between words and deeds can create major barriers to reform.

International actors, influences, and initiatives. International organizations and donors can strongly influence and promote anticorruption programs. In some cases, such as the corruption index threshold for the Millennium Challenge Corporation and World Bank conditionality, donors require serious demonstrations of a country's actions and intentions in fighting corruption as a prerequisite for larger loans and grants. Conversely, international actors can undermine anticorruption programs by sending mixed messages. Coordination and consistency among donors (as well as among various countries' diplomatic, development, and commercial actors) regarding intentions and priorities can make the difference between leveraging for common objectives and contradictions that undermine anticorruption investments. Other initiatives, such as the UN Convention Against Corruption and regional treaties, establish agreed standards for anticorruption efforts; some also involve review mechanisms to evaluate a country's progress in meeting those standards. Industry-based efforts like the Extractive Industries Transparency Initiative and Publish What You Pay campaigns also establish standards for anticorruption efforts in specific sectors, though the voluntary nature of all these initiatives means they do not guarantee adherence by countries that sign on.

The Corruption Assessment Framework

Assessments are used as vital input for decision making and programming. Corruption assessments can help to not only inform program directions but also support host country priorities and solutions.

While there are indices that currently exist to measure the general level of corruption in a country, they are measured largely on the basis of expert opinion or popular perceptions. Transparency International's Corruption Perception Index ranks countries by their perceived levels of corruption, as determined by expert assessments and opinion surveys. The Global Integrity Index rates accountability and transparency in civil society, elections, government administration, oversight, regulation, and the rule of law. The World Bank Control of Corruption Index monitors the extent to which public power is exercised for private gain based on opinion surveys of firms, individuals, and experts. These indices and surveys can offer useful country comparisons over time, but they usually do not provide sufficient detail to inform particular country programming.

The assessment framework presented here involves several practical tasks that progressively build a detailed analysis of the country's corruption problems and what can be done realistically to improve the situation. Figure 5.2 offers a graphic presentation of these tasks.

Early Steps

To ensure that the assessment team's time in country is well spent, a substantial amount of effort should be allocated to pre-trip preparation. Early review of existing information and formulation of working hypotheses is the best way to avoid repeating analyses that have already been conducted by others and to make the most effective use of time on the ground in the country.

Task 1: Team Planning Meeting and Initial Review of Existing Resources

Team planning meeting. The purpose of the team planning meeting (TPM) is to begin the task of preparing the assessment work plan, which is then refined as the team begins work. By setting aside time before the assessment team arrives in country, teams can make their time working together more efficient and productive. In addition, teams tend to function better when TPMs are held at the front end of an assessment. At a minimum, TPMs should address these questions:

1. Who is the client? Who are the stakeholders?
2. What is the task?
3. What are our team roles and responsibilities?

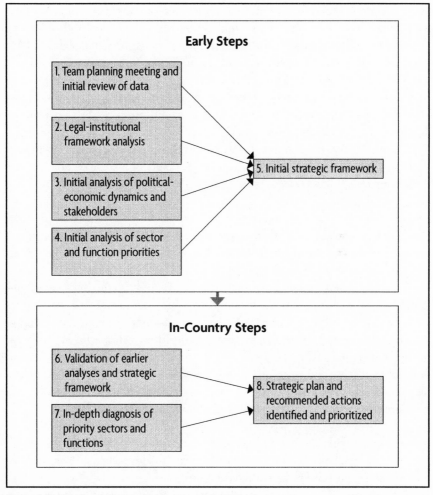

Figure 5.2 Flowchart of corruption assessment framework.

4. How will we best work together in terms of leadership and working styles?
5. What is our work plan?

An independent facilitator—someone who is not responsible for producing the work but who will shepherd the TPM process along—can be useful to conduct an efficient meeting.

Sometimes all members of the team may not be fully assembled until the assignment begins in country. While this presents a challenge for forming the team and beginning to work together, and it is optimal to be colocated, TPMs can be conducted with members in different locations through tele- or video-conferencing. Or it may be necessary to conduct two TPMs—before departure and upon arrival in country—to make sure each member has a common understanding of the team's objectives, timelines, and products, as well as his or her individual roles and responsibilities.

Initial review of existing resources. Given the growing quantity of anticorruption and related analysis that is publicly available, it is strongly advised that teams be given sufficient time prior to arrival in country to review documents, conduct initial analysis, and develop working hypotheses and preliminary priorities. The team should explore as many resources and materials as possible; many are likely to be available on the web (see resources in annex A). Impressions developed by the team at this early stage can be revisited and reassessed once team members arrive in country.

Host government and donor coordination. There is increasing interest and action in the development community to reduce duplication of assessments and improve coordination of assistance among donors and with the host government. In the 2005 Paris Declaration on Aid Effectiveness, donors and host governments pledged to take steps to reduce the burdens that donors place on host governments and to improve coordination between host country priorities and donor programs.[5] Good practice in this area is still developing, but a minimum standard for all teams should include the following[6]:

- work with donors and the host government to identify existing assessments and mine those documents for information that does not need to be collected again;
- identify host country anticorruption strategies, plans, and programs and evaluate the degree to which they represent a viable basis for future anticorruption programs; and
- come to agreement about the degree to which host country counterparts will be consulted, briefed, and otherwise included in the assessment process and the degree to which host country priorities will be reflected in recommended programs.

Task 2: Legal-Institutional Framework Analysis

Corruption is facilitated or inhibited by the legal and regulatory framework, how it is put into practice, and how it is enforced or monitored through governmental institutions. This analysis is meant to be conducted by one or more legal experts—usually in country—who are well versed in the current status of laws, regulations, and institutions that are typically considered to be the prerequisites of a comprehensive anticorruption regime. The categories of questions are listed in figure 5.3. The factors in the table include the categories addressed in the UN Convention Against Corruption.

1. **National Anticorruption Strategies and Plans**
   1.1 Anticorruption Strategy and Plans

2. **Anticorruption Enforcement Laws and Institutions**
   2.1 Explicit Anticorruption Laws
   2.2 Corruption Investigations
   2.3 Corruption Prosecution in Courts
   2.4 Money Laundering
   2.5 Asset Recovery
   2.6 Witness Protection

3. **Corruption Prevention Laws and Institutions**
   3.1 Executive Branch
      3.1.1 Asset Disclosure
      3.1.2 Abuse of Discretion
      3.1.3 Gifts, Favors, Abuse of Influence
   3.2 Legislative Branch
      3.2.1 Asset Disclosure
      3.2.2 Gifts, Favors, Abuse of Influence/Conflicts of Interest
      3.2.3 Oversight Responsibility
   3.3 Judicial Branch
      3.3.1 Asset Disclosure
      3.3.2 Gifts, Favors, Abuse of Influence/Conflicts of Interest
      3.3.3 Judicial Independence
      3.3.4 Accountability Mechanisms
   3.4 Civil Service
      3.4.1 Conflicts of Interest
      3.4.2 Asset Disclosure
      3.4.3 Codes of Conduct
      3.4.4 Whistleblower Protection
      3.4.5 Lobbying

      3.4.6 Public Hiring and Appointments
      3.4.7 Immunity
   3.5 Transparency and Accountability
      3.5.1 Ombudsman (public complaints unit)
      3.5.2 Freedom of Information
      3.5.3 Public Hearings Requirements
   3.6 Political Parties and Elections
      3.6.1 Political Party Financing
      3.6.2 Elections
   3.7 Public Finance
      3.7.1 Financial Management Systems
      3.7.2 Audits of Public Expenditures
      3.7.3 Public Procurement
      3.7.4 Budget Planning
      3.7.5 Taxation
      3.7.6 Banking System
   3.8 Private Sector Regulation and Privatization
      3.8.1 Business Regulations
      3.8.2 Privatization
      3.8.3 Business Sector Anticorruption Activities
   3.9 Nongovernmental Organizations and the Mass Media
      3.9.1 Civil Society Organizations
      3.9.2 Mass Media

4. **Cultural Dimensions**

5. **International Cooperation**

6. **Compliance With International Legal Instruments**

Figure 5.3 Categories covered by the legal-institutional framework analysis.

The legal expert should consider the following when completing the table:

- Describe the *formal provisions of laws* and provide brief, factual responses as to the nature and content of the laws, regulations, and institutions that exist, at least on paper.
- Provide insight on *how the provisions are implemented in practice* and provide their perceptions as to the operations, effectiveness, and adequacy of the legal/regulatory provisions and institutions in reality.
- Identify the categories or subcategories that are *the weakest or present the greatest vulnerability* to corrupt practices.

The results of the analysis should be summarized at the beginning of the assessment report by highlighting the weaknesses and gaps in the formal legal-institutional framework, as well as in the provisions put into practice. The completed and detailed table can be used in its entirety as an appendix to the report.

Task 3: Initial Analysis of Political-Economic Dynamics and Stakeholders

While knowledge of the strengths and weaknesses of laws and institutions is necessary for diagnosing corruption problems and proposing solutions, it is not sufficient. Understanding the dynamics of political and economic power that shape these factors is equally essential for developing a realistic strategy to address the problem. Michael Johnston's concept of "corruption syndromes" is offered in this framework as a potential tool to facilitate political-economic analysis and identify corruption patterns and tendencies in the target country.[7] Although political-economic analysis can be conducted in a number of different ways by the team, syndrome analysis is a potentially illuminating approach to categorize countries in terms of the patterns of corruption causes and symptoms that emerge from a country's particular economic, political, and institutional trajectories. While the syndromes are explained in detail here, this is because the approach is innovative, not necessarily because it should be the central feature of the assessment.

Corruption syndromes. A syndrome is defined as a complex of symptoms that indicate the existence of a condition or problem. A corruption syndrome is a distinctive and complex pattern of corruption problems reflecting the ways people pursue, use, and exchange wealth and power, as well as the political and economic institutions that facilitate and/or impede those processes. Through the lens of syndromes, corruption is viewed as the result of a confluence of many factors, not just as the dealings of "bad people," the result of poor legal or regulatory systems, or activities that can be punished or deterred in isolation from broader influences. In other words, the whole (corruption in a country) may be greater than the sum of its parts (legal, institutional, and behavioral weaknesses). The syndrome tool provides the assessment team with a more complex picture of the factors that facilitate corruption and what might realistically be done about it—from a "deeper" strategic perspective and in terms of specific countermeasures. Perhaps most important, the syndromes approach can often tell us what not to do; reforms that work well in one setting may be irrelevant, or even harmful, in another. Assessment teams will determine if it is feasible to apply the corruption syndrome approach.

Syndromes are shaped by the long-term political and economic developments a country has experienced and by more recent influences and events. For example:

- The nature and spread of corruption in established democracies with reputable political and economic institutions are likely to be of a different nature (and to be coped with differently) than in countries in a transitional stage of democratization with political institutions that are not firmly in control and markets that operate primarily in the informal sphere.
- Other countries might be characterized by excessive collusion among political and economic elites, thereby weakening governance institutions, reducing the rule of law, and limiting the independence of the judiciary to provide adequate checks and balances. In these countries, anticorruption reforms must seek to increase political and economic competition in various ways to reduce the overall influence of these controlling elite networks.
- Yet other types of countries might be dominated by a ruler, inner circle, or family, where personal power and loyalties operate systematically to weaken democratic and institutional capacity. In these countries the elite plunders the state with impunity. Anticorruption reforms here often need to be aimed at mobilizing the press and citizen groups to gradually develop meaningful political competition and accountability mechanisms.

This framework profiles four broad syndromes (see table 5.1), and these syndromes can characterize almost all countries. Since the syndromes

(continues on p. 92)

Table 5.1
Corruption Syndromes Described

TYPE 1: **Wealth Pursues Influence in Public Institutions**	TYPE 2: **High-Level Figures Collude to Weaken Political-Economic Competitors**
While politics and the economy are usually active, competitive, and well institutionalized, you also see • Efforts by private parties to buy influence within public institutions and official processes; • Static or declining political participation and trust; • Declining credibility of parliaments, parties, elections, and executives; • Growing economic inequality; • Corrupt influence used to short-circuit political and economic competition; • Demand for access to decision makers exceeds legitimate opportunities; • Civil societies stagnant or in decline.	• Elite figures in several sectors share corrupt benefits, maintaining political and economic dominance in the face of rising competition; • Top political and economic elites overlap and interlink; • Fraudulent, indecisive, or uncompetitive elections foster collusion among party leaders; • Large overlap between state and business, poor transparency; • Moderately weak institutions: public-private boundaries are porous, politicized, and manipulated, while bureaucracy and business are colonized by parties and political leaders; • Civil society and media lack independence and are orchestrated from above; • Competitors exist but face systematic disadvantages.

Wealthy interests seek influence over decisions, usually via their connections to political figures. Wealth is used to influence specific decisions, often involving the implementation of particular policies, not to dominate whole societies or institutions. Thus, a business might deliver significant funds to an elected official, party leader, or lobbyist who in effect is placing influence and access out for rent. Wealth may also be channeled through a variety of organizations such as foundations and pseudo-charities. At times, this sort of corruption leads to agency "capture," but the process is generally too competitive, and officials have too much autonomy, to make full-blown state capture likely. Strong institutions and competitive economies make access a valuable commodity: large benefits are at stake, and official decisions have major consequences. Economies tend to be open, and state intervention relatively light. Officials themselves may take the initiative in demanding payment, as exemplified by "pay-to-play" deals in procurement and contracting. Over time, this syndrome reduces political and economic competition—perhaps undermining public trust in democratic processes—and produces inflexible policy, as businesses buy advantages over competitors, and political figures spend more time seeking rents than contending over policy.

Illustrative examples: Germany, Japan, United States

Elites are connected by durable networks based on sharing major benefits of corruption, while excluding political and economic competitors, though competition is intensifying. Elites may include politicians, party leaders, bureaucrats, media owners, military officers, and businesspeople in private and parastatal sectors. Corruption is moderate to extensive but controlled from above, with the spoils shared and uniting elite networks. Leaders of nominally competing parties may share graft revenues while excluding competitors. Often marked by ineffective legislatures, extensive state presence in the economy, politicized banking and industrial policy, and mutual "colonization" among business, parties, and bureaucracy. Corruption underwrites *de facto* political stability and policy predictability, partially compensating for moderately weak official institutions. International investors may find the situation attractive. But tight-knit elite networks delay the growth of genuine political competition and, by preempting needed economic and policy changes, can build rigidity into policy and governance. Often features very large and complex corrupt deals.

Illustrative examples: Italy, Republic of Korea

(continues)

Table 5.1
(continued)

TYPE 3: Oligarchs Contend in a Setting of Pervasive Insecurity	TYPE 4: A Dominant Inner Circle Acts With Impunity
• Powerful figures and personal followings plunder both public and private sectors in a setting of very weak institutions and widespread insecurity; • Institutions, rule of law, property rights, and public-private boundaries are all weak; • Little orderly competition, and violence is a common substitute for institutions (e.g., protection rackets in place of police and courts); • Capital flight and weak banking sector, and foreign direct investment is made for short-term gains only; • Economic and political opportunities are plundered, making gains insecure; • Little state autonomy and credibility, and bureaucracy, courts, and police are hijacked; • Chronic revenue shortages and poor tax collection; • Very large corrupt deals involving both public and private assets, and phony privatizations are common.	• Ruler, family, or favorites make unchecked use of state power for enrichment and/or political control; • Weak boundaries separate economy from top elite exploitation; • *Personal* power and loyalties dominate society, and *official* roles and structures are weak; • Power flows top down; opportunities, corrupt or otherwise, controlled by dominant figures; • Elite impunity and little or no accountability; • Little or no political competition, and civil society is weak, intimidated, or nonexistent.

Corruption is complex, chaotic, highly disruptive, and often linked to violence. Pervasive insecurity is created by very weak institutions and the influence of rapacious figures and their followers. Both politics and the economy are rapidly opening up; power and wealth are up for grabs, and few rules govern the ways they are sought. Winners find it difficult to protect gains or enforce agreements, encouraging violence, protection markets, and large-scale capital flight. Domination by few very powerful figures; their influence extends across sectors of both government and economy. Public-private boundaries are weak to nonexistent, while law enforcement and courts are used to grab power and assets. Organized crime and leaders' own families are powerful. Loyalty to an oligarch is only as valuable as the stream of rewards provided, making followings unstable. High instability, unpredictability, and weakness of opposing forces. Investment may be extremely risky, property rights shaky, and democratic guarantees meaningless.

Illustrative examples: Mexico, the Philippines

Involves corrupt figures who put state power to personal use—often, the top figures in a regime or their personal favorites. Unlike Type I, where wealth intrudes into state functions, *here personally controlled state power intrudes into the economy,* including diversion of aid and investment. Often depends on the personalities and agendas of top leaders; some may be completely venal while others pursue more enlightened policies. Family networks may be particularly powerful. Top political figures may form alliances with favored business interests or colonize those interests. In smaller societies, such networks may be relatively simple and controlled on a national basis by a dictator, family members, and personal favorites. In more complex countries, such networks may be more fragmented along sectoral or geographic lines, particularly where economies are rapidly creating new opportunities. While some political liberalization may be in progress, countervailing political forces remain weak, turning opposition to corruption into confrontation with the regime. Serious corruption can be extremely unpredictable, exacting major costs in terms of democratization and open, orderly economic development.

Illustrative examples: Kenya (under Moi), Indonesia (during and following Suharto) are multidimensional by their very nature, a particular country might be largely described by one *primary syndrome* but also have some of the elements of another *secondary syndrome.* In addition, it is important to consider that syndromes that best describe a country might change over time, and in some countries different geographic regions might exhibit different syndrome tendencies, as might different government sectors.[8] See table 5.2 for a list of countries that have been designated into the four syndromes using a quantitative analytical approach conducted in 2006.

To use this tool, the assessment team should read through the syndrome descriptions in table 5.1 to detect particular characteristics that appear to ring true for the targeted country. Local experts should also be involved in this process. While some countries may fit perfectly in one and only one syndrome, most will be described well by a *primary syndrome* but also have some characteristics of a *secondary syndrome.* An early hypothesis about key political and economic dynamics and underlying causes of corruption can be drawn from initial syndrome conclusions and other analyses based on background reading and the team's existing knowledge of the country, and validated once the team arrives in country.

Using the syndromes approach along with other analyses that help in the understanding of political-economic dynamics of corruption, the team should draft a short narrative for the assessment report that elaborates on the *drivers of corruption* in the country. This can include discussion of the following topics:

- why corruption affects the country as it does;
- how power and wealth are used, by whom, within what institutional context, and with what effect;
- how political and economic institutions have developed;
- how open and accountable is participation in the political and economic process;
- how the corruption problem can be framed in general terms;
- the nature of administrative and grand corruption, as well as state capture; and
- the broad implications that might be drawn about different approaches to anticorruption reform.

The implications of each syndrome and the most appropriate strategies and tactics to address those types of corruption will be discussed in Task 5.

The application of the syndrome approach has yielded some practical tips:

Table 5.2
Empirical Designation of Countries Into Corruption Syndromes

Type 1: Influence Markets

Australia	Netherlands	Ecuador
Austria	New Zealand	El Salvador
Canada	Norway	Ghana
Denmark	Spain	Guatemala
Finland	Sweden	Guyana
France	Switzerland	Honduras
Germany	United	India
Iceland	Kingdom	Jamaica
Japan	United States	Jordan
		Kenya
		Madagascar

Peru
Philippines
Romania
South Africa
Sri Lanka
Tanzania
Thailand
Tunisia
Turkey
Uganda
Zambia

Type 2: Elite Cartels

Argentina	Israel
Belgium	Italy
Brazil	Korea, South
Chile	Latvia
Colombia	Lithuania
Costa Rica	Poland
Czech Republic	Portugal
Estonia	Slovak Republic
Greece	Slovenia
Hungary	Taiwan
Ireland	Uruguay

Type 4: Official Moguls

Algeria	Nepal
Bangladesh	Niger
Cameroon	Nigeria
Central African	Oman
Republic	Pakistan
Chad	Panama
China	Russia
Congo, Republic of	Rwanda
Egypt	Senegal
Gabon	Sierra Leone
Guinea-Bissau	Syria
Haiti	Togo
Indonesia	Trinidad and
Iran	Tobago
Ivory Coast	Ukraine
Kuwait	Venezuela
Morocco	Zimbabwe
Myanmar	

Type 3: Oligarchs and Clans

Albania	Malawi
Benin	Malaysia
Bolivia	Mali
Botswana	Mexico
Bulgaria	Namibia
Croatia	Nicaragua
Dominican Republic	Paraguay

Note. Analysis conducted by M. Johnston based on 1995–2006 data sources. The four types in this table correspond to the types described in table 5.1.

- Do not agonize over syndrome assignment; the point is to draw insights from the detailed descriptions and to compare them to what you already know about the country.
- Syndrome analysis may be best used at the beginning and the end of the assessment. First, identifying important characteristics

of a syndrome for the target country may help the team formulate initial hypotheses about areas that need further analysis.
Later, the syndrome may help the team members think about
programmatic possibilities that they had not considered initially.

- The name or label of the syndrome is not important. It is the
description of the corruption problem in the syndrome profile
and the implications of those problems to which the assessment
team members should pay attention to see if they match up with
their view of reality.

- If a single syndrome profile does not provide an accurate or
reasonable description of the country being assessed, consider
identifying a primary and secondary syndrome. The value of the
syndromes lies only in the extent to which they provide helpful insights for anticorruption strategies and programming (see Task 5
for each syndrome's implications). The team *may identify more
than one syndrome* for the country as a whole, different regions of
the country, levels of government, or parts of the economy.

Finally, corruption syndromes are used in this framework as one of several tools for diagnosing corruption problems and prescribing solutions. As
this framework has been tested in the field, teams have used syndrome analysis
along with more traditional tools of legal, institutional, political, and economic
analysis. Assessors are encouraged to use the syndrome analysis in this framework as a way to help them think beyond the more straightforward strengths
and weaknesses of laws, institutions, and practices to ask themselves what they
might be missing.

For example, in Ukraine and Rwanda, country experts came to a quick
consensus on a single syndrome that best described these countries at the
present moment: both Type 2. While Ukraine appeared to be a pure Type 2,
Rwanda exhibited some hybrid features. Experts placed Paraguay as primarily
a Type 4 syndrome, characterized by a corrupt figure who puts state power to
personal use, but secondarily as a Type 3, where a more complex, chaotic, and
disruptive corrupt environment is marked by pervasive insecurity. A mixed set
of implications could be drawn as a result. In Mozambique, the team was unable to agree on a common syndrome. Instead, it analyzed political-economic
dynamics by examining the factors that facilitate corruption (e.g., single party
dominance, the merger of elite political and economic interests, limited rule of
law, linkages to organized crime, weak accountability mechanisms, and social
legacies) and those that inhibit corruption (e.g., the new government, incipi-

ent anticorruption institutions, the decentralization program, and donor investments in public financial management systems). The emerging extractives industry was also analyzed as a critical driver.

Analyzing stakeholders. The readiness of stakeholders to promote and implement anticorruption reforms is a function of their political will and capacity to act. At this early stage in the assessment, it is important for the team to examine the major stakeholder groups in terms of those that are likely to demonstrate a commitment to reforms and those that are likely to oppose them.

Political mapping of stakeholders is a helpful way to illustrate relative support and opposition for anticorruption programs (see figure 5.4 for an example from Paraguay in 2008).[9]

Opposition	Conditional Support	Core Support	Conditional Support	Opposition
		APC	MPQ PPS	
			PLRA	
		POLITICAL PARTIES		UNACE
		PRES. LUGO	CONGRESS	
		Min Fin	CISNI?	State Enterp.
		CC–AC	Customs	
		GOVERNMENT SECTORS	Contraloria **JUDGES**	
			FISCALIA	POLICE
		MCC	IDB	
		USAID		
			WORLD BANK	
		EXTERNAL ACTORS		
MCNOC ONAC	CEJ INECIP		Transparency Paraguay Asoc. Rural CIP CAPECO UIP FEPRINCO	Contraband
Public Employees	Asoc. Liberal Mayors			**Narco-traffickers**
Teachers	Decidamos Semillas		Ultima Hora ABC Color	**Clandestine** industry
Health Workers	Contralorias Ciudadanas	PRESSURE GROUPS/NGOS	LAWYERS	
Asoc. Sin Techos				

Figure 5.4 Stakeholder map on anticorruption issues (Paraguay 2008). *Source.* Excerpted from *Assessment of Corruption: Paraguay* (Washington, DC: Management Systems International, July 2008).

Horizontally, groups are arrayed in terms of their support or opposition to anticorruption reforms. Vertically, groups are arrayed across four sectors as demonstrated in the chart. Overall level of support can be estimated by the number of groups in the Core and Conditional Support sectors. Larger size and bold fonts can indicate the more important groups in terms of resources and political influence. Where there are a relatively large number of important groups in the "core" support sector, there is likely to be greater political commitment for implementing difficult measures. Similarly, numerous important groups in the opposition sectors can signal lesser support and political will for difficult decision making and implementation. Placement of groups on opposite sides of the map indicates incompatibility of interests—groups that are unlikely to align or coalesce in support of a particular issue. Groups on the extreme outside boundary of the map are considered "antisystem"—they typically function outside the normal "rules of the game" and often use violence as a political resource.

While this map presents only a snapshot in time of the readiness and opposition of groups to deal with anticorruption reforms, it can provide a useful early assessment of opportunities and problems that future anticorruption programs may encounter—who may be called on as champions for change, who needs to be nurtured, who is ready to advocate, and who has vested interests in maintaining currently corrupt systems. This information is extremely valuable for informing decisions on where to focus assistance efforts. Assessment teams may want to use this tool early in the assessment, using background reading and their own knowledge of the country, and/or revisit the analysis later in the process.

Task 4: Setting Initial Government Sector, Function, and Institution Priorities

At the heart of the corruption assessment are in-depth analyses conducted "where corruption lives" in particular government sectors and functions. In many heavily corrupted societies, the problem is found almost everywhere; to decide what to do first, the assessment team must identify early where corruption hurts the most and where the best opportunities exist to remedy these problems. In this stage, the team can use several inputs to identify an initial set of sectors, functions, and institutions with the greatest corruption risks that are most ripe for resolution. These inputs can include the following:

- *Legal-institutional analysis.* The analysis in Task 2 can suggest possible sectors or functions where there are particular high-priority corruption weaknesses or vulnerabilities.

- *Syndrome profiles.* The syndrome profiles and political-economic analysis derived in Task 3 may also suggest particular government sectors or functions that are good candidates for further diagnosis. For example, in some syndromes it is recommended that conflict of interest laws, electoral systems, public finance management, and/or court systems need to be strengthened. Based on these profiles, these sectors and functions can be pinpointed for future in-depth analysis.
- *Stakeholder mapping.* This analysis of actors (Task 3) can identify where political will and opposition lie—by sector and function—for reform.
- *Recent research reports.* The team may be able to find recent research reports, analyses, assessments, and opinion surveys that highlight government sectors and functions that are particularly vulnerable to corruption or where there may be ready opportunities for reform (Task 1). Likely sources for such reports are the World Bank, Transparency International, Global Integrity, the U4 Anti-Corruption Resource Centre (www.u4.no), and others.
- *Donor priorities.* Donor priorities for the assessment will probably be outlined in the scope of work for the assessment. Activity reports and country analyses conducted by donors will identify other areas of interest or help rule out areas for further investigation.
- *Host government priorities.* Experience has shown that anticorruption programs are most effective when they support meaningful and committed efforts on the part of host country counterparts. Many countries have developed anticorruption strategies and action plans, and though they are not all of equal quality, such expressions of host government priorities need to be carefully considered when exploring programming options.

On the basis of these sources, the team should develop an initial list of priority sectors, functions, and institutions that ought to be diagnosed in greater depth in later stages of the assessment. The benefit of developing this list while the team is still preparing is that it allows it to begin collecting data on those sectors and functions, find appropriate local consultants, and start scheduling meetings and interviews prior to arriving in the country.

For example, in Jamaica, the team reviewed the annual report of the contractor general that identified vulnerable political bodies and assessed the relative readiness of these bodies to respond positively to anticorruption programs. Readiness was based on expert interviews and focus groups concerning the political will of reformers or champions within these bodies and the existence of new anticorruption procedures and legislation.

In Paraguay, the team delimited the number of sectors and functions by first identifying those most debilitated by excessive patronage, political influence, and insufficient resources. Among these sectors and functions, the team members highlighted the ones with the most operational responsibility to confront public corruption. They ultimately selected the judicial sector, law enforcement, audit, and customs. Running across all of these were two major dysfunctional crosscutting functions: public administration and budgetary frameworks. These were selected as well for in-depth diagnosis.

In Rwanda, the USAID mission and the government decided prior to the assessment that the health sector presented the greatest need to tackle corruption and was home to reformers with the political will to follow through on new initiatives. In Morocco, the team sought guidance from the USAID program office and several technical offices at the USAID mission for their priorities across the sectors and functions to pare down the list to a doable number.

Task 5: Initial Strategic Framework
On the basis of the previous steps, the assessment team should have sufficient insight into the country's corruption problems and anticorruption opportunities to sketch out a preliminary anticorruption strategic framework that can guide the more detailed in-country work that will follow.

"Strategy," in this sense, refers to sustained action against the underlying causes shaping a country's particular pattern of corruption, not to specific programs or controls aimed at particular practices. The team's strategic framework should reflect the team's understanding of the corruption problem at this early stage of the assessment, based on the preceding analyses in Tasks 1 through 4. It will be a "best guess" that can be adjusted as more is learned once the team is on the ground. This step does not necessarily require significant time, as it will likely be revisited later in the process. Still, having this framework at this stage will be very helpful to plan appropriately for conducting the in-country assessment tasks. The framework will provide team members with a set of working hypotheses that can be tested during their trip.

In this task, team members should attempt to integrate what they have learned into a short narrative that can be included in the assessment report and will help in elaborating a more complete strategic plan later in the assessment process.

- Analysis of the legal-institutional framework and the state of its implementation (Task 2) should have provided the team with an understanding of what are usually considered the prerequisites for effective anticorruption programs, including the gaps and deficiencies in the current context.
- From the political-economic analysis of Task 3, the team should have generated information about the underlying problems and causes of corruption and the anticorruption approaches that are likely to be helpful in developing a meaningful near- and long-term strategy.
- As well, the stakeholder analysis conducted under Task 3 should have identified likely opportunities and potential roadblocks in implementing an effective anticorruption program.
- The results of Task 4 provided the team with a layered understanding of *where* corruption vulnerabilities exist and must be addressed directly—by sector, function, and institution.

Together, these analyses provide the team with a wealth of information for this initial integrated analysis. The written narrative should include a discussion of the following:

1. The *core problems* that represent the underlying causes of corruption that have emerged from the initial analyses should be included. This ensures that the assessment does not deal merely with the visible symptoms of corruption but seeks to remedy problems that can have a more positive and long-lasting impact on the country. Core problems are usually described broadly and might include, for example, poor political accountability and competition, colonization of the civil service bureaucracy by political party loyalists, poor tax collection, weak governance institutions, or economic and political opportunities plundered by elite few. The syndrome profiles in table 5.1 provide particular problem statements that are common to each syndrome type and may be relevant to a particular country.
2. The *strategic goals* should be geared to specifically address the core problems. They propose broad basic approaches to remedy the identified problems. Core problem areas and key strategic directions common to particular corruption syndromes are included in table 5.3 on *syndrome implications*. These can include,

(*continues on p. 102*)

Table 5.3
Strategic Implications of Corruption Syndromes

TYPE 1: **Wealth Pursues Influence in Public Institutions**	TYPE 2: **High-Level Figures Collude to Weaken Political-Economic Competitors**
MAIN GOAL: Build capacity of citizens and civil society groups in the course of pursuing and defending their interests, punish corrupt officials and parties, and reward good governance with support, votes, and contributions. • Increase participation in, and credibility of, politics; build political trust; • Link corruption control to the interests of citizens and civil society groups; • Increase political competition of elections; • Increase legitimate access to decision makers; • Broaden base of funding election campaigns; • Combat deals to gain special access to officials and corrupt demands upon contributors.	**MAIN GOAL:** Increase political and economic competition at a moderate pace; link such opening-up processes to aid and other incentives. **CONSIDER:** • Monitor treatment and protect rights of emerging businesses, parties, and civil society groups; • Strengthen property rights; • Promote economic opportunities, political funding, and lending *not* dominated by elite; • Promote economic initiatives and investment from outside the country; • Promote conditionality linking aid to treatment of opposition groups and economic competitors, rewarding tolerance, transparency, and fairness; • Seek gradual pluralization of political system with new competing groups emerging based on open, vigorous, and broad-based economy; • Build independence and professionalism in the bureaucracy, courts, and legislative institutions.
CONSIDER: • Strengthening civil society and forces checking top politicians. Civil society efforts need not aim directly at corruption control but at effective voicing of group interests through politics; • Backing development of parties that represent real groups and interests rather than personal agendas and followings of top political figures; • Increasing political competition; • Monitoring bureaucracy's autonomy to prevent capture by politicians or private interests; • Where institutions, civil liberties, and rule of law are relatively secure, emphasize transparency in political funding and lobbying; • Use political finance systems to support competition and participation, not just to control flows of money; subsidies may be necessary.	**AVOID:** • Sudden political or economic threats to elites that may encourage repression or frantic theft; • Excessively fragmenting bureaucracy; • Starving the political process of funding; • Hope of quick results from strategic reforms; • Information-intensive reforms until competent and independent bureaucracy is in place; • Using conditionality and external resources to challenge regime directly; • Undervaluing unity and stability at top; remember that alternatives can be worse!
AVOID: • Starving politics of legitimate funds or inhibiting free expression and legitimate influence process; • Restricting bona fide constituent service; • Too much or too little bureaucratic autonomy; • Very technical and onerous political finance rules; • Stigmatizing self-interest or treating political parties as "civic" entities only; • Excessive public expectations about reform; • Forms of transparency that deter citizens; allow small anonymous contributions; • Free-rider problems; build on self-interest.	

(*continues*)

Table 5.3
(continued)

TYPE 3: Oligarchs Contend in a Setting of Pervasive Insecurity	TYPE 4: A Dominant Inner Circle Acts With Impunity
MAIN GOAL: Reduce insecurity and violence, build credible public and private institutions, and enable opposition to corruption to grow. **CONSIDER:** • Strengthening property rights; • Promote credible policies and implementation in a few areas (e.g., taxation, policing); • Promote stronger boundaries but easier and *legitimate* access between state and society; • Reduce "informal" economy, while making institutionalized markets more credible; • Promote predictable revenues for the state based on simple, effective, and fair taxation; • Protect citizens and small business from exploitation and abuse; • Over long term, reduce risks and unpredictability in markets; strengthen banking practices, bond and equity markets, and currency; • Over long term, promote stronger civil liberties, free and independent press, and honest elections. **AVOID:** • Anticorruption initiatives and agencies that can become weapons for rival oligarchs; • "Strong hand" options that create more insecurity; • Weak "ownership" of reforms that waste opportunities and credibility; • "Privatizations" that become licenses for theft; • Elections without socially rooted parties and procedural safeguards; • Massive public anticorruption campaigns that lack credibility; • Civil society strategies and elections until risks subside; • Sharp increases in competition that heighten elite insecurity; tolerate a degree of collusion.	**MAIN GOAL:** Gradual growth of political competition and independent power centers. • Credible official roles and institutions; eventual growth of "civic space"; • Accountability based on public, not personal, grounds; • Strengthen press and civil society gradually. **CONSIDER:** • Shielding private sector from official raids; create more secure property rights; • Establishing basic civil liberties rather than moving rapidly to full democracy; • Creating/strengthening incentives for officials to work for public, not political, patrons and gradually building social capacity to demand accountability, if not through elections then via organized groups; • Encouraging gradual emergence of a diverse national elite featuring a political class separate from top economic figures, where power and accountability rest on the rule of law; • Enlarging the scope of economic participation and decision making and offering existing elites economic rewards for accepting change. **AVOID:** • Rapid or sudden change; perceived threats to elites may put reform advocates and emerging civil society at risk; • Reforms and public morality campaigns that hide corruption or produce political reprisals; • Reforms (e.g., public management improvements) with short-term timelines: reforms require a long-term process; • Promoting civil society groups aimed solely at anticorruption and good governance agendas: their activities will be risky, and collective action problems may be severe; • Massive anticorruption campaigns and anticorruption agencies until it is clear they will not be personal tools of top figures.

for example, strengthening property rights, developing stronger boundaries between the state and business, decreasing the state's role in the economy, establishing systems for credible political competition and elections, generating systems of incentives for civil servants to work for the public good and not political patrons, developing an independent judiciary, and promoting an independent mass media.

As an example, the Senegal assessment team decided that the country was best described as a mixture of two corruption syndromes: Types 3 and 4, both characterized by weak institutions and increasingly centralized power personalized in a narrow leadership group. As a result, the strategic framework defined the core problems in terms of inadequate controls on executive decision making, a lack of accountability in delivering public services, a lack of transparency in government operations, and inadequate public demand and advocacy for change. Understanding the potential obstacles to reform at the central level, the team targeted its proposed strategic directions at promoting change through local government and civic participation, by building capacity in agencies that oversee public spending and procurement, and by applying pressure and conditionality by international and bilateral donors.

3. *Working hypotheses* should be formulated that reflect these core problems and strategic goals in a way that they can be tested—validated, refuted, or adjusted—by the information and insights collected by the team during its in-country activities. These hypotheses should get to the heart of why corruption plagues the targeted country and what broad approaches are likely to have positive impacts.

In-Country Steps

Task 6: Validation of Earlier Analyses

Upon arrival in country, the team should initially test the working hypotheses and preliminary strategic framework formulated during Task 5. Broad-ranging discussions with key observers of corruption, politics, and economics in the country, as well as more specific discussions with donor program and project managers, relevant embassy and international donor representatives, and key host government counterparts, should be planned in advance if possible and undertaken quickly. Individual interviews or focus group sessions are both effective. On the basis of these meetings, the team should assess whether the political-economic analysis, stakeholder mapping, and the strategic plan need to be adjusted.

During this task, it is also important to revisit the prioritization of sectors and functions that will be diagnosed in depth. Given the limited amount of time the team has in country, it is essential to bring the number of sectors and functions down to a reasonable number. To accomplish this, the team should systematically consider the following criteria:

- Are there major deficiencies and vulnerabilities, plus strong opportunities, in the sector or function?
- Does the sector or function fit into one or more of the core problem statements in the strategic plan?
- Is there strong political will and readiness among stakeholders in the sector or function?
- Are major programs already under way or planned by the government or donors in the sector or function?
- Do major obstacles to reform or internal resistance exist in the sector or function?
- Is there high donor priority for the sector or function?

Task 7: In-Depth Diagnosis of Sectors, Functions, and Institutions
Detailed diagnoses of risky sectors, functions, and institutions should be conducted based on document reviews, interviews, and focus groups with major stakeholders. The team can review existing sectoral literature for probing questions to ask in focus groups and interviews to pinpoint critical sector- or function-specific corruption weaknesses. This task will probably consume a major portion of the team's time in country.[10] The increasing number of corruption analyses produced by groups such as Transparency International and Global Integrity, as well as more specialized reports such as those on public financial management (www.pefa.org), may allow fairly detailed analysis of these sectors before the team even arrives.

As part of these detailed diagnoses, stakeholders within the sectors, functions, and institutions should be assessed to determine their support or opposition to reforms, their political will and capacity to act, and their leverage over others to make things happen. The stakeholder-mapping approach can be used again at the sector, function, and institution level, though teams do not necessarily need to produce detailed diagrams for each sector.

The diagnostic results need to be analyzed within the context of the initial strategic framework (Task 5), considering the key problem statements and priorities. For the report, a brief narrative analysis of each selected sector, function, and institution should be developed that includes an overview of the current situation, vulnerabilities to corruption, opportunities and obstacles to reducing these risks, and program option recommendations. These programmatic recommendations should be feasible within the country context and in concert with the overall strategic framework.

Task 8: Strategic Plan and Prioritized Recommended Options
In this last task, the initial strategic framework from Task 5 should be updated based on the sector, function, and institution diagnoses and developed into a strategic plan for an integrated anticorruption program. An illustrative structure for such a strategic plan is presented in table 5.4 that includes core problems, strategic goals, and implications for action. This table should be included in the assessment report to provide a rationale for the recommended programmatic options.

The proposed recommendations that were developed at a sectoral, functional, and institutional level need to be integrated and prioritized into a logical and reasonable plan in accordance with the strategy. There are likely to be some recommended options that are common across sectors or functions, for example, budgeting reform, procurement reform, and transparency activities. These might be bundled together as cross-sectoral options to avoid duplication of effort.

Many options usually arise during the course of discussions for the sector or function diagnoses. Other potentially innovative ideas can be gleaned by referring to international experience and lessons learned by donors, governments, and nongovernmental organizations in other countries. The assessment team should have access to relevant integrative reports that review and evaluate the track records and experiences of anticorruption programs in many countries across a wide range of sectoral and functional domains. An example of anticorruption recommendations derived from syndrome analysis and strategic goals developed in the assessment process is presented in table 5.5.

Typically, assessment teams generate too many recommendations across all sectors and functions for a donor to handle effectively. As a result, it is essential for teams to *delimit and prioritize* their recommendations. Several criteria are suggested to help the team pare down the number of recommendations and order them in terms of importance and likely impact:

Table 5.4
Illustrative Anticorruption Strategic Plan: Senegal 2007

Core Problems	Strategic Goals	Implications for Sectors, Functions, and Institutions
Core Problem 1: Inadequate checks on executive decision making	1.1 Strengthen judiciary and legislature 1.2 Strengthen local government	1.1.1 Take measures to reduce political interference 1.2.1 Widen the base of citizen participation in monitoring the budget
Core Problem 2: Lack of transparency in government operation	2.1 Promote high-level policy dialogue 2.2 Support selected oversight institutions	2.1.1 Address ways to develop independent regulatory and audit agencies 2.2.1 Establish independent watchdogs to monitor public contracts
Core Problem 3: Lack of quality and accountability in delivery of public services	3.1 Promote effective decentralization 3.2 Concentrate efforts in local-level key sector programs	3.1.1 Extend training in good governance to municipal officials 3.2.1 Establish professional codes of ethics in each sector
Core Problem 4: Ineffective public opposition to corruption	4.1 Support citizen oversight of government 4.2 Public education and diffusion of corruption's impact	4.1.1 Promote civil society analysis of good governance 4.2.1 Civic education via religious leaders and citizen movements

Source. Adapted from *Corruption Assessment: Senegal* (Washington, DC: Management Systems International, August 2007).

- Does the option satisfy the core problem statements in the strategic plan?
- Does the option satisfy existing or planned donor priorities?
- Does the assessment suggest likely success for the option?

Table 5.5
Implications of Syndrome Analysis for Strategy (for a Type 4 African Country Where a Dominant Inner Circle Acts With Impunity)

Guidance From Syndrome Analysis	Core Strategy Recommendations
Start with basic civil liberties and transparency.	Fix structural weaknesses in democracy and governance.
Without committed leadership, supply-side improvements have limited likelihood of success.	Focus on transparency in governance as a first step toward accountability.
Be careful about insecurity for advocates, and link public participation to concrete issues and possibly depoliticized ones.	Support demand-side capacity and activism, but look to groups active in other sectors (mainstreaming, local government).
Recognize the overall constraints of an unaccountable system: leaders may be more accountable to donors than to public.	Put heavy emphasis on donor or diplomatic role.

- Are there particular risks involved in proposing or implementing the option?
- How rapid is the likely program impact (near-, mid-, or long-term)?
- Is there political will and readiness among local stakeholders to embrace and implement the option?

Ultimately, the prioritized options need to fit in the overall strategic logic of the assessment's analysis, so they should be linked back to the core problems and strategic goals in the strategic plan. The final product of this task should be a well-considered integrated program for anticorruption action for the donor or host government to consider in the context of the overall corruption assessment report. Recommendations should be designated as short-, medium-, or long-term priorities. Each recommendation should be described briefly, major stakeholders and counterparts listed, potential obstacles to success recognized, anticipated impacts on corruption identified, and likelihood of success estimated. A sample recommendations table for the health sector in Honduras is presented in table 5.6. Depending on the donor's interest, resources required and/or recommended time frames may be important additions to such a table.

The accompanying narrative may need to explain why some potential program areas were *not* included as priorities, especially if they were of particular interest to the donor or the host government.

Other Considerations

Democracy and governance assessments. Democracy and governance (DG) assessments typically provide the broad political and institutional context within which a corruption assessment can be better understood. The corruption assessment examines governance, accountability, and transparency issues in great depth within the democracy and governance sector itself, as well as in other sectors and government functions. The DG assessment may in fact identify corruption as a key problem based on the confluence of weaknesses in the core characteristics of democracy, such as competition, rule of law, and governance. A corruption assessment should draw on the analysis in available DG assessments and go the next step by identifying the most promising and strategic ways of addressing the problem.

Fragile states. Corruption weakens governance practices, confounds the rule of law, and reduces government revenues that were meant to provide public services; these factors serve to promote fragility and deterioration of the state. At the same time, failing, failed, and recovering states operate within conditions that usually promote corruption; in fact, the use of corrupt practices may be the only way to get things done within a state that is incapacitated. The political-economic analysis within the corruption assessment framework views the state of institutional capacity as very important in framing the nature and spread of corruption; it establishes parameters for accountability and control of corruption. Fragile states and those rebuilding after conflict have greater hurdles to overcome than typical developing states.[11]

Gender considerations. There is some evidence that corruption affects men and women differently and that there are gender differences in the response to corruption. While conducting corruption assessments, especially during the detailed diagnostic phase (Task 7), the team should inquire about the following gender-related issues within sectors and government functions where corruption risks are deemed to be high:

- What is the variable impact of corruption on men and women? In each sector or function, are there significant differences in the extent to which men and women interact with potentially rent-seeking government officials? What are they? In each sector or

(continues on p. 110)

Table 5.6

Prioritized Recommendations: Honduras 2008

Anticorruption Program Option	Priority	Major Counterparts	Potential Obstacles	Anticipated Impact on Corruption	Likelihood of Short-Term Success
Strategic Goal 1: Depoliticize Government Institutions and Enhance Accountability					
Enhance Health Ministry capacity to make purchases of medications and other public health inputs more transparent.	Short term	Health Ministry (MOH), State Procurement Office, National Anticorruption Council	Bureaucratic inertia and interference by corrupt stakeholders to prevent reform.	Could close a grand corruption avenue with a substantial positive impact on health standards.	Potentially significant
Proactively incorporate corruption prevention interventions in health sector.	Medium term	MOH, National Anticorruption Council, Supreme Audit Agency	None if resources are available.	Significant if anticorruption practices introduced during the program design stage prove effective.	Not likely

Strategic Goal 2: Support Civil Society in Advocating for Anticorruption and Overseeing Government Agencies

Systematize and disseminate best social audit practices applicable to the health care sector.	Medium term	MOH, National Anticorruption Council, Supreme Audit Agency, municipal transparency committees, NGOs	Complexity of endeavor, resistance by local authorities.	Major in communities willing to become actively involved in the initiative.	Potentially significant
Decentralization of the management of financial resources for health.	Long term	MOH, National Anticorruption Council, Supreme Audit Agency, municipal administrative authorities, municipal transparency committees, NGOs	Difficulties in implementing decentralization process, particularly in light of weak local management capacity.	Considerable to the extent that the decentralization process is effectively implemented in a transparent and accountable manner at the local level.	Not likely in light of time required for program to be initiated and implemented across Honduras. Disparities in local management capacity will reduce possibility of short-term success.

Source. Adapted from *Honduras Corruption Assessment Report* (Washington, DC: Management Systems International, October 2008).

function, are there significant differences in the impact of corrupt practices on men and women in terms of degraded public services, lost income, and so on? What are those differences?

• What are feasible and promising approaches to address the differential impact of corruption among men and women? How much awareness exists of the differential impact of corruption among men and women? In each sector or function, are there significant differences in gender participation in citizen advocacy aimed at controlling corrupt practices? Can program options be developed that promote realistic gender participation in combating corruption and build on unique interests and opportunities for men and women to participate?

Case Studies

The following chapters present four case studies that applied this assessment framework—in Ukraine, Senegal, Honduras, and Timor Leste. These assessments were all conducted between 2005 and 2009.

Notes

1. Michael Johnston, Svetlana Winbourne, and Mary Liakos contributed to an earlier version of this chapter.

2. Management Systems International. February 2009a. *Corruption Assessment Handbook*. Washington, DC: MSI.

3. Bertram I. Spector, editor. 2005. *Fighting Corruption in Developing Countries: Strategies and Analysis*. Bloomfield, CT: Kumarian Press; J. Edgardo Campos and Sanjay Pradhan, editors. 2007. *The Many Faces of Corruption: Tracking Vulnerabilities at the Sector Level*. Washington, DC: World Bank.

4. Daniel Kaufmann. March 11, 2003. "Rethinking Governance: Empirical Lessons Challenge Orthodoxy." http://papers.ssrn.com/sol3/papers.cfm?abstract_id=386904.

5. Organisation for Economic Co-operation and Development [OECD]. 2005. "Paris Declaration on Aid Effectiveness." www.oecd.org/document/18/0,3343,en_2649_3236398_35401554_1_1_1_1,00.html.

6. OECD. 2007. "Policy Paper and Principles on Anti-Corruption: Setting an Agenda for Collective Action." Development Assistance Committee Guidelines and Reference Series. http://www.oecd.org/dataoecd/2/42/39618679.pdf.

7. Michael Johnston. 2005. *Syndromes of Corruption*. New York: Cambridge University Press.

8. For more detailed case studies that describe these syndromes, refer to Johnston (2005).

9. For more information on constructing macro- and micro-political maps, please refer to Derick Brinkerhoff and Benjamin Crosby. 2002. "Political and Institutional Mapping." In *Managing Policy Reform*. Bloomfield, CT: Kumarian Press.

10. See the USAID website for the "Corruption Assessment Handbook" and for its "Library of Illustrative Diagnostic Guides," which features 19 targeted sets of questions for assessing sector-specific corruption vulnerabilities (www.usaid.gov). For example, in the health care sector, diagnostic questions home in on corruption risks in (1) the provision of services by frontline health workers; (2) health care fraud; (3) procurement and management of equipment and supplies, including pharmaceuticals; (4) regulation of quality in products, services, facilities, and personnel; (5) the education of health professionals; and (6) hiring and promotion. In a very different sector, the elections process, diagnostic questions examine (1) the independence of the elections commission, (2) the institutional capacity of the commission, (3) accountability of the commission, (4) integrity mechanisms, (5) transparency of the process, (6) complaints and enforcement mechanisms, and (7) election fairness provisions.

11. Bertram I. Spector. 2011. *Negotiating Peace and Confronting Corruption: Challenges for Postconflict Societies*. Washington, DC: US Institute of Peace Press.

6

Ukraine 1 (2005)

In early 2005, after years of state control and systemic corruption, Ukraine appeared poised to adopt a Western-style market economy based on transparency, the rule of law, and fair competition. Much of this new optimism stemmed from the 2004 election of opposition leader Viktor Yushchenko, who won the presidency after massive public demonstrations, known as the Orange Revolution, protested suspect election results favoring his conservative competitor. Having achieved popular support with his promises of anticorruption policies and Western-style reforms, Yushchenko faced high expectations from both the local populace and the international community. "We will destroy corruption and bring the economy out of the shadows," he vowed to cheering supporters at his inauguration in January 2005.[1]

By the end of that year, however, the anticorruption promise of the Orange Revolution appeared to be fading. Ukraine lacked a clear strategic direction against corruption and accompanying programs to increase transparency, strengthen accountability, and build integrity. Citizens and businesspeople continued to experience widespread, visible corruption in their daily lives, and grand corruption continued extensively in higher levels of government, where substantial political influence and money were at stake.

In November 2005, the US Agency for International Development (USAID), among other donors, seeking to bolster the new regime and its lagging anticorruption objectives, commissioned a corruption assessment to pinpoint the underlying causes of corruption and its manifestations across sectors and to develop a plan for recommended action. This chapter presents the results from that assessment from late 2005.

Legal-Institutional Analysis

Ukraine's principal policy document on national anticorruption strategy—*The Concept on Fighting Corruption for 1998–2005*—provided general direction but failed to offer benchmarks and specific terms. The government also frequently drafted Plans of Action to Fight Organized Crime and Corruption, which were typically Soviet-style in their format and evaluation procedures, and often proved to be ineffective and even harmful. In 2005, President Yushchenko issued the first policy document by the new administration calling for strengthened measures in several corruption areas: on urgent measures to deshadow the economy and counteract corruption (No. 1615/2005). The decree touched on a number of important issues, but its measures appeared random, disconnected, and inefficient. For instance, three separate agencies were established to draft new national anticorruption strategies and concepts at the time: the Parliamentary Committee Against Organized Crime and Corruption, the State Security Service, and the Ministry of Justice. While the government seemed to be aware of these dispersed efforts, little had been done to consolidate these drafts into one document, though the parties appeared to be in favor of joining forces and were ready to start a dialogue.

In terms of anticorruption enforcement legislation, the principal existing laws included the Law of Ukraine on Fighting Corruption (adopted in 1995) and the Criminal Code (Part 17, in particular). Most experts and practitioners agreed that the anticorruption law needed further modification or outright replacement to harmonize it with modern international legal standards. Several draft amendments had been introduced in the Verkhovna Rada (parliament), including one submitted in July 2004 to replace the anticorruption law.

Enforcement of anticorruption legislation was problematic, however. It had often been used as an instrument of suppression or political retribution against lower-level officials. After the Yushchenko administration came to power, many investigations into high-profile corruption allegations were initiated, but there were few court hearings.

Several pieces of important corruption prevention legislation were also under consideration in late 2005, addressing public hiring and appointments, asset disclosure, and sunshine laws (requiring that meetings of boards or commissions must be open to the public). Several laws already existed to regulate public access to information, but implementation of the laws was very uneven, and several NGOs had found frequent abuses of citizen rights related to information access. Governmental bodies were obligated to have mechanisms to collect and respond to citizen complaints, and almost every governmental agency had recently introduced telephone and web-based hotlines. Presidential Public Reception offices had also recently opened in all oblasts and reported a mounting number of complaints. No whistleblower law existed, however, to protect public officials or civil servants who reported on corruption or misconduct in their agencies. In terms of conflict of interest issues, applicable laws were limited and generally did not apply to high-level public officials.

Ukraine had signed or ratified several international conventions, committing itself to join the Council of Europe Group of States Against Corruption (GRECO) and to implement its recommendations, and reactivating its cooperation under the OECD-sponsored Anticorruption Network for Transition Economies. Fighting corruption was also highlighted among the top three objectives of the Yushchenko administration's governmental program, Towards the People. However, after the administration had been in office for almost a year, no significant, consistent, and visible actions had been accomplished. High-level rhetoric about fighting corruption had not been translated into clear messages or deeds.

Coordinating Institutions

At the beginning of 2005, there was no single institution in the executive branch or any interagency institution responsible for fighting corruption in a comprehensive and cross-sectoral fashion. Thus, the agreement establishing the National Security and Defense Council (NSDC) as the anticorruption coordinator within the Ukrainian government signaled a starting point for real dialogue among governmental agencies. By November 2005, the secretary of the NSDC announced that an Interregional Commission Against Corruption would be established to coordinate anticorruption-related activities of the Security Service of Ukraine, Ministry of Internal Affairs, prosecutor general, and representatives of the court system. The commission would also include representatives from the legislature and civil society organizations.

The other institution that was poised to play a substantial role in anticorruption efforts was the then recently established Presidential Commission on Democracy and the Rule of Law, chaired by the minister of justice. The major objective of the commission was to align Ukrainian policy with the Copenhagen criteria regulating membership to the EU and to implement an EU–Ukraine action plan. There were several activities under the action plan that directly or indirectly related to fighting and preventing corruption.

Oversight Institutions

There were several governmental institutions whose mission it was to oversee the executive branch, and some of them were directly involved in overseeing corruption abuses. The parliament, for one, had maintained oversight over corruption issues since 1992, when the first Temporary Parliamentary Commission was established. Since 1994, the parliament had a permanent

Parliamentary Committee Against Organized Crime and Corruption, which reviews governmental and other annual reports on corruption, among other functions. The committee was very active in promoting anticorruption policies and initiating new legislation. It drafted an anticorruption strategy on its own initiative, an action that its committee head described as setting a positive example while pushing the executive branch to develop and implement a national anticorruption policy.

The Ombudsman Office did not play a significant role in fighting or preventing corruption. While it collected thousands of citizen complaints, it did not analyze this information to identify problem trends but rather acted on a case-by-case basis and rarely passed this information to the offending governmental institutions to bring their attention to abuses and violations. The Ombudsman's Annual Report to parliament primarily contained statistics on complaints and complainers but no systematic analysis or recommendations for reform.

The Accounts Chamber was an independent governmental oversight institution that was empowered to conduct performance and financial control and analysis of all governmental programs and institutions and to review how legislation was implemented. The chamber was proactive in its efforts to reach out to governmental institutions to improve legislation and practices. It cooperated with the Prosecutor's Office and monitored the further development of cases it passed to the prosecutor for investigation. In 2004, the chamber uncovered the misuse or ineffective use of budget and extra-budgetary funds totaling over US$1.5 billion.

The Main Control and Revision Office of Ukraine under the Ministry of Finance conducted financial audits of budget expenditures. It performed such audits for over 15,000 organizations and agencies funded from the public budget on an annual basis. During the first nine months of 2005, the office uncovered the unlawful use or misappropriation of public funds in the amount of about US$200,000, recovering about US$71,000.

Law Enforcement Institutions

Most of Ukraine's law enforcement agencies (e.g., police, tax police, Prosecutor's Office) that had responsibility to fight corruption were typically rated as being the most corrupted governmental institutions in public opinion surveys. In 2005, law enforcement reforms were being developed, but it was too early to tell how the new policies would affect internal controls and law enforcement effectiveness in fighting corruption.

In March 2005, the president issued an order to establish a working group that would draft a concept to create a National Bureau of Investigation with responsibilities to investigate high-profile crime and corruption. An attempt to establish such a bureau in 1997 had failed, in part, because of a disagreement among law enforcement agencies about the role of the bureau and the division of responsibilities. Since then, there had been at least seven drafts to establish a new bureau. This latest idea was forcefully debated, though many experts believed that strengthening and reforming existing agencies would be more effective.

Other Governmental Institutions

The Main Department of Civil Service of Ukraine became very engaged in 2005, issuing guidance on how to prevent and detect corrupt behavior in the civil service system at all levels and jurisdictions. However, there appeared to be no attempt to establish indicators to assess the effectiveness of these measures and to monitor implementation.

The Tax Administration adopted an Anticorruption Action Plan for 2004–2008. This plan established a code of ethics, a special Anticorruption Department, and regulations on job responsibilities. The Anticorruption Department issued monthly reports on internal investigations and results and posted them on its website. For the first eight months of 2005, regional branches conducted 2,259 internal investigations, of which about 30% were triggered by citizen complaints. This resulted in administrative sanctions against 1,078 employees, including 142 who were fired. The department also conducted preventive measures through training Tax Administration staff and conducting public outreach programs.

The Customs Administration aggressively pursued a campaign against corruption and abuses of power in its operations. By 2005, it removed or rotated executive staff members, conducted about 100 internal investigations resulting in over 200 dismissals and administrative sanctions, opened a hotline for citizens, imposed a set of rules and restrictions for its personnel, and set limits for the amount of cash officers could carry while on duty. One-stop shops for processing freight customs clearances were also introduced to reduce business-government interactions and opportunities for bribe taking and bribe giving. It issued a "Stop Card" that businesses could use against customs officers who created unjustified delays or other barriers during customs procedures. Officers who received these cards were investigated by internal control units.

Civil Society Organizations

Civil society organizations and business associations are potential sources of demand and pressure on government for reform. The number of NGOs in

Ukraine is on the upswing, from 25,500 in 2000 to approximately 40,000 in 2004, of which only about 10% are considered to be active.[2] According to a 2003 report, the largest percentage of Ukrainian NGOs was involved in training, advocacy and lobbying, and information dissemination.[3]

Despite the incredible force they exerted during the Orange Revolution, Ukraine's civil society and businesses do not appear to offer a cohesive and mature platform to push for change. There are few strong advocacy or watchdog groups, and they have limited access to information about government operations and limited experience using information as a tool to force government action. These deficiencies can be attributed to NGO avoidance of highly charged policy debates, their underdeveloped management capacity, and their overdependence on foreign donors. For its part, the business community was poorly organized, with only about 25% of businesses belonging to associations. Most businesses expressed deep skepticism about their associations' willingness and capacity to provide services to members and represent member interests.

There did exist, however, a number of local and national NGOs and business groups that conducted very effective advocacy and watchdog functions related to anticorruption reforms. For example, the All-Ukraine Network for People Living With HIV/AIDS gathered difficult-to-access cost data on pharmaceutical procurements conducted by the Ukrainian Ministry of Health (MOH) and compared them with similar procurements conducted by the Global Fund to Fight AIDS also in Ukraine. They uncovered extremely wide cost differentials, with MOH procurements as high as 27 times the cost that the Global Fund paid for the same medications. Apparently, collusion, special deals, and kickbacks between the MOH procurement commission and vendors were producing very unfavorable results and depriving needy patients of their required drugs. The network presented its results to the MOH, the Ombudsman, the Prosecutor's Office, and international donors. Further investigations were launched to validate the network's findings, and donors halted their contributions to the MOH.

Other groups, such as the Laboratory for Legislative Initiatives, conducted very professional watchdog monitoring activities of Rada deputies. The laboratory maintained a "report card" website that contained deputies' campaign promises, their complete voting records, their links to business interests, and whether they had kept their campaign promises.

Among business associations, the Coordinating Expert Center of the Entrepreneurs' Union of Ukraine, uniting over 60 business associations, had been successful in promoting business-friendly legislation. Another strong voice for business interests was the Council of Entrepreneurs, the advisory body to the

Cabinet of Ministers. Although it was established by government decree, it became very active in monitoring regulatory reform implementation and serving as a channel for direct dialogue between the government and the business community.

Mass Media

With certain exceptions, the mass media in Ukraine was deficient in investigative reporting, a major channel by which journalists can serve as effective public watchdogs. The media suffered from the lack of public access to government information and from a poor understanding of the linkages between the law, the judicial system, and corruption. Since the Orange Revolution, however, the clans' and cartels' strong control of media outlets was reduced, and repressive actions against these outlets were relaxed.[4]

Political-Economic Analysis

Several factors facilitate the spread of corruption throughout a wide range of sectors and government functions in Ukraine. As indicated earlier, the basic legal framework as it relates to corruption, transparency, accountability, and integrity required major revisions, amendments, and additions. Drafts of many of these legal changes had been on hold in the parliament for years, with little accompanying public discussion. Existing laws and regulations were selectively enforced, however, as they were subject to political and business influence and corrupt practices. Excessive discretion was exercised by public and elected officials at all levels.

The national government also wielded undue influence over the economy, with excessive regulation that provided numerous opportunities for corrupt behavior. The government cultivated close ties with the country's economic elite in a mutually advantageous system that provided enhanced political influence to those with lucrative business interests. Moreover, the highly centralized nature of the government's operations and decisions—and its adamant resistance to decentralization—helped to maintain these collusive practices among the elite.

These types of activities flourished in the general absence of checks and balances traditionally provided by other government branches. The judicial and executive branches possessed little independence and oversight capacity. The civil service was highly subject to political manipulation due to extensive clan influence in hiring, low salaries, and minimally adequate candidates for bureaucratic positions due to the low salaries. The absence of a strong ethic of professionalism and enforced performance standards within the bureaucracy, along with unclear regulations and poor procedures, created opportunities for excessive discretion and abuse of office.

Civil society also generally lacked the capacity to serve as an effective accountability mechanism. There were few citizen watchdog groups that monitored and oversaw government departments and their use of the public budget. Moreover, investigative journalists, often natural watchdogs of government operations, had not been a major force for transparency and accountability. As a result, transparency in government decisions and activities was uneven, with inadequate public access to information.

The excessive power of the executive branch was further exacerbated by infrequent internal and external audits and inspections and little authority within judicial or administrative systems to impose sanctions even when abuses were identified. As a result, corruption was generally viewed as a low-risk activity for most public officials, who believed they could act with impunity.

Even in this kind of environment, if political will existed at the top levels, some positive actions could have been taken by executive decree at a minimum. However, many of the presidential decrees that had been put forth had served primarily as rhetorical platforms and had not yielded real change. Recent presidential directives on corruption issues sent to several ministries and top-level agencies seemed to only cause confusion, with several agencies drafting uncoordinated national anticorruption strategies and proposed structural changes.

Despite this discouraging picture, many factors in Ukraine had the potential to inhibit corrupt behaviors and facilitate the promotion of good governance, assuming the necessary commitment on the part of leaders. For one, the Orange Revolution had mobilized popular frustration about corruption, and President Yushchenko had pledged to deal effectively with the problem. The sacking of the cabinet in fall 2005, primarily over corruption problems, seemed like an indication of political will to follow up on the president's rhetoric. Yushchenko had also directed several ministries and agencies to develop a national anticorruption strategy and to formulate a new Anticorruption Commission.

The Presidential Secretariat had also recently released a memorandum outlining successful actions taken over the past year to deal with the problem of corruption.[5] These included reforms in the State Customs Service that resulted in large increases in collected revenues, several State Tax Administration workshops for officers on corruption issues, and increased activities by the Central Department of the Civil Service to enhance the legal literacy of public officials. In addition, adherence to recruitment procedures for civil service applicants was made much more stringent.

On the basis of this analysis and use of the assessment methodology described earlier in chapter 5, Ukraine could be categorized as an "elite cartel" syndrome in 2005 (Type 2), where top political and business figures collude behind a façade of political competition and colonize both the state apparatus and sections of the economy (see table 5.1 in chapter 5). From the early 1990s onward, powerful officials in Ukraine's government and politics acquired and privatized key economic resources of the state. Shadowy businesses, allegedly close to organized crime, became powerful economic forces in several regions of the country.[6] Over the course of the following decade, these business groupings—or *clans*, as they were called—grew into major financial-industrial structures that exerted their influence over the government, political parties, mass media, and state bureaucracy in order to enlarge and fortify their control over the economy and other sources of wealth. They used ownership ties, special privileges, relations with government, and direct influence over the courts and law enforcement and regulatory organizations to circumvent weaknesses in governmental institutions. Their tactics and their results can be viewed as a clear exercise of *state and regulatory capture.*

A 2004 report by the World Bank refers to this clan-based elite cartel syndrome in Ukraine as a "closed insider economy" that can be an obstacle to future sustainable economic growth and integration into the EU and world economy.[7] It hinders fair competition, encourages under-the-table deals and collusion between state officials and business, promotes rent-seeking behaviors, discourages foreign investment, and decreases adaptability over time.

In more recent years, several Ukrainian clans have grown and subdivided, increasing the number of clans that compete with one another for wealth and power and establishing what appears to the Western eye as an incipient competitive market economy. Sometimes, for convenience, these clans coalesce on political issues.

After the Orange Revolution, the network of "bosses" within the government bureaucracy who could "make things happen" for the clans was partially destroyed by Prime Minister Yulia Tymoshenko, resulting in instability and uncertainty and a slowdown for major businesses. It was unclear, however, if the Yushchenko government would be able to seize the opportunity to create new administrative procedures and institutions based on fair and equitable rules and a professional, meritocratic, and disciplined bureaucracy.

To move elite cartel countries such as Ukraine away from corruptive clan practices, state, political, and social institutions need to be strengthened, and existing trends toward increasingly open political and market competition must continue on a *gradual* path. The behind-the-scenes collusion, favoritism, and colonization of bureaucracies and economic sectors that mark elite cartel corruption suggest that the "consensus package" of liberalization, improved public management, and enhanced transparency may be productive, as long as change is accompanied by institution building in the state, political, economic, and social realms.

Proposed Strategic Directions

The preceding analysis suggests several strategic directions for future anticorruption progress in Ukraine. The following core strategies establish specific goals.

Support establishment of the prerequisite conditions for effective anticorruption programs. The legal, policy, and institutional frameworks for the government and civil society to pursue major and comprehensive anticorruption programs are not fully established. Since the Orange Revolution, it appears as if the political will and trajectories exist to upgrade or revise these frameworks to establish a strong foundation for future activity. Donor support is warranted to bring these frameworks to the required levels of competence.

Support the development of strong demand-side pressure for anticorruption reforms. The revolution clearly demonstrated the power and inclination of Ukrainian civil society and media to make their voices heard and demand reform. More capacity building is needed, as well as organizational coordination across civil society organizations, to establish them as a permanent and forceful source of external demand on government. Support for watchdog and advocacy activities should be provided.

Support supply-side institutions contingent on visible demonstration of their political will. There is much rhetoric by government leaders about their desire to reduce and control corruption but little demonstrated action or progress. Major donors can be encouraged to enhance their dialogue, coordination, and messages to the government. Moreover, they can develop a set of clear benchmarks and initiate a monitoring and evaluation program by which positive actions and results demonstrating the government's sincere commitment to anticorruption goals can be measured and tracked. If demonstrated progress can be presented, then the government should be rewarded with appropriate technical assistance and resources.

Mainstream anticorruption activities throughout the portfolio of donor programs. Donors should seek ways to inject anticorruption objectives and activities into all their programs in Ukraine—across all sectors and functions. This mainstreaming approach will yield a more comprehensive and visible assault against corruption. Donors should encourage the Ukrainian government and civil society groups to do the same.

Intermediate initiatives to achieve these core strategies include the following:

Support implementation of transparency initiatives. Many Ukrainian laws and regulations mandate transparency, publication of government information, and openness in government operations. However, implementation of these requirements does not always meet the necessary standards. Donors should apply pressure to government agencies to achieve their transparency objectives quickly. Where technical assistance is reasonably required to meet these goals, it can be offered. Demand from civil society for improved government transparency should be generated and supported.

Support programs at the central and local levels. While the drama of the Orange Revolution and political pronouncements against corruption occurred in Kyiv, much can be done to deal with the problem at the regional and local levels, where the effects of corruption are felt most personally. As a result, donor programs should be targeted at both central and subnational levels to allow for trickle-down and trickle-up effects.

Promote an independent judiciary and improve access to information. Support programs for court reform would ensure a separation of powers that will reduce executive interference in judicial decision making. A major objective of donor support should be not only to strengthen public and media access to information but also to build the capacity of civil society, business, and the media to *use* the information to which they gain access to effectively monitor and oversee government functions.

Promote a professional bureaucracy. Emphasize efforts to shore up administrative quality, autonomy, and professionalism in the civil service, and sustain them over the long run.

Support economic competition. Strengthening and expanding ongoing programs to enhance economic competition will reduce opportunities for state capture by monopolistic forces. The subdivision of business-administrative groups into competing units is a positive sign that will dilute the influence of each particular elite group. Promoting economic and political competition at all levels will reduce the extent of state capture by economic elite over time.

Promote anticorruption programs in key sectors and functional areas. This and other assessments have shown that corruption in Ukraine is widespread and affects almost all government sectors and functions. Since donors cannot direct their anticorruption efforts against *all* sectors and functions, this assessment identifies and analyzes a small number of key areas where corruption weaknesses are high, but opportunities to deal with the corruption problems are available and strong.

Promote high-level diplomatic dialogue and multidonor pressure. Since the revolution, anticorruption efforts have risen on the Ukrainian political agenda to the highest level. To capitalize on this status, high-level diplomatic dialogue and multidonor pressure are needed, along with anticorruption donor programming, to mobilize Ukrainian counterparts and ensure that there continues to be strong movement forward.

Analysis of Key Sectors

The assessment team asked six Ukrainian experts to rate a large number of government sectors and functions in terms of the extent of corruption, the existence of an adequate legal and regulatory framework to deal with corruption problems, and the adequacy of implementation mechanisms. Sectors that ranked high were validated against open-ended interviews conducted with additional Ukrainian specialists. Here, we summarize the assessment results for the judicial sector, public finance, the private sector, and subnational government.

Judicial Sector

In public opinion surveys, the judicial system typically scores as one the most highly corrupted institutions in Ukraine. The sector lacks necessary independence from the executive branch of government, suffers from excessive discretion on the part of judges and court administrators, lacks sufficient internal controls to effectively reduce abuse of power, and is not sufficiently transparent in its procedures and decisions. Many of these issues stem from inadequate legal, regulatory, and institutional frameworks, which are compounded by chronic underfunding of the judicial budget.

In 2005, several draft laws were under consideration in the Verkhovna Rada to correct some of these problems. Adoption of these laws, followed by meaningful and rapid implementation, would demonstrate the government's political will to reduce corruption in the judicial sector. One law that was enacted established a registry of judicial decisions.[8]

Major points of vulnerability to corruption in the judicial sector include the following:

Judicial selection. Despite a thin veil of merit-based competition for judicial recruitment and appointments, there were extensive corruption problems in the selection process. Patronage from the Heads of Court (who were appointed by the president) was essential to get appointed to a court seat. In larger cities, where competition was greatest, seats on the general jurisdiction courts could allegedly be bought for US$2,000 from the Head of Court. In addition, the process of testing in the Qualification Commissions was not transparent. The Presidential Secretariat, which had no role in the appointment process by law, had inserted itself into the process and could remove or instate judicial candidates at will. The result of these problems was a judiciary plagued by favoritism, nepotism, and political influence.

Judicial discipline. There was minimal monitoring and oversight of judicial conduct. Disciplinary investigations, hearings, and punishment were very infrequent. In this atmosphere, judges tended to believe that they could act with impunity.

Court procedures and administration. Interference in judicial decision making by the executive and parliamentary branches, higher-level judges, and businesspeople was common. At the same time, the Heads of Court maintained strict control over case allocation, vacation vouchers, bonuses, and equipment and facility budgets; there was little control over their discretion on these matters. Court clerks received minimal oversight. Another problem was a lack of transparency—there were few open trials in Criminal Court or oral hearings in Commercial Court, and court decisions were not published regularly. As a result, the law was applied unequally or with excessive discretion.

Budgetary dependence. Financial and administrative autonomy was also compromised, as the State Judicial Administration, whose head and deputy were appointed by the president, was responsible for the court system's budget, facilities, and logistics. This arrangement placed the judicial system in an overly dependent position relative to the executive branch.

Enforcement of judicial decisions. Enforcement of judicial decisions was the responsibility of the Ministry of Justice's State Enforcement Department, which was not extremely effective and allegedly subject to corrupt practices.

The Environment for Reform

At the time of the assessment, certain conditions and developments affected the environment for judicial reform in both positive and negative ways. Several key actors in Ukraine's government appeared receptive to reform. The Rada Committee on Legal Policy had established a working group to synthesize 15 draft laws into a single draft amending the 2002 Code on the Judicial System, which it hoped would be discussed and adopted by the Rada immediately after the 2006 legislative elections. Ukraine's justice minister, Serhiy Holovaty, was seen as a genuine reformer and was leading a national commission to develop a strategy addressing rule of law and judicial reform issues. In addition, the Council of Judges, a self-governing body of judges, could be called on to handle executive independence issues that plagued the judiciary.

Recent administrative and policy changes represented positive steps in the anticorruption effort. A major salary increase for all judges was scheduled to go into effect January 1, 2006, with the intent of eliminating bribe taking due to low wages. The Rada had also just approved a new law to establish a registry of judicial decisions, publicizing court rulings for the first time and increasing accountability for judges. In addition, an Administrative Court had recently been established to offer a new venue for citizen-government problems. However, the court was operating without an Administrative Procedures Code, its planned regional and appellate division expansion was not sufficiently funded, and its judicial selection procedures suffered from the same problems as the other jurisdictional courts.

Extreme case overload was also a continuing problem, largely because of the fact that over 1,500 judicial positions were left vacant. Judges often had inadequate training, and excessive political and economic influence over judges was difficult to control. The basic ingredients of an effective judicial system were also lacking—the court system budget was wholly inadequate, barely covering salary costs, and there was extensive leakage of funds in the distribution of the budget to the courts. Moreover, the Criminal Procedure Code was an outmoded holdover from Soviet times and badly needed modernization.

Recommendations
Given this analysis, a set of recommendations to address corruption problems in the judicial sector was developed. Many of these suggestions were contingent on the adoption by parliament of effective judicial reform laws and implementation of technical assistance promised by donor organizations. Some of the highlights are presented below.

Judicial Selection
- Provide technical assistance to the Qualification Commission to design criteria, improve testing procedures, develop merit-based assignment procedures, and conduct training programs at the Academy of Judges.
- Institute control mechanisms to reduce the influence of the Heads of Court in the selection process.

- Set up an electronic registry to track judicial candidate processing and support the assignment and placement of judges.

Judicial Discipline
- Adopt a preventive approach, randomizing case allocation and strengthening the Code of Judicial Conduct, with associated monitoring and enforcement of the code by the self-governing body of judges (the Council of Judges).

Court Procedures and Administration
- Transfer authority over the State Judicial Administration to the Supreme Court, and support the design of the administration's internal regulatory framework and its organizational and budgetary training.
- Publish court decisions systematically on the Internet. This will help make judges more accountable for their decisions.
- Develop and adopt alternative dispute resolution mechanisms to reduce case overload.
- Strengthen and clarify court administration procedures and make them more transparent. Provide training in these procedures to court management staff.
- Develop and enact civic education programs for high schools that include, among other topics, the workings of the judicial system.

Enforcement of Judicial Decisions
- Reinforce the bailiff function, and develop stronger control and oversight mechanisms.

Public Finance
Vulnerabilities related to public finance typically emanate from three weaknesses: a poor legal and regulatory framework, weak capacity (technical, organizational, and human resources), and a lack of transparency and oversight. Specific technical problems exist (e.g., Ukraine uses the cash basis of accounting rather than the more appropriate accrual basis), and strengthening government capacity might have a positive impact.[9] Likewise, while the legal and regulatory framework is far from ideal (at the time, there was no freedom of information law, for example), a number of existing laws, decrees, and regulations do provide for obligatory transparency and accountability, notably in the

budget and procurement areas. Ukraine has experienced the following deficiencies in the public finance sector.

Budget. In 2005, the legal and technical aspects of the budget process in Ukraine generally complied with international standards and were consistent with EU requirements. There were, however, two concerns. First, the Ukrainian government did not appear to offer extensive opportunities for citizen involvement in the process at either the national or the local levels. While there were some public hearings or opportunities to present testimony or analysis to the Verkhovna Rada, there was little evidence that such input had any impact on the budget.

Second, and more important, the transparency of the budget and its execution were quite low. While the government did, indeed, provide extensive information to the public (posting the budget proposal on the Verkhovna Rada website, for example), it did not necessarily include amendments or the legislature's discussions of them. Many budget numbers were available only in summary form. Interbudgetary transfer calculations used complicated formulas that often lacked justification. Variances from the budget on either the expenditure side or the revenue side were typically not reported, even when the variance was significant. Annual reports lacked important information on certain assets, and there were no longer-term budget forecasts.

Budget information for the social funds was particularly opaque,[10] as were subnational government budgets. Even information that is required by law to be made public was often not provided. As one report noted, "Officials use excuses like 'the information is not available temporarily,' 'the requested data has not been collected yet' and 'the data cannot be disseminated because of technical difficulties.'"[11]

Procurement. The procurement review board did not include nongovernmental actors, and there was little citizen input into what items and services were procured. Moreover, the policies for contesting a procurement decision were weak. The practice of competitive tendering was relatively new to Ukraine at the time, and a large portion of public expenditures was still spent through a multiple-bid system that fell far short of full and open competition. This indicated a system inherently susceptible to political or corrupt manipulations.

Taxation. The State Tax Administration administered all taxes in Ukraine. The main revenue sources were personal and business income taxes, VAT, and excise taxes on items such as alcohol, tobacco, and certain entrepreneurial activities. At the time of the assessment, tax laws and regulations were not always clear, changed often, contained numerous loopholes, and could conflict internally. Administrative procedures for tax collection and management were likewise unclear. This resulted in a high level of tax evasions, very large collections arrears, and an extremely large shadow economy.[12]

In addition, citizens complained that taxpayers' rights were routinely violated. Tax exemptions or tax breaks were typically granted by the legislative branch as a result of lobbying—a clear manifestation of state capture by influential business. In 2004, a tax reform was implemented with the intent of reducing tax rates, simplifying legislation, and eliminating many loopholes and exceptions. It lowered the profit tax for enterprises from 30% to 25% and introduced a flat 13% tax on personal incomes.

Audit. The Ukrainian government has the appropriate internal and external audit agencies. External audits were performed by the Accounting Chamber of Ukraine (ACU). It was independent, reported to the parliament, and appeared free from political and operational interference. The internal audit function was managed by the Chief Control and Auditing Administration, reporting to the Ministry of Finance. Both of the bodies appeared to possess significant technical capacity. They conducted not only financial audits but also various types of compliance and performance audits of government programs.

The ACU typically reported its findings to the parliament and the agency being audited and made recommendations for improvements. However, compliance with these recommendations by the audited entity was not high. The ACU also published extensive data on its website, including the detailed findings of certain audits. However, the results of sensitive audits were often not published or were released only in summary. Audits of the four social funds, thought to be particularly susceptible to corruption, were typically not released.

The Environment for Reform

The relatively free press and growing business community, together with the capacity of NGOs, are important forces that can advocate for improved public finance transparency. Points of access for information that are already in place (such as the parliamentary website) indicate that organizational structures and capacity do not have to be created anew. In addition, some governmental institutions, such as the Tax Administration and Chief Control and Auditing Administration, have demonstrated their willingness to strengthen performance and implement reforms.

Certain procurement problems were addressed in a 2005 amendment to the procurement law that sought to create a more competitive public procurement process and more transparent procedures. In particular, it included provisions covering publication of procurement plans on the Internet, electronic tendering, guarantees of nondiscrimination for participants, and equal access to procurement information. The law also contained provisions against unfair acts of bidders and participation in procurement committees by close relatives and associates of bidder's representatives and officials of consolidated companies. In addition, the law established a new independent controlling body, the Tender Chamber, a nonprofit union of NGOs.

The tax system was being examined in a more systematic way by a newly established Presidential Secretariat, which drafted a new Concept to Reform the Tax System. This document suggested a further reduction in the tax burden and a stabilization of the tax system, making it more transparent and streamlined. The concept was being discussed broadly among stakeholders. In addition, a National Commission on Developing Main Directions for Tax Reform in Ukraine had been established in 2005 with representatives from the business community and government. The commission drafted a Charter on Tax Relations, which was opened for public discussion. Ukraine's Tax Administration was also considering tax reforms after the roughly $1 billion VAT refund scam of 2004, in which tax officials were suspected of receiving kickbacks of 30% to 50% of the amount refunded. One proposal under review would establish a list of "low-risk" firms that would be allowed to file electronic VAT returns.

Recommendations

Reform in the public finance sector requires both a top-down and a bottom-up approach. The top-down aspect involves building political will among Ukrainian government officials through concerted donor coordination and focused dialogue on the need for increased transparency. The government also requires assistance in policy implementation to comply with its transparency obligations under current law. The bottom-up aspect involves mobilizing interested constituencies to increase their advocacy efforts through direct engagement with government actors and collaboration with activist coalitions. Specific recommendations for the public finance domain follow.

Budget

- Promote implementation of the OECD Best Practices for Budget Transparency policies in budget planning, implementation, reporting, and monitoring.[13] In particular, limit possibilities for discretion in budget and revenue planning and the interbudgetary transfer system by introducing clear formulas and promoting performance-based budgeting.

- Consider establishing a budget advocacy organization, such as those supported by the International Budget Project in other countries, to lobby for greater participation and transparency in the national budget.[14] Such an NGO could also provide training and technical assistance to sectoral NGOs to assist them in advocating for similar reforms in their sectors.

Procurement

- Separate functional responsibilities for implementation and monitoring. Consider establishing an internal supervisory body to support documentation and communication systems and e-procurement activities.
- Monitor implementation of the recent amendment to the procurement law requiring better transparency, conflicts of interest management, and external oversight. Involve business associations in public procurement monitoring.

Taxation

- Support ongoing efforts to reform the tax system to ensure that it reduces incentives for tax evasion and limits the discretionary power of tax officials.
- Reform regulations on VAT refunds to make it impossible to create bogus firms, to eliminate opportunities for extortion by tax inspectors evaluating tax return claims, and to streamline tax return procedures for reliable businesses.

Audit

- Support efforts to improve enforcement of recommendations from the Accounting Chamber and the Chief Control and Auditing Administration.
- Promote greater transparency and detail in audit institutions' reports.
- Support NGOs and the media in conducting watchdog activities to monitor and investigate public abuses in public funds spending.

Civil Society

- Form coalitions (such as an "access to information" coalition) among existing civil society groups or strengthen existing coalitions around anticorruption issues. Such alliances might ultimately seek the passage of a freedom of information law, but in the short term could mobilize actors across sectors and in the media to push for greater transparency on specific issues.

Private Sector

Widespread corruption has prevailed in the business sector, due in part to flaws, loopholes, and inconsistencies in legislation but largely to failures in interpreting, following, and enforcing the law. Reviews of business-related legislation uncovered over 5,500 regulations that did not comply with state regulatory policy or were outdated, contradictory, or excessive. As a result of such regulations and wide discretion, 82% of businesses made unofficial payments to public officials, and 84% of businesses operated in the shadow economy and failed to pay their taxes in full.[15] Corruption in this sector occurred on a petty, grand, and state-capture level. While small businesses paid frequent rents to bureaucrats, millions of dollars were embezzled from larger firms through lucrative procurements, privatizations, or massive VAT scams.

The business community was very poorly organized, with only 25% of businesses belonging to trade associations. These business associations were not prepared to provide their members with necessary services or advocacy support. Businesses, particularly small ones, generally lacked legal knowledge of their rights or of constantly changing regulations.

In the late 1990s, the government of Ukraine undertook some steps toward improving the business environment and simplifying business regulations, but these efforts soon faded. The new administration that came to power in 2005 revived and reinforced this course. Within a very short period of time, an effort to review all business regulations was initiated. Mandatory streamlining of procedures for business registration and the issuing of permits in hundreds of municipalities was conducted, a new procurement law was passed, customs reform began, and a business advisory council was reactivated, among other reforms. At the time of the assessment, it was too early to determine the impact of these efforts on reducing corruption, but the initiatives were a step in the right direction. There remained, however, many gaps and priorities that needed to be addressed in order to prevent and reduce corruption in business-government transactions.

A number of surveys showed that corruption ranked as one of the most significant problems hindering business development. According to the International Finance Corporation (IFC) survey of 2004, 75% of businesses identified corruption as the second major barrier, after unstable legislation.[16]

Corruption had an almost 25% increase in significance in comparison with the 2002 survey and almost a 30% increase since 2000.[17] The 2005 European Bank for Reconstruction and Development–World Bank Business Environment and Enterprise Performance Survey (BEEPS) report placed corruption among the top 4 significant problems for Ukraine out of a list of 21 business development obstacles.

Petty corruption—extortion, bribery, speed money, influence peddling, and favoritism—was common practice in most business-government transactions, including business registration, permits issuance, inspections, and leasing of public property. These forms of corruption had the greatest impact on small- and medium-sized businesses, which felt insecure and helpless in confronting authorities and bureaucrats.

Corruption in the Tax Administration was especially pernicious, occurring as a result of extensive flaws in legislation and discretion in implementation practices. Businesses considered their interactions with the Tax Administration as being excessively burdensome, complicated, and contradictory, while also being extremely flawed and unstable. Existing tax legislation created numerous opportunities for abuses: offering postponements of tax payments and a wide range of fines that could be imposed for the same violation, among other flawed provisions. Large-scale corruption was also suspected in the 2004 VAT refunds scam that caused long delays in legal VAT refunds to law-abiding exporters.

At the same time, tax evasion in the amount of just US$350 (about two months' average salary) could be subject to criminal investigation and prosecution. On such charges of tax evasion, the tax police had the right to occupy a firm's office, abuse its employees, seize all of the firm's assets and documents, and essentially destroy the business. Allegedly, this right had been widely abused both for suppressing political and economic competitors and for mere harassment.

In addition, tax privileges were granted to some companies and localities, allegedly in exchange for kickbacks. Tax evasion and VAT manipulation that involved public authorities were also well known and well documented. Lucrative property and enterprises were frequently privatized behind closed doors and involved kickbacks and other illegal financial and nonfiscal transactions. Certain industries (such as vehicles, sugar, and vegetable oil) achieved a special protected status by allegedly buying votes in parliament. In the 1990s, business-administrative groups (or clans) emerged in control of vital industries, influencing political leaders by allegedly buying votes and favorable government and court decisions, financing election campaigns, and populating the legislature and civil service ranks with allies. The absence of effective conflict of interest policies was a major problem, resulting in business and political leaders easily crossing the line of propriety.

Governmental initiatives to improve the business environment, promote small businesses, and deregulate business operations enjoyed some initial success but quickly stalled and became highly bureaucratized. The new administration reviewed 9,866 regulations at all governmental agencies and identified about half that needed to be eliminated or modified. The Customs Service, for example, demonstrated its intentions to introduce new internal policies and procedures to prevent corruption; this resulted in a significant increase in customs revenue collected during the last quarter. However, unrealistically short deadlines set by the central government may have jeopardized the quality of future reform legislation.

The Environment for Reform

Central government. The Yushchenko administration declared an aggressive course of action regarding business deregulation using several presidential decrees. The State Committee of Ukraine for Regulatory Policy and Entrepreneurship (SCRPE), which was at the vanguard of this effort, had a long history of promoting regulatory reform and supporting business development. With support from the president and the Cabinet of Ministers and with clearly defined objectives, SCRPE had been successful in reaching out to governmental agencies at all levels and jurisdictions. The current "guillotine" reform program (to eliminate regulations that are not reformed within a certain time period) aimed at improving the legal framework, removing major barriers, and reducing opportunities for corruption.

Local government, represented by three different jurisdictional branches— local self-governmental bodies, regional administrations, and local branches of the central executive government agencies—often manifest divergent interests. The dual subordination of some executive branch departments and the resource dependency of local elected self-governmental bodies on regional administrations made it difficult to mobilize all parties toward common goals, such as anticorruption. There had been some successful examples of anticorruption initiatives at the local government level, but these often depended on the personalities of local officials.

The *business community* remained poorly organized and very passive, especially the smallest firms. However, as a frequent victim of corruption and abuse, small businesses were looking for opportunities to address this problem, and business associations had the potential to be instrumental if further developed. The Council of Entrepreneurs, an advisory body to the Cabinet of Ministers, had recently undergone a change in leadership and renewed its focus on pursuing business interests. The council was proving to be an effective mechanism for public-private dialogue but risked being captured by government interests. Another example of effective mobilization of the business community was the Coordinating-Expert Center of the Entrepreneurs' Union of Ukraine, which united over 60 business associations, two-thirds of which were regional associations. The major mission of the center was to promote business interests by commenting on laws and draft laws.

In the meantime, the Yushchenko administration had opened the door to positive improvements in the business environment. The central government quickly advanced certain deregulation reforms and issued a number of laws and presidential decrees that demonstrated political will to address the flaws in the system. In addition, the prospects for WTO and EU accession offered opportunities to build coalitions for increased transparency, trade liberalization, and limited special privileges. The need to increase social spending was used as an excuse for eliminating tax privileges. Similarly, the need to maintain price stability was successfully used for advocating for trade liberalization.

The main obstacles to effective private sector reform centered on both the development and the enforcement of anticorruption legislation. Laws promoting stricter divisions between public and private interests, greater transparency in government-business transactions, and an improved business environment (enhancing privatization, taxation, inspecting agency incentives, etc.) were likely to face stiff opposition from interest groups that stood to lose from more transparent practices. Inspection agencies in particular, motivated by quotas for fine collections, were invested in punishing infractions rather than preventing them. Even if legislation was successfully enacted, there was substantial risk that it would not be properly enforced. Unless business associations developed into a force capable of effective monitoring, there would be little pressure to enforce legislation.

Recommendations

Progress in this sector relies on the development and enforcement of effective legislation and policies, at both the governmental and the corporate levels. Recommendations for private sector anticorruption reform include the following.

- Draft and implement new legislation that separates public and private interests and improves transparency in government.

- Draft, approve, and implement conflict of interest legislation to prevent biased decision making and collusion among public and private interests. The legislation should be applied to public officials at all levels, including members of parliament.
- Draft, approve, and implement legislation regulating lobbying activities and reducing opportunities to buy parliamentary votes, as well as other corrupt practices influencing legislation, and ensuring that essential governmental information is available to the public in a timely and comprehensive fashion.
- Support development and implementation of specific regulations to promote a better business environment.
- Develop and implement transparent and fair regulations and controls for further privatization of state-owned enterprises, land, and other kinds of state and municipal property.
- Support policies to change the incentives of controlling and inspecting agencies from collecting revenue through fines to promoting better business compliance with regulations.
- Improve the regulatory framework for taxation to reduce incentives for tax evasion and to limit the discretionary powers of tax officials. Reform VAT refund regulations to make it impossible to create bogus firms to scam VAT refunds, to eliminate opportunities for extortion by tax inspectors evaluating tax return claims, and to streamline tax return procedures for reliable businesses.
- Support the monitoring of legislation and reforms.
- Support regulatory reform policy that will improve the business environment and make laws and regulations consistent, straightforward, enforceable, and fair.
- Implement the Law on State Regulatory Policy requiring all draft laws to be broadly discussed by all interested parties prior to adoption, cost-benefit and social impact assessments to be conducted, indicators of effectiveness to be established, and monitoring mechanisms to be developed. Consider including requirements to assess draft laws on their "corruption risk" and their likely impact on reducing corruption.
- Ensure proper implementation of the recently passed legislation to improve public procurement practices that amended the Law of Ukraine "On Procurement of Goods, Works and Services at Public Expense."

- Implement programs to strengthen business associations and promote corporate governance practices.
- Support development of business associations that advocate business interests, government transparency, and accountability. Train and provide support to business associations in advocacy and lobbying and in providing services and legal support to association members.
- Draft and implement a corporate governance law and introduce corporate governance practices in large businesses.

Subnational Government

Ukraine's highly centralized government provided an excellent vehicle for retaining strong control throughout the country, transmitting instructions to the local level, and manipulating decisions. As a result, corrupt practices at the central level often were adopted at the subnational and local levels as well. Although greater responsibilities for service delivery have been delegated to local officials over the past several years, financial dependency on the center has increased, along with the risk of corruption.

Levels of corruption are highly uneven throughout the country, as are anticorruption efforts. In most instances, integrity levels depended on the political will of local leaders. Civil society and the business community in the majority of municipalities remained weak and unsophisticated in terms of developing demand pressure and advocating for reforms.

While decentralization in government can produce decentralization of corruption as well, it also offers another level at which to fight corruption and motivate constituencies for reform. In 2005, the status of decentralization reform in Ukraine was ambiguous; after extensive discussion in parliament, it was postponed awaiting further developments.

A strongly vertical executive power structure served as a perfect means by which to extend central policies and practices to subnational levels. Appointed from the center, oblast and rayon heads often overshadowed elected regional councils' authority and exercised complete control over their regions. The subnational level mirrored national-level corruption patterns: state capture, embezzlement, kickbacks in procurement and privatization, nepotism, patronage, and so on. But in addition, corruption arose in specific subnational-level functions, such as service delivery, local business regulation, taxation, and health care.

Local branches of the central controlling and law enforcement agencies, such as the Tax Administration, inspection agencies, police, prosecutor, and courts, were viewed by the public and businesses as the most corrupt institutions at the local level. Quotas to collect fines established at the central level for most inspection agencies established additional incentives to harass local businesses and extort bribes. Local courts, the prosecutor, and the police could be very selective in their actions and judgments because of their financial dependency on the center, and local budgets could supplement deficient allocations. Local departments charged with fighting economic crime were given a quota, and they often turned anticorruption programs into witch hunts.

In addition, the formula for intergovernmental transfers was not completely transparent, making it difficult, if not impossible, for cities to hold the central government accountable for the revenue they received (or failed to receive). As a result, many municipalities and rayon-level governments were not provided sufficient funds for the vital services and responsibilities delegated to them. Allocation of budget funds at the local level was often influenced by vested interests, and funding distribution was typically subject to shadow deals and favors across all levels.

Elected local and municipal governments were freer to make independent choices on policies and practices. However, a lack of accountability, a passive civil society, and ineffective law enforcement bred temptation among some mayors and councils to consolidate complete control over all aspects of financial and administrative matters. This could easily result in excessive abuse of power in property leasing, privatization, issuing of permits, granting of tax benefits, and so on. But this was not necessarily a widespread practice. Some mayors increasingly appeared to recognize the value of increased citizen participation and greater government transparency, in terms of both legitimizing their own mandates and the overall improvement in decision making that resulted.

Still, low salaries and low professionalism among municipal public servants often resulted in low performance and widespread abuses. Town mayors sometimes drew a salary lower than the official minimum monthly wage in Ukraine (about US$70)—yet even these types of positions were frequently bought or transferred through nepotism or clientelism. These unfavorable conditions led many talented and qualified professionals to seek employment elsewhere.

Some reforms to improve transparency and accountability of local administrations had been implemented in the previous two years: the local budget was published in the local media and discussed at public hearings in many cities, city council meetings were open to the public, public councils were established as advisory bodies within administrations, and business registration was simplified. However, many aspects of governmental functioning remained closed to citizens, reinforcing public perceptions of potential wrongdoing.

Overall, civil society and the business community remained weak in most municipalities and did not mobilize demand for government openness and accountability. The media was often controlled by the local administration.

The Environment for Reform

Local civil society and citizens' groups, along with the emerging small- and medium-sized enterprises, were the logical champions for reform. However, mayors and other city officials who recognized the political benefit they could derive from being seen as supporting transparent, participative, and accountable operations were perhaps the most important allies. The Ukrainian Association of Cities was another potential anticorruption force to be explored.

Political leadership at the municipal level, in some localities, seemed keen to embrace more European approaches to local governance and saw in them a comparative electoral advantage. The inflated expectations that arose during the revolution, and the resultant disappointment, provided the potential to convert dissatisfaction into demand for reform.

The extensive involvement of the central government in local affairs threatened to hinder subnational institutions' attempts to implement reform measures contradicting the interests of corrupt forces within the national government. Even decentralization, measures then under consideration, presented a potential hindrance to effective reform at the rayon level. Another problem was the significant cost and complexity of incorporating anticorruption safeguards into decentralization laws. And as always, successful development and implementation of legislation depended on political will, which was often lacking at both the local and the national levels.

Civil society and watchdog groups, potential monitors of reform implementation, generally lacked the capacity and professionalism to play a truly active part in anticorruption efforts. When they did engage in government affairs, there was always the risk they would adopt a purely adversarial role rather than one of constructive dialogue and action.

Recommendations

The most effective way to address corruption on a local level is to involve both government and nongovernment sectors. Nevertheless, action requires political will and readiness on both sides. In situations where there was little or no political will on the part of governmental officials, the assessment team recommended that programs focus on building local civil society capacity to effectively demand reforms from government. If the government does possess political will, the team advised efforts to align government activities with the priorities of the local community by establishing effective dialogue programs.

Local Government
- Implement professional administrative management practices: promote professionalism by establishing job requirements and offering training; develop and implement programs to eliminate conflicts of interest; introduce performance-based incentives, internal control, and reporting requirements; and implement computerized reporting and decision record systems.
- Implement reforms to standardize and simplify administrative procedures and provide better services to the public. Conduct public service report cards.
- Develop and implement effective and proactive transparency policies and involve citizens in decision-making processes.
- Promote effective public-private dialogue mechanisms that involve all local stakeholder groups in coordinating efforts to address corruption.

Civil Society
- Support civil society programs that encourage citizens to monitor the quality of service delivery and make demands for greater transparency. Promote establishment of citizen watchdog groups to conduct professional monitoring of governmental institutions and functions (such as budgeting, procurement, service delivery, etc.).
- Improve citizens' legal literacy of their rights and the government's responsibilities.
- Establish independent legal support offices to provide legal services and legal education to victims of alleged corruption and excessive bureaucracy.

Decentralization
- Assist government in decentralization reform to ensure that it will not breed "decentralized corruption" but rather establish a clear division of responsibilities and resources. Call for transparency. Introduce strict checks and balances. Ensure citizen participation in government decision-making processes.

Epilogue

The 2005 corruption assessment for Ukraine was conducted at a particularly delicate time in the nation's political history. In the aftermath of the Orange Revolution, there were promising signs of political will that could be instrumental in implementing true anticorruption reform. At the same time, disillusionment with the Yushchenko administration was rapidly beginning to spread. It was unclear at the time of the assessment which direction Ukraine's political circumstances—and attendant anticorruption initiatives—were headed.

Before long, the answer became clear. Months into Yushchenko's presidency, a number of high-ranking government officials resigned, charging the administration with widespread corruption. Yushchenko responded in September 2005 by dismissing Prime Minister Yulia Tymoshenko, Yushchenko's former Orange Revolution ally, and her entire cabinet. In subsequent parliamentary elections, the president's party suffered humiliating losses, enabling Yushchenko's one-time bitter rival, Viktor Yanukovich, to gain the post of prime minister. Over the course of the next two years, Yushchenko would dissolve parliament twice, attempting to regain control of a political environment in which he was increasingly losing favor. In the presidential elections of 2010, Yushchenko failed to advance past the first round, and Yanukovich assumed office in February 2010, later appointing Russophile technocrat Mykola Azarov as prime minister.

Amidst this political turbulence, progress on anticorruption issues stalled. Although Yushchenko's administration introduced a number of decrees and initiatives aimed at increasing transparency and accountability, they were largely unsuccessful.[18] Intransigence in parliament and inherent flaws in legislation hindered effective reform, but perhaps the biggest impediment was a lack of monitoring and enforcement. This stemmed from endemic problems in anticorruption agencies, the judiciary, and civil society, among other sectors.

A major source of anticorruption funding for Ukraine materialized in 2006 with the US Millennium Challenge Corporation's (MCC) Threshold Program—nearly US$45 million over two years.[19] These resources addressed corruption in five priority areas: the justice sector, higher educational institutions, construction and land regulations, ethical and administrative standards in government, and civil society advocacy—and achieved some measurable results. Anticorruption efforts in other key sectors found mixed success. Several donor organizations sought to address problems in the judiciary, private sector, public finance sector, and subnational government through a variety of programs implemented at or since the time of the initial corruption assessment. Although certain projects demonstrated promising results, the true impact of these efforts can be determined only in the long term. A brief discussion of the anticorruption situation in the sectors discussed earlier—five years since the assessment was completed—is presented below.

Judiciary. The judicial sector has generally been slow to reform, although a few high-profile cases have targeted corrupt judges. In early 2009, the head of the Lviv Administrative Appeals Court, Ihor Zvarych, was arrested on charges of abuse of office, bribe taking, and fraud. Preliminary investigations into the actions of Zvarych and other Lviv Administrative Appeals Court judges resulted in the confiscation of $2.9 million.[20] Although the number of criminal cases against Ukrainian judges has increased steadily in the past few years, few cases ever reach trial because of the highly complicated procedure for removing a judge's prosecutorial immunity, which requires parliamentary approval.[21] Among other flaws are excessive interference from the executive branch, conflict of interest issues, and extreme case overload.

A three-year MCC Threshold project—Combating Corruption and Strengthening Rule of Law in Ukraine—was launched in 2007 to address problems in the judiciary. Its main goals were to establish a registry of court decisions, develop and implement a uniform random case assignment system in selected courts, implement effective and transparent processes for judicial appointments and disciplinary procedures, and create an operating system for regional administrative courts. The project involved a wide variety of partners, including the Verkhovna Rada, the State Judicial Administration, the Council of Judges, the Ministry of Justice, the High Qualifications Commission of Ukraine, the High Council of Justice, and the Regional Qualifications Commissions.[22]

Part of an "EU-Ukraine action plan" designed to enhance political and economic relations between the two entities included reform efforts aimed at Ukraine's judiciary. This included strengthening the sector's administrative capacity, implementing recent reforms of various codes and procedures based on European standards, continuing reform of the prosecution system in accordance with a Council of Europe action plan, and improving the training of all judicial officials, especially on human rights issues.[23] In November 2009, this action plan was replaced by an "EU-Ukraine Association Agenda," which continued to emphasize improvements in the efficiency and independence of Ukraine's courts. It focused particularly on the importance of training for judicial officials and the implementation of civil, criminal, and administrative codes based on European standards.[24]

Despite these efforts, commentary in the media five years later noted that since the Yushchenko administration took power, corruption was perceived to have gotten even worse in the judicial sector. "Ukrainian lawyers and international monitoring organizations [have noted] a sharp rise in corruption among judges and prosecutors in the last five years," stated a scathing op-ed.[25] In this period of political crises and instability, political elites increased pressure on judges and prosecutors to produce outcomes favorable to their side, greatly undermining the judiciary's status as an independent institution.

Public finance. Just before the Orange Revolution, the World Bank launched extensive, multiyear projects addressing problems in Ukraine's public finance system. The Ukraine Public Finance Modernization Project involves an International Bank for Reconstruction and Development (IBRD) loan of US$50 million to improve public financial management capacity, efficiency, and transparency at various government levels.[26] Scheduled for completion at the end of 2010, the project is on track with many of its objectives, having implemented new statistical systems, improved public electronic access to data, updated computer infrastructure, and an integrated information processing system.[27]

The tax system was also targeted for reform, with a project running from 2003 to 2012. Aimed at improving the administration of the State Tax Service, as well as voluntary compliance with tax legislation, this initiative is close to meeting many of its goals. For one, a risk-based audit selection system has been initiated, reducing the total number of audits and improving audit effectiveness. An automated invoice matching system and increased use of e-filing mechanisms has also improved overall VAT performance. Many similar key performance indicators have demonstrated progress under this project.[28]

Private sector. The Yushchenko administration made several steps in the right direction in the area of private sector reform. These included mandatory streamlining of business registration and permit-issuing procedures, a new procurement law, customs reforms, reviews of all business regulations throughout the country, and the reactivation of a business advisory council.[29] Many critical flaws in business-government transactions remain, however, and it is unclear the extent to which the new Yanukovich administration will take action to combat these problems.

Donor programs in this sector have met with some success but were stymied in recent years by Ukraine's economic problems and the global economic crisis of the late 2000s. In 2006, the World Bank initiated a project aimed at improving access to financial services for small- and medium-sized enterprises (SME), particularly in rural areas. Although two dozen SMEs received lines of credit through this initiative, the banking crisis of 2008 jeopardized the project's viability to the point where the majority of the loan had to be cancelled.[30] The World Bank had also supported private exporters with enhanced access to capital, but the substantial progress of a few years slowed considerably with the onset of financial turmoil in Ukraine's banking sector.[31]

USAID and the UN Development Programme (UNDP) have also played an active role in promoting Ukraine's business development. In 2005, USAID launched the Capital Markets Project, a five-year initiative designed to bolster the capacities of Ukraine's financial regulators and pension fund providers and establish effective financial instruments for portfolio investment. It also included a program to enhance private enterprise competitiveness in a broad three-year "Local Investment and National Competitiveness Effort."[32] UNDP created the Blue Ribbon Commission Analytical and Advisory Centre in 2005 to support policies and regulations that would improve the business environment for small- and medium-sized enterprises.[33]

In addition, the MCC made a significant investment in improving Ukraine's business environment by allocating US$8 million in 2006 to a "Trade, Investment and Business Acceleration" (TIBA) project.[34] Since its inception, this project assisted in drafting amendments to Ukraine's Regulatory Policy Law (RPL) that aimed at improving its clarity and effectiveness while eliminating loopholes. It then helped draft amendments to the Rules of the Cabinet of Ministers and 21 other laws to bring them in line with the new RPL. It is also helping to develop proposals for rapid deregulation in areas such as construction, land, permits, and tourism.[35]

Subnational government. Corruption vulnerabilities within local government have received significant attention from international donors. In 2008, USAID initiated a three-year project to strengthen the financial capacity of Ukraine's municipal governments and promote the development of municipal utility companies. City governments received training in capital budget planning based on performance program budgeting, and on the national level, the project sought to create a regulatory environment that would facilitate local governments' ability to attract financing for infrastructure development.[36]

UNDP has been working since 2004 on a program to decentralize national government fiscal and administrative responsibilities in favor of local authorities. In support of this goal, local governments and communities received capacity-building assistance to help them develop and deliver public services and social and economic development programs. Through a variety of workshops, conferences, training programs, grants for local development projects, and pilots of public-private partnerships, among other methods, the

"Municipal Governance and Sustainable Development Program" was on track with many of its objectives, and the program was slated to run until the end of 2010.[37]

Local financial management capacity also received a boost from the World Bank. One of its projects, under the umbrella of overall public finance reform, helps local governments improve policy evaluation and decision-making processes through modernization of their data collection and computer systems. Another project, initiated in 2008 and slated to run until 2013, recently implemented automated accounting and reporting software as part of its larger goal of improving the efficiency and transparency of subnational authorities' financial management operations.[38]

Notes

1. This chapter is adapted from the assessment written by Bertram Spector, Svetlana Winbourne, Jerry O'Brien, and Eric Rudenshiold, for Management Systems International, under a USAID contract.

2. Vera Nanivska. 2001. *NGO Development in Ukraine*. Kyiv: International Center for Policy Studies; 2004 NGO Sustainability Index for Central and Eastern Europe and Eurasia, 8th ed. (USAID, 2005).

3. Counterpart Creative Center. 2004. *Civil Society Organizations in Ukraine: The State and Dynamics (2002–2003)*. Kyiv: Counterpart Creative Center.

4. *Nations in Transit 2005*. Washington, DC: Freedom House.

5. Presidential Secretariat, General Information on Measures on Combating Corruption in Ukraine in 2005.

6. Roman Kupchinsky. January 12, 2003. "Analysis: The Clan From Donetsk," RFE/RL Poland, Belarus and Ukraine report, http://www.ukrweekly.com/Archive/2003/020304.shtml.

7. World Bank. August 2004. *Ukraine: Building Foundations for Sustainable Growth, A Country Economic Memorandum: Volume 1*.

8. See the recent assessments of the judicial system by J. T. Asscher and S. V. Konnov, *Ukraine Justice System Assessment Report* (TACIS, June 2005), and David Black and Richard Blue, *Rule of Law Strengthening and Anticorruption in Ukraine: Recommendations for USAID Assistance* (USAID, May 2005) for more detailed reviews of the judicial sector and potential reform options.

9. Institute for Economic Research and Policy Consulting. 2003. *Diagnostic Report: Fiscal Transparency and Openness in Ukraine*. Institute for Economic Research and Policy Consulting, 17.

10. Ibid. "Documents of [the] pension fund are not fully available to the public; only general figures on budget execution and the amount of arrears are published."

11. Ibid., 81.

12. Estimated by the Ministry of Economy and European Integration at 42.3% of GDP.

13. OECD Best Practices for Budget Transparency policies, http://www.oecd.org/data oecd/33/13/1905258.pdf.

14. www.internationalbudget.org.

15. IFC 2004.

16. Ibid., 6.

17. IFC 2003, 17.

18. USDA Agricultural Economy & Policy Report—Ukraine. February 2009. http://www .fas.usda.gov/country/Ukraine/Ukraine Agricultural Economy and Policy Report.pdf.

19. Millennium Challenge Corporation, "Millennium Challenge Corporation Board Approves Anticorruption Initiative in Ukraine."

20. Global Integrity Report, Ukraine. 2009. http://report.globalintegrity.org/Ukraine/ 2009/scorecard/44.

21. Kiev Ukraine News Blog. May 17, 2009. "Despite High-Profile Arrests, Corruption Still Dogs Courts," http://news.kievukraine.info/2009/05/despite-high-profile-arrests-corruption .html.

22. MCC-USAID Year 2 Workplan, "Combating Corruption and Strengthening Rule of Law in Ukraine Under the MCC TCP."

23. EU–Ukraine action plan, undated.

24. EU–Ukraine Association Agenda. November 2009. http://ec.europa.eu/external_ relations/ukraine/docs/2010_eu_ukraine_association_agenda_en.pdf.

25. Taras Kuzio. April 8, 2010. "Judges Mock Justice With Their Useless or Corrupt Rulings." *Kyiv Post*, http://www.kyivpost.com/news/opinion/op_ed/detail/63477/print/.

26. World Bank Project Description: Ukraine Public Finance Modernization Project, http://web.worldbank.org/WBSITE/EXTERNAL/PROJECTS/0,,contentMDK:21606893~ pagePK:41367~piPK:279616~theSitePK:40941,00.html.

27. World Bank, "Status of Projects in Execution—FY 09," http://siteresources.worldbank .org/EXTSOPE/Resources/5929620-1254491038321/6460830-1254491059045/Ukraine .pdf.

28. Ibid.

29. Global Integrity, "Ukraine: Integrity Indicators Scorecard," 2009, http://report.global integrity.org/Ukraine/2009/scorecard/81.

30. World Bank, "Status of Projects in Execution—FY 09."

31. Ibid.

32. USAID, Capital Markets Project, http://www.capitalmarkets.kiev.ua/.

33. UNDP website, "Ukraine: Prosperity, Poverty Reduction and MDGs," http://www .undp.org.ua/en/prosperity-poverty-reduction-and-mdgs/38-prosperity-poverty-reduction -and-mdgs-/631-blue-ribbon-commission-analytical-and-advisory-centre.

34. USAID/TIBA website, About USAID/TIBA, http://www.tiba.org.ua/eng/about/ PressRelease.

35. USAID Ukraine website, Economic Growth, Accomplishments, http://ukraine.usaid .gov/accomp_econ.shtml.

36. USAID Ukraine website, Economic Growth, Programs, http://ukraine.usaid.gov/ukraine_economic.shtml.

37. UNDP website, "Ukraine: Municipal Government and Sustainable Development Programme," http://www.undp.org.ua/en/local-development-and-human-security/37-local-development-and-human-security-/613-municipal-governance-and-sustainable-development-programme.

38. World Bank, "Status of Projects in Execution—FY 09."

7

Ukraine 2 (2006–2009)

Many public opinion surveys were conducted as part of the US Millennium Challenge Corporation's (MCC) Threshold Program (2006–2009) with the objective of assessing trends in citizen perceptions and experience with corruption. While this is a very short period of time in which to observe significant impacts of recently implemented reforms, some interesting results were uncovered. These are presented in this chapter, especially those targeting results in the key sectors addressed by the 2005 assessment presented in the previous chapter.

Overall National Trends

In 2007 and 2009, identical national surveys were conducted to assess the impact, if any, of anticorruption initiatives adopted as part of the MCC's Threshold Country Plan (TCP). The surveys measured changes in the public's perceptions of and experiences with corruption.[1] Overall, the survey findings showed that between 2007 and 2009, the incidence of actual corruption *experiences* gradually decreased, while *perceptions* of widespread corruption levels increased (see figure 7.1). This phenomenon of increasing corruption perceptions at a time of decreasing corruption experiences is not uncommon. Because of initiatives like the TCP, citizens were increasingly aware of corruption scandals and anticorruption efforts, as these issues received considerable attention in the media and the public agenda. As a result of rising expectations, Ukrainians' negative perceptions increased, despite the positive effects of anticorruption interventions.

Between 2007 and 2009, corruption remained one of the five top problem areas identified by a wide majority of Ukrainians. Over 93% of citizens pinpointed government corruption, the high cost of living, the high cost and low quality of health care, crime, and unemployment as major problems facing Ukrainians. In fact, most Ukrainians perceived corruption levels as increasing

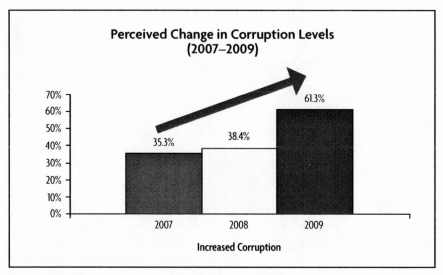

Figure 7.1 Perceptions of corruption levels in Ukraine (2007–2009).

sharply: 35% of respondents said that corruption was on the increase in 2007, while 61% said it was on the increase in 2009. This corresponded with a significant 6% decline in public trust in government structures between 2007 and 2009.

In 2009, Ukrainians believed there was more widespread corruption in more sectors and institutions of government than in 2007. Corruption was perceived to be significant in 14 out of 20 sectors and institutions in 2009—most prominently the state auto inspection, the court system, the police (*militzia*), health care, the Prosecutor's Office, universities, land privatization and ownership, government permit authorities, and the tax authorities. Across all sectors and institutions, Management Systems International's cumulative Corruption Perception Index increased from 35% in 2007 to 38% in 2009.

This perceived growth of corruption in Ukraine was not a problem that could be attributed solely to growing greed among government officials. A majority of Ukrainian citizens (51%) believed that the use of corruption was sometimes or always justified to "get things done" and solve personal problems. Thus, corruption in Ukraine was a *two-way street*, where citizens and government officials would initiate corrupt transactions.

In terms of *actual experiences* with corruption, although a relatively high 62.5% of citizens reported having at least one corrupt transaction over the past 12 months, this actually represented a decline of 4.5% (from 67% in 2007)

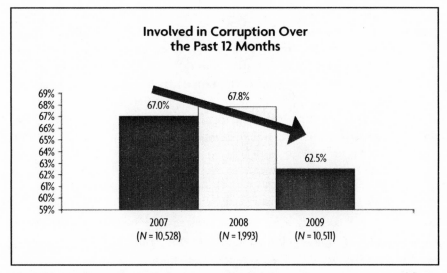

Figure 7.2 Ukrainians experiencing corruption over the past 12 months.

(see figure 7.2). Experience with extortion decreased from 25.6% in 2007 to 22.1% in 2009, while voluntary bribe giving declined from 13.1% in 2007 to 9.9% in 2009. The reported use of personal connections also decreased, from an average of 23.4% in 2008 to 13.7% in 2009.

Judicial Sector

Although the judiciary was still perceived as among the most corrupt sectors in Ukraine, actual corruption experience in this sector decreased between 2007 and 2009. Perhaps because of the significant attention this sector's corrupt activities had received in recent years, 20% more respondents stated that they viewed corruption in the court system as "widespread" in 2009 as in 2007. In key experience areas, however, corruption was trending downward. While encounters with court extortion dropped slightly over the two years, both voluntary bribe giving and the use of personal connections dropped 5 percentage points each since 2007. This could also be a consequence of the enhanced focus on judiciary corruption: citizens may have felt more indignant about initiating corrupt activities and more apprehensive about being caught if they did.

Significant problems remained, however. Among citizens and businesses, the biggest difficulties in dealing with the court system continued to be long delays in court proceedings and the impunity of judges. For the majority of lawyers and prosecutors, the key problem in the judicial system was clearly the impunity of judges; this belief had grown stronger between 2007 and 2009.

Lawyers and prosecutors perceived that corruption was widespread within all stages of the judicial process, and this perception had increased significantly since 2008 (from 32% to 41%). In particular, they believed that corruption was particularly pervasive at the pretrial inquiry stage. Among citizens and businesses, more than one-third of them were strongly suspicious that their counterparts in court cases had attempted to influence the court decision in the form of a gift, service, or bribe.

Despite these beliefs, companies that reported experiencing corruption within the court system had dropped from 37% to 24% between 2008 and 2009. Citizens also experienced a decrease, though smaller, in their overall encounters with corruption in the court system over that same time period (from 19% to 16%). The most common type of corruption experience among citizens was extortion initiated by judges.

Lawyers, prosecutors, and company representatives were the best informed about the Unified Registry of Court Decisions, a TCP initiative. Since January 2008, there was an increase in the share of respondents who knew about the registry and had experience using it. Of those who used the system, a majority (56% on average) believed that it generated greater transparency in judicial decisions and thus would reduce corruption in the courts.

Public Finance

Forty percent of citizens surveyed in 2009 perceived that corruption was widespread among tax authorities (virtually unchanged from 2007), placing it ninth out of 20 sectors as the most corrupted government function in the public's mind. But trends in citizen experience with tax authorities suggest a slowly improving situation with regard to corruption. Incidents of extortion declined from 24% to 20%, bribe giving declined from 15% to 14%, and the use of personal connections decreased from 18% to 14% between 2007 to 2009.

Private Sector

Corruption perceptions and experiences with business regulation and inspection were mixed. While the perception of widespread corruption increased in 2009 (to 29.3% from 27.6% in 2007), the actual use of personal connections was also on the rise, from 23% to 25%. However, corruption experiences of bribe giving (from 22% to 20%) and extortion (from 41% to 35%) declined with regard to business regulation and inspection transactions.

Businesses that sought construction and land permits from government using traditional regulatory procedures perceived a significant increase in widespread corruption. In sharp contrast, those businesses using the new one-stop shops that streamlined construction and land permitting regulations perceived a dramatic decline in the level of corruption. Businesses encountering corruption using the services of the traditional permit authorization system increased by 6% (for land permits) and by 8% (for construction permits) between 2008 and 2009. Meanwhile, corruption experiences for companies using the new one-stop shop services significantly decreased (by 18% for land permits and 7% for construction permits) between 2008 and 2009. These TCP-supported one-stop shops were significant not only in reducing incidents of corruption but also in increasing efficiency. By cutting in half the number of visits required to get permits and slashing the average number of days required, the opportunities to interact with corrupt officials were also reduced.

Customs is another major regulatory sector affecting the private sector. Businesses perceived a decline in the spread of corruption (from 43% to 39%) and also small reductions in actual experiences with corruption in the customs field: extortion down from 37% to 30%, bribe giving down from 18% to 17%, and use of personal connections down from 16% to 14% between 2007 and 2009. In both 2007 and 2009, the most corrupted stage of customs procedures was perceived to be at border crossings. However, corruption when paying official fees was perceived to have decreased significantly between 2007 and 2009.

Subnational Government

Lower-level government enjoyed generally higher degrees of public trust than other government entities, though this was faint praise considering the low favorability ratings other government branches received with regard to corruption. Citizens viewed corruption as less widespread at the city (or village) and oblast level than at any other government level, though there was a perception that signficant corruption had spread at the subnational government level since 2007. In general, city and village governments emerged as the most positively perceived government entity in several categories.

In terms of the perceived prevalence of corruption, 47% of respondents thought that corruption was widespread at the oblast level in 2009 (up from 38% in 2007), and 39% thought the same about city or village governments (up from 32% in 2007). Nevertheless, citizen views of national-level government were significantly worse: 65% believed corruption was widespread in the national parliament, and the president and secretariat, as well as the Cabinet of Ministers, did not fare much better.

City and village governments also ranked above other government entities in citizens' perceptions of which branch was most willing to deal with the problems of corruption. Oblast governments received a middling ranking, though fewer citizens perceived that oblast governments and city and village governments were dedicated to overcoming corruption in 2009 as in 2007. These results occurred in the context of deep distrust of the government at all levels to meaningfully fight corruption. (The president and secretariat in particular experienced a steep drop in citizen confidence, with only 7% of respondents in 2009 believing that this branch was willing to overcome corruption, as opposed to 21% in 2007—testament to the failure of the Orange Revolution.)

Subnational governments received comparatively less recognition for anticorruption efforts, however. City and village governments and oblast governments ranked sixth and seventh, respectively, out of eight levels in terms of awareness by citizens of anticorruption activities initiated. At the same time, the effectiveness of the city and village government programs rated relatively high; 17% of respondents thought that programs initiated at this level were effective, higher than for any other. This did, however, represent a 5-percentage-point drop from 2007. Interestingly, the effectiveness of anticorruption efforts at the oblast level was considered among the lowest of any sector, with only 5% believing in the success of these programs.

These results indicated that trust in government anticorruption efforts, while low across the board, tended to increase the more local the institution. Oblast heads, for instance, were appointed by the national government and thus often lacked a sense of accountability to constituents. At the city and village level, elected officials were often more responsive to anticorruption sentiments, recognizing the political advantage of being seen as addressing a widespread public concern. Commitment to fighting corruption was highly dependent on political will at the subnational level.

Overall, these survey results suggest small, but encouraging, improvements in the corruption situation in Ukraine in general and across most sectors analyzed in the 2005 assessment. On the basis of the assessment, as well as other analyses, the government and donor organizations promoted reform initiatives in these and other sectors that went into effect relatively quickly. Even over the short-term, these activities appear to have had positive impacts on reducing the corruption problem. The sustainability of these reforms is a matter that requires continuing monitoring.

Note

1. Management Systems International. June 2009b. *Corruption in Ukraine: Comparative Analysis of National Surveys: 2007–2009*. Washington, DC: MSI (under contract to USAID).

8

Senegal (2007)

In 2000, Senegal experienced a major regime change that ousted the incumbent president and his party and brought Abdoulaye Wade and a broad coalition of opposition parties to power. Wade and the Senegalese Social Democratic Party (PDS) had vowed to liberalize the country's economy, modernize its bureaucracy, and fight the systemic corruption that plagued the highest levels of government and the daily lives of many citizens.[1]

In the ensuing years, the government took a number of steps to address corruption and increase transparency. It created new institutions, such as the National Program for Good Governance (PNBG), the National Commission Against Non-transparency, Collusion and Corruption (CNLCC), and the Good Governance Ministry; passed new laws to reform the public procurement process, such as the 2007 Code de Passation des Marchés Publiques; and promised to institute a more thorough and independent internal auditing process through the General State Inspectorate and the Cour des Comptes. Yet, long after these reforms had been implemented—and Wade won a second term in February 2007—there were still few concrete results.

While several indicators show that public perceptions of corruption have improved slightly in recent years, citizen surveys demonstrate that corruption nevertheless remains a major occurrence. Senegalese respondents reported that they encountered administrative corruption on a daily basis when obtaining routine government services from the police, courts, land titling agency, and service delivery agencies, such as the Ministries of Health, Education, and Water and Forestry. For many, including the media and the educated elite, the most disturbing form of corruption and mismanagement was grand corruption involving the use of state funds and foreign loans in government contracting, particularly in large public works projects.

After a movement toward a more decentralized and pluralist set of institutional arrangements led to the incumbent leadership's defeat in 2000,

President Wade steadily concentrated power in the executive branch and in the president's office in particular. The effectiveness of the new reform measures was thus subject to the political will—or lack thereof—at the top of Senegal's government. As a result, many laws and institutions suffered from serious gaps and limitations, were heavily oriented toward maintaining executive power, offered few checks on abuse of executive power, and contained few provisions for ensuring the autonomy of regulatory institutions. Moreover, the state still controlled most of the formal economy and increasingly conducted its operations through semiautonomous agencies that were formally outside direct government control and regulation. The combination of these developments produced an environment in which nontransparency and corruption still flourished.

Legal-Institutional Analysis

While Senegal possessed a substantial body of law to oppose corrupt practices, many of these laws were incomplete, infrequently applied, or easily thwarted. There were also significant legislative gaps on key anticorruption provisions. For instance, no laws existed to protect witnesses and whistleblowers, establish ethical standards for public officials, or regulate gifts and hospitality in return for political favors.

There were laws requiring disclosure of assets, but they applied only to the president and members of the Cour des Comptes. The law concerning the president in particular was unclear and contained no sanctions. Investigative legislation was similarly incomplete, as few agencies possessed the autonomy to conduct or initiate investigations. On paper, major contracts were procured using a competitive bidding system, but in reality there were many exceptions, and information about most contracts were not made publicly available. Legislation also existed to prevent or punish conflict of interest situations and general corrupt practices, but it was rarely applied.

Circumventing the law altogether was another common practice. Although regulations prohibited illegal means of personal enrichment, assets were frequently transferred abroad, out of reach of Senegalese authorities. Funding was also frequently brought in from abroad, for such purposes as election campaigns, without being made public. This practice and other means of obtaining political funding were illegal according to a 1981 law limiting political party funding, but there were no resultant audits or sanctions. Laws defining and sanctioning conflicts of interest also technically existed but were often thwarted through proxy companies or third-party involvement.

Institutions are important both in the way they structure incentives and in the way they reflect power realities. In Senegal, many of the institutions that could have countered the power of the executive branch did not do so because the structure of authority within government did not give them sufficient ability to impact policy and pursue violators.

Financial and budgetary controls, while theoretically in place, had little impact. Although parliament was required to approve the national budget on an annual basis, it was limited in this capacity by a general lack of technical competence necessary to comprehend the highly complex budgetary provisions. No budget reconciliation law had been passed in the past seven years, and in practice the president could obtain funds virtually without limitation.

Agencies ostensibly charged with overseeing aspects of the budget were hindered by a lack of independence. The General Inspection of Finance had no autonomy from the Ministry of Economy and Finance, and its reports were not made public. The Financial Control Mechanism was controlled by the president's office and had no authority over National Assembly expenditures. In addition, the Cour des Comptes was hampered by limited material and human resources and questionable independence from the Ministry of Finance. It generally imposed only weak sanctions for violations.

The judicial sector also suffered from autonomy problems. Although an independent judiciary existed in theory, the president exerted strong influence over the Magistracy High Council, which controlled judges' careers. When the judiciary did review administrative decisions, it was mainly in the form of regional tribunals. As for corruption within the sector, the penal code did apply to judges, but few were ever prosecuted. Only one judge had ever been dismissed on corruption charges, and two had been given warnings.

Other checks and balances within the government operated with mixed success. The Autonomous National Election Commission (ANEC) under the Ministry of Interior supervised elections while nominally independent from political parties. An ombudsman existed and appeared to maintain real autonomy despite the fact that his reports were submitted directly to the president. It was often very difficult, however, to obtain information from government agencies. A national anticorruption program had been created in the form of the PNBG, but it lacked a comprehensive action plan, and its only concrete action had been to create the CNLCC. This technically independent anticorruption commission was not empowered to initiate investigations, and its reports were referred to the president and not published.

While the weaknesses of independent institutions could be partly ascribed to deficiencies in the law, they were also a result of the powerful influence that some civil servants exerted on institutions. This related not only to the judiciary but also to such control bodies as the State General Inspectorate (IGE). This control was often used to cover up embezzlements rather than fight corruption and bad governance. One example of this was the investigation by the Inspectorate of the Administration and Justice in a case against several judges. This investigation resulted in convictions and symbolic punishments against the judges who took bribes, but those who offered the bribes have yet to be judged.

The president could also unduly influence the judiciary. Since he maintained de facto power over the appointment and promotion of judges, it was difficult for judges to pass rulings that would not find favor within the executive branch.

The judicial and legislative branches both suffered from insufficient human and financial resources. Many parliamentarians, for instance, lacked the skills, staff, and information necessary to initiate legislation on their own or to evaluate laws initiated by the executive branch. These inadequacies affected other control institutions, such as the Cour des Comptes. For this reason, monitoring of government institutions and personnel was often carried out on a much more limited sample of public services than it should have been. The uncertain nature of monitoring mechanisms reduced the risk of being identified, and therefore prosecuted, for corruption offenses.

Official immunities and judicial privileges often presented a challenge to the effective deterrence and prosecution of corruption. The president enjoyed the greatest degree of immunity and could not be prosecuted except in the case of high treason. While governmental officials could be prosecuted, they were judged only by the High Court of Justice, an institution extremely susceptible to political interference. National Assembly deputies could also be prosecuted, but the judicial proceedings could be hampered by the National Assembly itself, which had to approve the prosecution of any sitting deputy.

Beyond the shortcomings noted within various control bodies, there was a general lack of coordination among the various bodies in Senegal responsible for curbing corruption, and notably between the IGE and the Cour des Comptes. Redefining the mission of these organs would help streamline the control process. If this were done, the Cour des Comptes would probably be the sole governmental agency with judicial authority in cases of public financial corruption.

There was also a need for better coordination between the CNLCC and the National Centre for the Processing of Financial Information (CENTIF), given that there were clear connections between corruption and money laundering. For example, every case of corruption that the CNLCC investigated could also be brought to the attention of CENTIF for investigation. Since the state prosecutor was authorized to act when cases were brought to him by CENTIF, this coordination would make the fight against corruption more effective.

Anticorruption Stakeholders

Despite the widespread existence of corruption in Senegal, forces exist that have a stake in reform and that, under the right circumstances, can assist in bringing it about.

External forces. Donors certainly promoted governance reform in recent years, in terms of both their policy dialogue with the government of Senegal (GOS) and their assistance to finance good governance, economic governance, and public management reform programs. Conversely, donors did not *directly* target corruption as a major issue. Many of the international donors, including the World Bank with its lead role in the National Program for Local Development, the US Agency for International Development (USAID) with DGL-Felo, and Canada, Germany, Switzerland, the Netherlands, and Luxembourg, decided to focus their governance assistance on decentralization and training of local elected officials. In addition to the bilateral and multilateral external actors who supported governance reform, Senegal benefited from a good deal of nonstate foreign assistance, called "decentralized cooperation," nearly all of which focused on local-level governance and infrastructure. Recently, several of these donors shifted their approach to include national-level activities as well, following their analysis that working only at the local level was insufficient to promote system-wide change. Several even resumed direct budget support as part of their governance portfolio.

In terms of policy dialogue, the major donors jointly addressed their concerns to the prime minister and president on several occasions. Interviews with these actors indicated that they did not feel that the GOS had been particularly responsive to these appeals. While donors indisputably constituted a force for reform, many of them felt frustration about their level of impact on the policies and behavior of the central state and the overall quality of donor coordination in the area of good governance and anticorruption. The most significant achievement to date had been the passage of the 2007 Public Procurement Law, with its accompanying monitoring capability in the Agency for the Regulation of Public Markets. The mobilization for this took several years and significant donor cooperation, without which it is very unlikely that the bill would have passed. It remains to be seen, however, how the law will be implemented.

Internal forces. Some Senegalese strongly support governance reform, and they are generally found in specialized agencies such as the CNLCC, the PNBG, and the control organizations (the IGE and Cour des Comptes). In all of these agencies, many civil servants expressed the desire for more authority and resources to do their jobs properly. There was no indication, however, that they possessed much capacity to influence decision making.

Perhaps more promising was evidence that there were civil servants within technical ministries who want to reestablish the credibility and professionalization of their services and who took seriously recent studies that recommended changes in the ways these services operate. This group has the potential to become a force for change within the state.

Even more pro-reform sentiment can be found at the level of "decentralized" state institutions, such as among Regional Assembly members and regional support organizations. However, they tend to suffer from an extreme lack of resources and authority that frustrates their efforts.

The most dynamic pro-reform force within the state is at the level of local government.[2] Although local elected officials are subject to many of the same governance problems as found in higher office, their capacities in areas such as planning, monitoring, and contracting are improving, due largely to decentralization programs sponsored both by donors and by nonstate organizations through decentralization cooperation. Swiss, German, and Dutch, as well as USAID, programs are notable in this regard, as are programs sponsored by foreign NGO partners, such as Le Partenariat (France).

Societal forces. Civil society is well organized in Senegal and constitutes a potential force for reform. Specialized NGOs such as the Transparency International affiliate—Forum Civil—and Aide Transparence are potential sources for mobilizing broader public awareness and demand for better and less corrupt governance. Their links to the scholarly community through such organizations as the Institut Fondamental d'Afrique Noire group in Development and Poverty Reduction are especially critical in producing the kinds of data that can provide the grist for public debate and discussion. Other groups are less clearly focused on corruption and governance reform but are emerging as concerned parties, especially when their interests are directly affected. Associations, such as the Conseil National de Concertation et de Coopération des Ruraux (which represents agriculturalists), connect with and can potentially mobilize many people at the base. Typically, unions and student associations have not played a significant role in anticorruption advocacy because they were highly politicized. There were indications, however, that that is changing, as evidenced by recent protests by the Customs Workers Union.

Private sector business groups have also been absent from the forefront of anticorruption advocacy, in part because of their precarious position vis-à-vis the state. Some of the smaller and less formal firms have, however, revealed a strong concern for governance reform and a fairer, less-biased playing field.

The media, both print and electronic, is free in Senegal and plays a major role in sensitizing public opinion to corruption and mismanagement. Though it is limited by its weak resource base and limited audience, it continues to be a major advocate for reform.

Political-Economic Analysis

At the national level, competition for political power and capture of the state is intense, and the stakes are very high. Corruption involves not only personal enrichment and the enrichment of family, loyal supporters, and clients but the generation of resources to win and maintain power. A major battlefield is national elections, particularly the presidential election, where contenders need significant resources to attract and keep supporters. Grand corruption involving the allocation of state resources and the awarding of contracts, particularly in the public works and construction sector, serves to fuel political competition and potential domination. This corruption involves clan leaders, religious leaders (*marabouts*), government officials, and entrepreneurs who are vital parts of the political machine. The dominant form of linkage between the state and the population in this neopatrimonial system is based on personal relationships through which resources and privileges flow from person to person rather than from state to citizen or community. Grand corruption in Senegal appears to be growing in the fastest liberalizing sectors of the economy, especially mining and extractive industries, construction, and land ownership.

Secondary forms of corruption involve officials at all levels who are able to use their discretion and the slow, awkward functioning of the bureaucracy—particularly public service delivery and access to courts—to generate additional income. Since lower-level officials are not well paid, they tend to see these forms of administrative corruption as routine supplements to their income, while victims often regard these payments as conveniences to facilitate favorable decisions and avoid onerous expenses (such as the repair of vehicles that would not otherwise pass inspections). These forms of corruption help to undermine confidence in the regime and reinforce the sense of separation of the state from its citizenry.

Opposition to corruption in Senegal is growing, but it has not been very effective. At the elite level, the effort to reduce corruption is gaining momentum, particularly through public presentations and discussions by the Forum Civil. Although public expression of opposition to corruption is growing on the part of the business community, Senegalese firms remain heavily dependent on the state for contracts and business opportunities, a situation that creates favorable conditions for corruption. At the mass level, opposition to corruption is weak and disorganized. Public opinion polls reveal that the people are quite tolerant of corruption and accept it as the norm for doing business with the state and as part of a system of governance that ignores their interests.

The nature of Senegal's prevalent corruption can be described by complex political-economic dynamics. Senegal is characterized by the transitional nature exhibited by the regime since the 1990s and through the early 2000s: Senegal clearly changed over the years from a closed and authoritarian (hierarchical or vertical) regime to a more open and democratic regime, thanks to a wide range of political and economic liberalization measures. It still exhibits characteristics of the pluralism that made the alternation of power at the top possible.

At the same time, Senegal shows strong elements of a very different dynamic, described in terms of the centralizing trends and personalization of decision making that has become increasingly prevalent since the early 2000s (see Type 4 syndrome in Johnston's typology in chapter 5, table 5.1). Characteristics of the emerging regime that fit this second type are as follows:

- There is increasing domination of the regime by a single figure—the president—who is recognized as both the initiator of policy and its final arbitrator.
- The hierarchical nature of decision making is expressed through the combination of control over initiatives and decisions. This type of governance reinforces the powers of the executive over the legislative, leaving only marginal room for social mediation by institutions like the Council of the Republic.
- There is extension of executive power over institutions that previously had some characteristics of pluralism, such as the ANEC and the Haut Conseil de l'Audiovisuel (HCA: High Council for Broadcast Media). These institutions have lost much of their visibility and credibility.
- There is consolidation of power by a single party (the PDS), which now maintains control over parliament and most local government institutions.

- There is dominance by the president simultaneously over both the ruling party and the state, leaving him in a position to alter and rearrange institutions and to appoint and dismiss leaders as he sees fit, with little open discussion or debate.

Some of these characteristics reflect the leadership style of a very dynamic and popular leader who often acts as though he is the sole force capable of rapidly energizing a weak and unresponsive state bureaucracy and modernizing at least some sectors of the economy. Others derive from contemporary constitutional law and French centralization models inherited from the colonial era, which supports the concentration of power in the executive branch of government. Certainly, the constitution of January 2001 accorded the president an extraordinary legal capacity to accumulate power. Moreover, cultural patterns of power incorporating the personalization and concentration of power in the ruler or superior has not given way completely to more pluralist Western notions of democracy.

Senegal, however, retains many of the characteristics of newly democratic regimes, and its people appear to be highly supportive of how its democratic system works.[3] The current president himself has come to power through open competitive elections in 2000, which ousted the party that had been in power since independence.

Political competition has remained vigorous. The 2007 presidential elections were very competitive, and although the opposition had hotly contested the result, there was relatively little political violence. The president's personal popularity, populist style, and effective use of clientelism, as well as the fragmented nature of the political opposition, seem to have accounted for his victory rather than repression and massive electoral fraud. And, although in decline, the political opposition demonstrated some strength in mounting a relatively successful boycott campaign during the June 2007 legislative elections. The low turnout pointed to limited public interest in parliamentary elections and growing dissatisfaction of many Senegalese citizens with the regime.

Civil society is much more developed and tolerated than what might be expected in a highly centralized and personalized regime. Freedom of association, expression, and the press is still strong in Senegal. The government does not repress trade unions but seeks to control them through co-optation and patronage. Civil society organizations and the media are free to openly criticize the regime, and in some cases public opinion and lobbying by civil society organizations has obliged the president to limit or reverse unpopular policies, practices, and abuses of power. Despite some incidences of intimidation, the press continues to express a variety of opinions and to inform the public about corruption and misuses and abuses of government power.

In Senegal's context, corruption appears to be a rational, calculated behavior. As a profitable practice, it meets a strong need for funding desired lifestyles and clientelistic networks. For many of those involved in petty corruption, it offers the opportunity to earn a minimally acceptable income and meet basic family needs. Corrupt actions such as the abuse of power or rent-seeking behaviors are not very risky because prosecution and punishment are infrequent and unpredictable. Management and supervision, internal and external audits, and checks and balances are relatively weak in most sectors and functions of government, making it possible for public officials to engage in corrupt activities with impunity. At the same time, the public's high tolerance and acceptance of corrupt practices, coupled with the low priority given to corruption when compared with the struggle for survival, make it even more difficult to enforce norms and controls.[4]

Beyond the inherent logic of corruption, there appear to be a number of factors that contribute to the widespread growth of corruption and the limitations of control mechanisms. The following factors are framed within a culture that has limited respect for the rule of law.

Laws without teeth and inadequate enforcement mechanisms. Despite the generally adequate formal legal framework for dealing with corruption, there are still laws in force that permit the government to evade monitoring and control. This is most notable in the stipulations of a May 2002 law that provide for noncompetitive awards of contracts. A new law making it more difficult for government to award contracts without public competitive bidding has been approved but has not yet come into force. Other laws also need to be revisited, such as the legal framework for the CNLCC, which has little power to initiate investigations or subpoena officials.

Inadequate application of existing laws. Anticorruption laws that are on the books are often either selectively invoked for political reasons, ineffectively invoked because the instruments of control (auditing agencies, courts) are underresourced, or not invoked at all. According to the Forum Civil, more than 28 laws need to be modified or adapted. Drafts of many of these legal changes have been on hold in the parliament for years, while public discussion and debate on these necessary reforms have been limited.

The politicization of the state bureaucracy and its inability to effectively deliver basic public services. Although these characteristics were present in the previous regime, the situation has been exacerbated under the Wade government.

Politicization of the bureaucracy, coupled with rapid turnover of ministers and other senior officials, among other factors, has fostered institutional instability and undermined the ability of the state bureaucracy to deliver public services efficiently and in a nonpartisan manner. While it is common in democratic presidential regimes to base many high-level appointments primarily on political criteria, this is usually accompanied by an effort to recruit people meeting merit standards for the post. With his populist style and suspicion of the state bureaucracy inherited from the Diouf regime, President Wade has reduced the autonomy of the administration and chosen ministers and high state officials who often lack the administrative experience and technical skills needed to effectively run their departments. The neopatrimonial nature of the administration also encourages clientelism based on political loyalty and personal relationships in determining access to public services, reinforcing conditions for corruption at all levels. The high degree of politicization, lack of incentives for efficiently delivering public goods and services, and low salaries of local level officials all combine to undermine these officials' professionalism and resistance to corruption.

Weak accountability mechanisms. The government has few effective internal accountability mechanisms. The ones that exist are concentrated in the presidency and the Ministry of Economy and Finance, which have few institutional checks on their activities. External guarantors of accountability through *a posteriori* audits and sanctions are weak and ineffective. Internal and external audits and inspections are conducted infrequently and are not sufficiently funded. When abuses are actually identified, there is minimal follow-up authority within the judicial or administrative systems.

In addition, supervision and management within the civil service are generally ineffective. Citizen watchdog groups that monitor and oversee government departments and their use of the public budget barely exist. Investigative journalists, the natural watchdogs of government operations, often lack sufficient knowledge of the law and legal system to make their case effectively. They do not play a major role in the effort to achieve transparency and accountability.

Uneven transparency. Transparency in government decisions and activities is inconsistent. The public has access to some types of information, but not all. Even where there is public access, citizen awareness and interest in directly participating in monitoring and evaluating public sector performance is low, especially at the local level. The involvement of the Forum Civil and other national-level civil society and private sector organizations in advocating for more transparency are the exceptions to the rule.

Resistance to decentralization. Government operations and decisions in Senegal are highly centralized, which help to maintain collusive practices among national- and local-level political and economic elites. Although the 1996 Decentralization Code transferred considerable formal powers and authority to local government units to manage and deliver public services, this has not been accompanied by the transfer of adequate financial and human resources to permit local governments to fulfill their new roles. The trend toward centralization of political and administrative power in the hands of the president also explains the failure to move more rapidly to implement the 1996 decentralization reforms. Moreover, the president's strategy of providing key local government officials with cars and increased personal financial resources provides attractive incentives for them to abandon their political neutrality.

Limited scope and capacity of civil society organizations involved in anticorruption activities. Senegal has thousands of community grassroots voluntary associations and hundreds of national, urban-based civil society and private sector organizations, which operate across all sectors of society. Few, however, specifically focus on good governance issues or on exposing and controlling corruption. In the past decade, civil society groups like the Forum Civil have expanded their capacity to monitor and document bad governance practices and launch campaigns to inform the government and the public about their findings. Despite their efforts, these groups have little impact on influencing government policy and the behavior of corrupt officials. They also fail to reach and mobilize people at the grassroots level to participate in anticorruption campaigns or change the widely prevalent public tolerance of corruption in Senegalese society. In terms of mobilizing public opinion, the groups generally do not conduct sufficient outreach to grassroots urban and rural Senegalese, whose interests and concerns are focused on concrete problems directly affecting their daily lives rather than on grand corruption at the state level. Moreover, the way these groups frame corruption issues often means little to less-educated members of the public.

Widespread public tolerance and acceptance of corruption based on cultural and social norms and traditions.[5] Patrimonial modes and norms of governance based on clientelist relationships between rulers and ruled have been deeply rooted in Senegal's precolonial past and are not easily transformed. Control over the state, rather than productive economic activities, provides the best means for generating personal wealth, and rulers are generally expected to use state power for this purpose rather than to provide state services.[6] At the same time, leaders are expected to be very generous to their immediate entourage and followers as the best means of retaining their loyalty. President Wade's concentration and personalization of power, coupled with a populist style that reflects little interest in rationalizing state bureaucratic institutions, spark resurgence in the kind of warrior (*ceddo*) behavior found in Senegal's precolonial states. In this kind of system, generosity in bestowing resources on clients trumps hostility to corruption.

Although most Senegalese acknowledge that corruption is widespread and detrimental to society, only 1% of those polled in Forum Civil's 2001 corruption survey identified corruption as a major problem. Moreover, nearly a quarter of respondents maintained that corruption was acceptable as long as those involved redistributed some of their gains.[7]

Proposed Strategic Directions

The preceding analysis points to certain core problems in Senegalese government and society that facilitate the spread of corruption and to strategic directions that can help reduce corruption and its consequences. These problems are listed below, along with key recommendations to address these issues.

1. There are inadequate checks on executive decision making.
   - Strengthen capacities of local government to more effectively participate in controlling resources.
   - Mainstream good governance programs in different sectors (health, education, natural resource management) so that they become part of community-wide participation in financial management and control.
2. There is a lack of transparency in government operations.
   - Support the CNLCC to educate the public about public expenditures.
   - Create an independent watchdog center to monitor public contracts and publicize its findings.
   - Initiate and sustain ongoing policy dialogue at the highest level concerning lack of transparency, private sector rules, taxation policies, and development of independent and functioning regulatory and auditing agencies.
3. There is a lack of service orientation in the delivery of public services (health, education, forestry, water, etc.).
   - Support the involvement of government officials and employees in workshops to discuss the costs to the public and the

nation resulting from petty and grand corruption and to promote professionalism and professional ethics.

4. There is ineffective public opposition to corruption.
   - Develop a culturally relevant concept and approach to understanding and resisting corruption.
   - Support civil society's capacity to produce studies and collect data that can be used to generate discussions in various fora. Involve media and the university community in these discussions to advocate for better control of public expenditures.

Overall, reform efforts should be prioritized according to the following principles:

- Focus on program options that clearly relate to one or more of these core problems.
- Select an approach that is context specific (deal with the current and near-term character of corruption).
- Choose options that are logically linked to one another because they offer the possibility of addressing issues at different levels or sectors that are interlinked.
- Incorporate options that are based on best practices, approaches that have already been shown to produce some positive effect in the Senegalese context.
- Choose options that can build on, and are compatible with, the major existing concerns of donors and of the GOS as expressed in the Accelerated Economic Growth Strategy, the National Poverty Reduction Strategy (PSRP-2), and the National Program for Local Development.
- Choose programs that work with state, nonstate, and external stakeholders who demonstrate political will and interest in supporting reform.

On the basis of these criteria, a comprehensive anticorruption program in Senegal can focus on the following objectives:

1. Strengthen local governance through the development of culturally relevant concepts and tools.

2. Mainstream transparency and corruption control into existing sectoral programs by adopting a more community-wide (*cadre de concértation*) approach to addressing specific problems like forestry management, school maintenance and management, and health center management, thus adding value to existing governance aspects of these programs.

3. Strengthen citizen demand for better governance, a more plural and balanced state decision-making process, and transparency and corruption control through a grant program to develop data, impact analysis, cost analysis on state financial expenditures, and public market procurement. Also involved would be grants to widely diffuse the findings of these studies and the sponsorship of a series of debates and workshops at the national, regional, and community local government levels.

4. Improve the quality of governmental services by assisting with the reprofessionalization of civil servants involved in service delivery. This would be done in two ways: by involving them in workshops and debates on the transparency and corruption problems identified and documented in various studies and by assisting in the development of ethical and professional codes and the commitment of groups of government workers to maintain these norms.

5. Support the government's anticorruption program by involving the CNLCC where possible in the public dissemination of these studies and in subsequent debates and workshops.

6. Support greater transparency in public market allocation through one or more of the following mechanisms:
   • support and monitor the work of the tripartite Agency for the Regulation of Public Markets,
   • support the establishment of a politically and economically autonomous watchdog center for the tracking of public contracts at various levels, and
   • support the proposed electronic database project and website to track public market contracts.

7. Continue high-level policy dialogue with regard to transparency in budgeting and procurement and in laws, rules and tax structures governing state and private sector business.

Analysis of Key Sectors

The assessment team identified several key sectors for immediate action, among them health, local government, natural resource management, and the private sector, where major opportunities to reduce corruption exist.

Health Sector

The health system is an ideal breeding ground for corruption at all levels.[8] Scarce health resources are allocated in accordance with complex and rigid rules. Clients are desperately in need of these services but lack the information and skills to control the process. Health service consumers are generally seen to be in a socially and economically inferior position, and thus are in a dependent relationship with health care providers. Given widespread cultural norms that emphasize the display of gratitude for such services and respect for authority, corruption has become the principal way to obtain health care. Corruption is pervasive at every level of the system, and this situation has created a national crisis in health care.

The legal structure underpinning the provision of public health care in Senegal is generally adequate. The major problem is that many of these laws are not effectively implemented. This leaves health workers and those in need of health services in a world of informality in which all practices are conducted outside the law. The poor and the ill are the biggest victims of this informality. The "winners" are elaborate networks that colluded in order to benefit collectively from corrupt behaviors; these link support staff and nurses at the community health level to medical and administrative personnel and hospitals at the highest levels of medical care.

This system is fed, paradoxically, by both shortage and abundance. The health sector is in need of an estimated 3,000 additional trained medical personnel, and there are communities in greater urban Dakar where no health facility is available for more than 100,000 residents. On the other hand, funds from governmental and nongovernmental donors earmarked for programs like HIV/AIDS prevention and treatment provide ready sources of funding and materials that are often misallocated for personal benefit.

At the heart of this crisis are two major issues: an almost total lack of control and accountability for resources from the top down and a culture of corruption that seems to have displaced any sense of professional responsibility and obligation to the public. A National Forum on Health took place in 2006 in which health workers and officials gathered to discuss these issues and to see what remedies and reforms might be put into effect. A reform program based on three principles was affirmed there. This consisted of a multisectoral approach in which there would be a shift to a more customer-focused orientation, and citizens would be encouraged to participate in health planning and monitoring. Thus far, this program seems to be no more effective than previous efforts. The health system is still marked by a near total absence of effective participation on the part of organized health service users or socio-professional organizations that might be capable of checking, at least in part, the power and authority of highly corrupt medical professionals.

A recent and extensive study involving months of field observations documented a variety of corrupt practices at three levels of the medical system: the public hospitals, the health centers, and the local-level health posts.[9] Not only did this study identify particular vulnerabilities, it also contended that corruption at all levels was not an unusual practice—it was linked to underground networks that operated in the interest of health service personnel at all levels (although those higher up were often better protected against direct observation of their corruption).

According to this study, at the hospital level, the following vulnerabilities are prevalent: A triage racket exists, in which patients are charged illegal fees to be seen and even charged depending on how ill or fearful they or their loved ones appear to be. Low-level staff members extract fees for beds and other basic services and provide no receipts. Patients are overcharged or even double-charged, with the staff pocketing the difference. Health certificates for a variety of administrative requirements are for sale (such as to get a driver's license). Food and drugs are stolen for private use. Gifts for services are solicited and accepted.

At the health center level, the following vulnerabilities exist: There is overcharging for medicines not used. Illegal charges are made for treatments offered by unqualified personnel. Illegal charges are made for a variety of birth delivery services. Health certificates are up for sale. Public equipment is used by chief medical personnel for private consultations. There is a general failure to provide free public services.

At the health post (community) level, the following problems exist: Local influential religious leaders and their families are given preferential treatment and access in exchange for gifts. Foreigners, often followers of a *marabout* from a different area or country, are treated at higher-than-posted rates. Medicines that are supposed to be distributed for free are on sale, often on the open market by petty merchants. Services are overcharged or double-charged. There is misappropriation of HIV/AIDS subsidies.

Because of decentralization of administrative services and its implication in the Bamako (user fee) system, the health post level has become the most important for consumers of health services. The 2005 study contended that the major dysfunctions at this level were due to a number of factors: the operation of corrupt practices and networks at higher levels of the health system, the near total lack of transparency in the allocation of health resources and lack of effective monitoring and control from above, and the limited success in making use of community health committees as a way of fostering participation and improving accountability. According to that study, these committees rarely involve more than one or two local notables, who often collaborate with the health post nurse and the chief doctor at the district level to keep access to information limited. This allows the racket to continue for the benefit of those few in a position to know and influence how health resources are actually being used.

The Environment for Reform

Given the nature of corruption in the health sector, there is likely to be strong resistance to reform. The medical corps sees corruption as a well-tested and accepted survival strategy that is actually an extension of societal values and obligatory reciprocity in an environment marked by scarcity and inequality. It is likely to be difficult to persuade the medical corps to change its ways. Getting the state to allocate more resources to the health sector and reduce the shortage of available health care professionals could help, but it would have to be part of a general reform of public sector budget management and control. It is not at all clear that the GOS is ready to take on this level of administrative reform and budget transparency.

Recommendations

Given the systematic, collective, networked, and highly entrenched nature of corruption in the health system, there are no quick fixes that are likely to impact corruption in this sector over the short run. The following recommendations can nevertheless contribute to an improvement in the situation, if they are implemented effectively:

- Increase involvement of organized civil society and socio-professional groups in the implementation of reform at all levels.
- Clarify roles and authority between the national, regional, and community levels and increase formalization of rules and procedures, while still respecting the principles of decentralization.
- Adopt a multisectoral planning approach to health involving a broad stratum of the population in health planning and monitoring (recasting Health Committees as Commissions of Local

Government rather than autonomous local bodies attached to a particular technical service).

- Promote a code of ethics and clarify the status of health care professionals.
- Maintain stricter penalties and zero tolerance for corruption.

Local Government Sector

There are great differences in local governance styles due to the variety of local government institutions and differences in local conditions and populations. The levels and forms of corruption and anticorruption activities also vary considerably and depend on several factors: the political will of local leaders, the degree of interest and participation of local citizens in municipal and rural government, expectations concerning the delivery of public services, and the degree of politicization of local government institutions. It is common, however, for local presidents and mayors to possess highly concentrated power, largely unchecked by the limited authority of regional, municipal, and rural councils. In addition, courts at this level are fairly rare, and citizens do not often use them to resolve conflicts.

Although the national regime is highly centralized, it exercises little direct control over local government institutions, especially in rural areas. Since national anticorruption institutions like PNBG and CNLCC do not represent local government, only the local government section of the Cour des Comptes can monitor and audit finances at this level, and it generally lacks the personnel, resources, or will to do so effectively.

At the same time, the central government does not transfer adequate human and financial resources directly to local government entities to enable them to carry out their mission. While this reduces the potential for grand corruption at the local level, it also limits the power of local institutions. For instance, major projects affecting larger cities like Dakar and Thiès are controlled by the central government, often without consulting local government officials. Large-scale sectoral donor programs also often operate with minimum involvement from local government.

Municipal communes are highly politicized in Greater Dakar and in the larger cities, where high levels of political patronage and corruption prevail. In the Dakar metropolitan area, urban civil society elites focus primarily on national-level corruption and grand corruption rather than get directly involved with local government (with rare exceptions).

The Regional Councils and Commune d'Arrondissement Councils, originally created in 1996, lack the human and financial resources needed to carry out their missions. The Regional Councils tend to be dominated by major political leaders from the ruling party closely allied with the president. Although the mayors of the communes d'arrondissement are also politicians, they are often more representative of their constituencies.

Rural communities vary markedly in population size, area, level of financial resources, and degree of politicization and partisan politics. Senegal's rural councils generally have few resources and no professional staff outside of community secretaries. The presidents of these rural councils tend to be more representative of their communities than the mayors of municipal councils, and their smaller resource base offers fewer opportunities for corruption at the local government level.

Although donors in Senegal do not have local government anticorruption programs per se, they are increasingly sponsoring programs to enhance citizen participation in local government planning and training on local government issues, including references to transparency and accountability as necessary for good government. USAID has been supporting decentralization efforts since the mid-1990s and has supported good governance practices in its sectoral programs as well.

Although decentralization often entails replication of corruption patterns found at the national level at the local government level, it also provides opportunities for citizens to control corruption at this level, since citizens are often closer to their local elected officials than to their national officials. Civil service recruitment is highly politicized, especially in large cities, which leads to hiring on the basis of political criteria rather than merit and the use of public office to reward political supporters and enhance the political position of the party controlling local government. Once in office, mayors and council presidents possess a high degree of concentrated power, and weak municipal and rural councils have little ability to counter their authority.

The frequent and large turnover of local government officials, coupled with the lack of knowledge of local government rules and procedures by local officials and local inhabitants, opens the way for manipulation of the rules and misuse of power. In addition, limited public interest and participation in local government affairs, especially in Dakar and larger towns, reduces checks on abuses of power.

Public acceptance of certain forms of petty corruption—for example, payoffs for getting public services or for reducing taxes and fines—is relatively high. The exchange of money for services is often regarded as a normal part of doing business with local officials, an attitude that makes it difficult to fight corruption at the local level. This is compounded by the failure of the government to sanction the actions of corrupt public officials. In addition, cultural norms relating to mutual reciprocity, solidarity, and obligation related to family, kin, friends, and political allies promote corruption in hiring and favoring of family and friends, providing gifts for services, and reluctance to impose sanctions when called for.

Although agents of deconcentrated technical government services are theoretically under the authority of local government, local officials have few levers with which to exercise controls and sanctions for poor performance and corruption by local technicians (such as forestry agents, health workers, school teachers, etc.). As long as their salaries are paid by the state and their career paths determined by their superiors in the central technical ministries, local technical officials have few incentives to become more accountable to elected local government officials and local communities.

The Environment for Reform

The legal framework contained in the 1996 Local Collectivity Code provides specific mandatory mechanisms for ensuring transparency, accountability, and public participation in decision making. Surveys show that the public has more confidence in local government than in national-level political institutions such as the National Assembly and political parties. Local government in rural areas is also more likely to remain nonpartisan than national government and more responsive to its constituents. Moreover, the number of civil society activists elected to local government offices has been steadily increasing.

As a result of decentralization reforms, citizens and elected officials are acquiring greater understanding of how local government ought to work. They are becoming more aware of the costs of petty corruption at the local level and the fact that certain forms of corruption—such as *ger*, or imposing payment for services that should be given free—violate cultural norms.

Donors are increasingly recognizing the importance of good governance and citizen participation at the local level as essential for effectively implementing antipoverty and local development programs. They are providing resources for training local government officials and citizens at local levels and collaborating in preparing local development plans. Pro-reform elements promoting good governance at the local level include national-level associations representing and lobbying for local government, such as L'Union des Associations des Élus Locaux (UAEL); the Direction of Local Government in the Decentralization and Local Government Ministry; representatives of local civil society concerned with improving good governance at local levels; national media and community radio stations reporting on corruption at local levels;

local government officials committed to the development of their communities; and elements within technical services promoting professionalism.

Effective mechanisms for promoting good governance and reducing corruption include establishing *cadres de concértation* between different levels of government and civil society organizations (in Saint-Louis), participatory budgeting involving citizen participation in elaborating and monitoring the budgetary process (in Fissel), and depoliticization of local government operations (in Gorée).

Recommendations

Several recommendations are offered in support of anticorruption reforms at the local level:

- Extend training and information concerning the functioning of local government to include municipal and rural councilors and local civil society.
- Support participatory budgetary processes developed in Fissel.
- Support and strengthen mechanisms like *cadres de concértation* (Saint-Louis) to promote greater collaboration between different levels of local government, local civil society, and local media (such as community radio).
- Tailor local government anticorruption interventions to local political, social, cultural, and economic contexts.
- Promote and support participation of national urban-based elites in local government in their areas (e.g., *Mouvement Citoyen*).
- Support integration of anticorruption components in health, education, and natural resources programs.
- Develop mechanisms to ensure sustainability of anticorruption programs at local government levels after completion of projects.
- Work for better harmonization and coordination of local government components in local development and antipoverty programs.

Natural Resource Management Sector

Like most sub-Saharan countries, Senegal has experienced an unprecedented environmental crisis caused by the persistent degradation of natural resources: forests, fisheries, wildlife, arable land, biological diversity, and mining resources.[10] Progressive degradation of the environment has taken place despite the adoption of numerous codes—for example, Wildlife (1986), Forestry (1998), Environment (2001), and Mining (2003) codes—and regulatory mechanisms, accompanied by the government's increased commitment to implement sustainable development strategies to protect the environment.

Effective management and regulation of Senegal's natural resource base is not only vital to avoid damage to Senegal's physical environment but also critical to sustain and develop the Senegalese economy and the provision of livelihoods for the country's rapidly growing population. Fishing and mining constitute two of Senegal's leading export sectors. Declining fishing resources and mismanagement of Senegal's major mining sectors (such as Industries Chimiques du Sénégal) threaten the future of these two sectors, while rapid deforestation caused by growing demand for charcoal in urban areas and arable land in rural areas reduce soil fertility and productivity, undermining the rural economy. Growing demand for increasingly scarce urban land for housing is pushing up land prices, sparking speculation, and making it more difficult for Senegalese of modest means to pay for decent housing.

The 1996 Decentralization Code transferred authority to local government units for managing natural resources. Although local government, theoretically, has legal responsibility in this area, in practice, the state continues to play the dominant role in regulating access to, and use of, most of Senegal's natural resources and imposing sanctions on those violating the law.

Overall, the combination of increasingly fierce competition for access to scarce natural resources, inadequate and nontransparent control and regulatory mechanisms, inadequate understanding of the complex laws and regulations governing natural resource use, and the high costs of degrading the environment provides a propitious climate for corruption.

As in many other sectors, there is a wide gap between the law and the application of the law. Senegal's diverse natural resource codes are generally well written. However, there is a severe shortage of personnel and resources to ensure enforcement of the codes and punishment of those violating the law. For instance, there are not enough forestry agents to patrol all the protected forests, inland waterways, and national parks and wildlife reserves or enough maritime agents and boats to adequately patrol and prevent overfishing of Senegal's offshore fisheries. The insufficient number of personnel decreases the chance of catching violators of the law.

The level of corruption in this sector is directly related to the economic stakes involved. Grand corruption is more likely to be found in areas where the economic stakes are high, such as large-scale mining industries, major offshore fishing activities involving well-equipped foreign fishing boats, and the allocation and titling of large tracts of urban land. Petty corruption is also widespread and results from illegal agreements between natural resource users and government officials charged with regulating access to and use of land, forestry resources, wildlife, and so on.

The politicization and lack of transparency of different government ministries and departments managing natural resources, coupled with a high degree of discretionary power on the part of ministers and department heads making decisions concerning quotas, licensing, and punishment for violators of the rules, offer temptations to engage in corrupt practices. For example, the allocation of charcoal quotas is still conducted at the national level despite the fact that quotas have been officially abolished and responsibility for allocating licenses has been transferred to the presidents of the rural councils.

Opportunities for corruption exist at many levels because government regulations are costly for entrepreneurs seeking to reduce their costs of doing business and increase their profits by exploiting natural resources. Petty corruption occurs when officials accept bribes for not enforcing rules concerning the use of illicit fishing nets, overloading trucks with firewood and charcoal, hunting and grazing in protected areas, removing species from the protected list, and operating without licenses. Corrupt officials also impose fines on those caught violating the rules and keep the money collected for themselves or sell confiscated goods for personal profit. Land speculators have been known to bribe officials to gain title to coveted property in urban areas, while urban mayors sometimes favor their electoral supporters in allocating lots.

As in other sectors, ordinary citizens caught violating the law or seeking to reduce their transaction costs see little harm in engaging in petty corruption, viewing it as a necessary part of life and often essential to their economic survival. Moreover, many civilians and enforcement agents do not fully understand the existing laws or keep abreast of new changes in the law. Citizens are therefore often unaware of their rights or the appropriate procedures to take when these rights are violated.

The Environment for Reform

Given the political climate in the country, the best opportunities for reducing corruption lie in working at the local government level and facilitating greater citizen participation to manage natural resources. The 1996 Decentralization Code and the 1998 Forestry Code, for example, provide a solid legal framework for community management of local forests. Local communities can also work in other areas involving management of grazing lands, inland fisheries and fishponds, wildlife reserves, road construction materials, and so on.

Although local government and community regulatory and management mechanisms entail relatively small-scale activities and simple control mechanisms, they can have a major impact on reducing petty corruption at the local level and lead to more efficient management of resources and greater economic returns to the community. Local communities often possess a large stock of indigenous knowledge about their natural resources and traditional management methods that can be adapted to changing conditions and technologies. What is needed, however, is more training of local government officials, technical agents, and citizens in understanding the new rules governing natural resource management and their rights to manage these resources.

Consciousness is growing on the part of the government, private sector, and national-level civil society concerning the importance of preserving the environment and the economic damage caused by corruption in this sector. This signals an opportunity to build support for reform by supporting studies documenting trends and highlighting the costs of mismanagement and corruption. These results can be widely disseminated.

Recommendations

The following recommendations are based on the assumption that community management of natural resources is the best approach toward ensuring good governance practices and curtailing corruption at the local level. This approach seeks to build partnerships between all the different stakeholders—state, local government, concerned technical services, private sector, community, and resource users—to ensure rational management of existing resources and consensus as to how resources should be used and benefits distributed. These recommendations include the following:

- Involve local populations and local government in negotiations concerning sectoral policies related to access to, use of, and distribution of benefits and the types of sanctions to be imposed in case of violation of the rules.
- Adapt and harmonize existing laws to eliminate contradictions and to be more in line with local strategies and practices. Local conventions that reflect these strategies should be recognized as binding and their legal status strengthened.
- Advance the decentralization process by strengthening the role of local communities in decision making for the use of resources and in the distribution of profits resulting from their management. Efforts should also be made to strengthen the capacity of local government officials and community stakeholders to manage local resources more efficiently.

- Reinforce control mechanisms by investing more in human resources and providing greater material and financial support.
- Strengthen collegiality and collaboration among different state administrative and technical services charged with regulating the natural resource environment.

Private Sector and Economic Growth

During the first two decades of independence (1960–1980), the Senegalese formal private sector was rudimentary and tightly managed by the state, while the economy was dominated by French and Lebanese business interests. Corruption was moderate. At that time, the small Senegalese formal private sector was heavily dependent on state contracts and licenses to function.

The 1980s saw the expansion of the formal private sector, the rise of larger-scale and modern industrial and service enterprises, and the emergence of a strong informal sector that challenged the dominance of Lebanese and French firms in the commercial sectors. Despite the steady movement toward decreased state regulation of the economy and greater privatization of government enterprises under a series of structural adjustment programs, the Senegalese private sector remained highly dependent on the state for contracts and business opportunities and therefore more vulnerable to corruption.

Since the mid-1980s, the Senegalese private sector has become increasingly modernized and better organized. The private sector has increased its demands for greater transparency and speed in government operations and played a larger role in elaborating Senegalese economic growth strategies. Three major business associations represent the interests of the Senegalese private sector: Conseil National du Patronat du Sénégal (CNP), representing some of the older large-scale industrial and service groups; Confédération Nationale des Employeurs du Sénégal (CNES), a more vocal actor criticizing the government's slow pace in implementing transparency measures; and Union Nationale des Commerçants et Industrielles du Sénégal (UNACOIS) representing the so-called informal sector.

Although President Wade and the Senegalese private sector express their strong commitment to liberalizing the economy, it is not clear that the private sector or the president want a wide-open market economy in which the state plays a minimal regulatory role. The president has concentrated a great deal of discretionary power in agencies attached to the office of the president, which has been able to avoid competitive bidding on major public works and infrastructure projects. For their part, the three main private sector organizations have expressed the need to receive some protection from foreign investors. UNACOIS is concerned about competition from Chinese merchants and investors, while the other two associations that together cover most of the modern formal Senegalese sector want at least to be guaranteed subcontractor status on government contracts with foreign investors or protection against foreign investors competing in the same area.

One of the major changes in Senegal in recent years has been the willingness of the state to publicly acknowledge that corruption is a serious problem hindering economic development and the growth of the private sector. Surveys conducted of Senegalese enterprises identified corruption as particularly serious in the areas of tax collection, access to credit, and obtaining permission to create a new business.[11] There was also a strong perception among the general public that there was significant corruption involved in public sector–private sector contracts, although there was little direct evidence that this assertion was accurate, since by nature this form of corruption would be carefully hidden by both parties. This perception had been fueled by the high degree of government contracts escaping public bidding. The IMF reported that over 90% of public contracts in the first quarter of 2007 did not entail competitive bidding, as compared with 56% of contracts in 2006.

The state, rather than the Senegalese private sector, remains the dominant economic actor. Despite liberalization measures, the government continues to highly regulate private sector economic activities through taxing, licensing, and customs regulations, while the massive inflow of foreign aid and sharp increases in government revenues and investments in infrastructure make Senegal's private sector heavily dependent on the state for contracts and economic relief.

Corruption vulnerabilities take several forms.

A high degree of dependency by many private sector enterprises on government contracts. State officials can demand kickbacks while businesses offer bribes to obtain contracts. Interviews indicate that bribes range from 10% to 30% of the value of the contract. In a difficult economic climate, failure to offer a bribe could mean bankruptcy for firms experiencing economic difficulties. This phenomenon occurs at all levels and scales of activity.

Lack of transparency and information concerning terms of contracts and criteria for awarding contracts. It is difficult and politically risky for Senegalese private sector firms to openly challenge the lack of transparency when it occurs in agencies attached to the presidency. Foreign investors dissatisfied with the lack of transparency can more easily look elsewhere.

Inadequacy of existing institutional corruption control mechanisms within ministries. Institutional instability caused by rapid turnover, as well as the politicization of top-level government posts, makes it difficult to control middle- and low-level corruption involving kickbacks and bribes for speeding up procedures to obtain licenses, reducing taxes, and faking invoices for imported goods, for instance.

A culture of tolerance of corruption in business affairs. Businessmen generally accept corruption as part of doing business and factor this into their accounting. Grand corruption by those in power is also tolerated by the general public as long as some money is spread around.

Onerous tax and customs duties. These make it difficult for small- and medium-sized informal sector enterprises to survive if they pay the official rates levied on them. For example, paying taxes on volume of sales rather than on profit margins threaten the viability of enterprises with low profit margins.

Lack of knowledge of regulations concerning taxes, customs, official bookkeeping norms, registration procedures, and so on. Informal sector entrepreneurs are often unaware of this information, making them vulnerable to corrupt government officials and discouraging them from entering the formal sector.

Limited understanding by judges of commercial law. This hinders fair decisions in conflicts involving the private sector and between the public and the private sectors.

Petty corruption: extortion, bribery, speed money, influence peddling, and favoritism. This is a common practice in most business-government transactions, starting from business registration, issuing of numerous government permits, inspections, and leasing of public property. These forms of corruption have the greatest impact on small- and medium-sized businesses, which feel insecure and helpless in confronting authorities and bureaucrats.

The Environment for Reform

Senegal has several constituencies that seek reform to different degrees:

- private sector umbrella organizations, such as CNP, CNES, and UNACOIS;
- civil society organizations, such as Forum Civil, Aide Transparence, and the coalition of civil society organizations formed in 2003 to monitor public sector activities;
- women's groups, such as the Association of Women Entrepreneurs involved in preparing the Diamniadio Industrial Platform and women's entrepreneur associations seeking equal access to economic opportunities;

- the media, which has widely reported and exposed private-public corruption;
- government agencies interested in reform, such as PNBG, CNLCC, and Agence Nationale Chargée de la Promotion de l'Investissement et des Grands Travaux (APIX); and
- USAID and other donors interested in improving Senegal's business climate.

All three of the major business umbrella organizations have a common and direct interest in promoting greater transparency in public markets. Relatively conservative organizations like CNP prefer to battle corruption by emphasizing good governance and creating a business environment that makes it more difficult for corruption to flourish. Both CNP and CNES are consulted by the government to discuss Senegal's accelerated growth policy. UNACOIS, which has been the most vocal in attacking the government's private sector policies and corruption, also needs to be involved in efforts to lobby for greater transparency. To the extent that the lack of transparency has prevented some foreign investors from coming to Senegal, APIX can also have an interest in promoting greater transparency to attract foreign and Senegalese investors. PNBG and CNLCC, in addition, can act as government allies in support of this kind of program.

While the business community needs to take the lead, civil society associations, women's entrepreneurial associations, and the media also have a stake in launching efforts to lobby for greater transparency and generating greater public support for anticorruption activities.

Recommendations

The fight against corruption constitutes a major theme toward improving the business sector, increasing growth, and accelerating Senegalese enterprise competitiveness. Given the political realities, the following recommendations can be considered:

- Support the establishment of a national "observatory" that would monitor public markets and the application of the new procurement code.
- Provide training and technical assistance to informal sector enterprises to enhance their understanding of government rules and regulations and their bargaining power vis-à-vis the government.

Also, offer the prospects of becoming formal private sector enterprises.

- Provide support for creating mechanisms of collaboration between the private sector, civil society organizations, and the media to investigate, document, and share information concerning corrupt practices in private-public sector relationships and measures to combat them.
- Provide training in commercial law and best practices to judges and state officials involved in hearing cases and mediating private sector conflicts and conflicts between the state and the private sector.
- Encourage high-level diplomatic dialogue with the president concerning the need to accelerate good governance reforms and combat corruption more vigorously.

Epilogue

Since the 2007 corruption assessment in Senegal, concerns have grown about President Wade's centralization of power. Although a 2001 constitutional amendment limited the president to two five-year terms, the National Assembly recently approved a new amendment eliminating term limits and re-extended the presidential mandate to seven years. Wade then announced his intention to run for president again in 2012, at the age of 84. In addition, the president appears to be grooming his son, Karim, as his possible successor for the presidency. After an unsuccessful bid in 2009 for the position of mayor of Dakar, the younger Wade was appointed by his father to the highly powerful post of minister of state for International Cooperation, Urban and Regional Planning, Air Transport, and Infrastructure.

Other actions have added to the perception that Senegal increasingly resembles a "family-run patrimonial state," in the words of one opposition leader.[12] In particular, Wade's spending habits have created "huge confusion between his own resources—he was not wealthy—and the country's resources," according to a local advocacy group.[13] The president frequently travels with a large entourage, spending lavishly on accommodations and other perquisites, and became embroiled in a minor scandal in September 2009 after gifting a departing IMF official with US$200,000 in cash.[14] In April 2010, the government unveiled an enormous "African Renaissance Monument," a pet project of Wade's that drew criticism for employing North Korean, not African, laborers and costing US$27 million in a time of economic crisis. (Wade, moreover, claims a share of the profits made from visits to the statue, as he maintains he contributed artistically to the monument's conception.)[15]

Although opposition parties made a strong showing in local elections in 2009, Wade's party continues to enjoy a significant majority in the National Assembly. These legislators are generally quite susceptible to influence from the executive branch, and opposition forces are fractionated. As the 2012 presidential election approaches, some of Senegal's many political parties are attempting to devise a common platform to unite opposition to the president. They are likely to face a bigger challenge, however, in deciding on a single candidate to represent them in the upcoming elections.[16]

In September 2009, Senegal received a US$540 million grant for economic growth programs from the Millennium Challenge Corporation (MCC), having successfully completed the five-year eligibility process.[17] The US State Department acknowledged "signs of slippage" in Senegal's governance but asserted that the award was meant to "press the Government of Senegal to make needed improvement in good governance and fight corruption."[18]

While corruption is perceived as on the rise in Senegal, there has been some progress in certain key sectors, with donors and NGOs finding a degree of success in health, local government, natural resource management, and private sector development programs.

Health Sector

Many anticorruption programs in the health sector focus on local service delivery issues and supportive civil society capacity. A five-year, US$11.5 million USAID program that began in 2006 assists Senegal's Ministry of Health in developing policies and tools to improve the health system but also works to build capacity and responsibility for health delivery at the local level. These efforts facilitate decentralization of institutions by strengthening local management capacity. In particular, the program assists local officials and civil society organizations in developing and implementing annual health plans, funded by both local revenues and decentralized funds from the national government. In 2008, 172 communities received assistance in creating these health plans and budgets, with over 2,580 individuals participating. USAID also worked to establish mutual health organizations, community-based health financing schemes that covered 76,000 community members in 2008.[19]

Transparency issues are addressed through evaluations and training of local health providers. In many communities, budget expenditures, health results, and even prices for common services and supplies are not publicized. In the Malem Hoddar District of Senegal's Kaffrine province (population roughly

83,842), USAID support led to district health teams deciding to post service and supply prices publicly, to issue monthly health committee financial reports to the public, and to integrate good governance indicators into monitoring and supervision activities.[20]

Support was also provided at the national government level in the areas of policy reform and dialogue and overall health governance indicators. USAID was requested to provide additional support in the development of a new 10-year strategic plan for the health sector, which would include an important governance and accountability component.[21]

Other health programs also target local and civil society involvement in health issues. A World Bank HIV/AIDS program running from 2002 to 2010 worked to strengthen civil society and community organizations in their efforts to prevent and treat the virus. Through these initiatives, interventions among key vulnerable groups had increased significantly, particularly in rural and remote areas.[22]

Local Government Sector

The World Bank has devoted significant attention to issues of decentralization and, along with USAID, is implementing programs aimed at strengthening local government and civil society capacity. These ongoing projects have met with reasonable success, and plans are under way for continued efforts toward decentralization and good governance.

Two World Bank projects were launched in 2006 to develop the management and financial capacity of local authorities. The first, worth US$82 million, was on track with a number of core objectives achieved by its midterm evaluation. The percentage of the budget for infrastructure and maintenance allocated through local authorities was 7.84% in 2008, almost twice the targeted percentage. The number of municipal budgets approved was 98.5%, with repayment of municipal loans at 92.6% (also exceeding target percentages).[23]

The World Bank's second project established a framework for participatory local development and decentralization. Resource transfers to local governments and communities have increased. Three development partners joined the government in financing its national program, and several small-scale infrastructure projects have been created or upgraded. Still, implementation of development plans by local governments and community organizations has been delayed, necessitating a two-year extension of the project end date.[24]

Similar initiatives are being implemented by USAID, which characterized Senegal as possessing a "highly centralized government where weak checks and balances undermine good governance."[25] In December 2009, it launched a

"Decentralization, Governance, and Transparency" project in Senegal designed to improve public administration at the central and local levels and administration and service delivery of municipal governments in five pilot regions.[26] A US$20 million program was also recently approved to increase transparency and accountability in certain public institutions and state organizations and to strengthen civil society groups' capacity to fight corruption. Another goal of the four-and-a-half-year program is to help ensure free and credible 2012 elections, through empowerment of Senegal's autonomous electoral body and advocacy organizations.[27]

Natural Resource Management Sector

Sustainable management of natural resources is gaining attention as an issue critical to Senegal's environment and economy. The World Bank and European Union in particular are devoting significant resources to rural development programs, of which a large component involves increasing the sustainability of the fishing industry.[28] As increasing numbers of destitute West African fishermen began immigrating to Europe in search of better livelihoods, the European Union (and Switzerland) developed a US$25.5 million integrated fisheries project package to boost the economies of coastal fishing communities by improving fisheries management and rehabilitating local ecosystems.[29] The World Bank has also instituted a US$16.49 million, seven-year Integrated Marine and Coastal Resources Management Project, which aims to increase the sustainability of fisheries through improved management techniques by 2011.[30]

In 2004, the World Bank launched a US$10.75 million project intended to develop fisheries management capacity in three pilot areas over the course of seven years, thereby conserving the local ecosystem and its marine and coastal resources. The project required restructuring in 2009 to simplify its institutional structure. Since then, however, it has made important progress in improving biodiversity management and increasing community involvement in the target areas.[31]

Four years later, the World Bank established a similar project to reduce pressure on fishing stocks in the central coastal areas. The initiative focuses on improving governance of these fisheries, rehabilitating local ecosystems, creating alternative livelihoods for those in the fishing industry, and strengthening capacity to manage and monitor the fisheries. The effectiveness of this four-year project, with US$3.55 million allocated so far, has yet to be determined.[32]

In another area of natural resource management, the World Bank is seeking to promote sustainable energy sources in rural areas with the use of efficient cooking stoves (including wood fuel stoves) and lamps and improved methods for carbonization and natural resource and sustainable forest management. It has made considerable progress toward meeting its goals and has strengthened the capacity of the rural executive agency (ASER) in clean development mechanisms.[33]

Many of USAID's and MCC's programs related to this sector tend to focus on agricultural and livelihood development, but some incorporate aspects of sustainable natural resource management. For instance, USAID expanded its "Wula Nafaa" program enhancing livelihoods through export-oriented activities to include an ecological region along the coastal areas of the Casamance and Sine-Saloum delta, to address growing problems of overfishing and mismanagement of other maritime resources in these areas. The project works with participating local collectives and community organizations to encourage the adoption of good governance practices.[34]

Private Sector

Programs aimed at enhancing private sector productivity tend to also include support for policy and regulation reform. Engagement with the government was a critical part of two recent major programs aimed at developing Senegal's private sector, which met with varying degrees of success. The World Bank's Private Investment Promotion project, initiated in 2003, is a US$50 million, six-year effort with four major components. The first aims to improve the investment climate with strategic reforms in the legal, judicial, and tax systems and the regulation of infrastructure. It also seeks to eliminate administrative and trade barriers and facilitate private-public consultations. The second component involves support to Senegal's National Agency for Investment and Infrastructure, which includes matching grant programs, capacity-building efforts, and the divestiture and oversight of certain public entities. Third, the project supports economic sectors with untapped potential, such as information technology or tourism, through the promotion of investment and policy reform. The last task involves ensuring the project's sustainability through local capacity building, most notably for the Steering Committee under the Ministry of Finance. As of 2009, the World Bank reported that the project was on track with its objectives and recording measured improvements, though it was scheduled to be restructured before the end of 2009 to increase operational effectiveness.[35]

The World Bank's Private Sector Adjustment Credit project, which operated from 2004 to 2009, attempted to engage the GOS in a variety of market-oriented reforms. A US$75 million project, its goals were to implement an investment-friendly private tax enterprise regime, restructure the edible oil sector to stimulate competition, and enhance the sustainability and corporate governance of the pension system. However, the project fell short of many of its objectives, largely because of lack of political and financial commitment on the part of the national government. While the administration lowered certain taxes and fees on private enterprise, it failed to allocate a portion of this revenue to a matching grant fund as required by the program. The government also continued to interfere inordinately in the groundnut and edible oil sectors and failed to provide adequate political or monetary support to both the postal and the pension reform efforts. The World Bank rated the overall project's outcomes—as well as the Senegalese government's performance—as "unsatisfactory" and concluded that in the future, the World Bank should not mistake action plans for true willingness to act.[36]

USAID is also heavily involved in private sector reform efforts, though the effectiveness of its 2005 Economic Growth Project is unclear. The seven-year project provides US$60 million toward private enterprise development through promoting regulatory reforms, improving the environment for business, and increasing private investment for delivery of public goods and services. However, the ultimate success of its objectives depends heavily on the political will (or lack thereof) at the national level.[37]

Notes

1. This chapter is adapted from the assessment written by Robert Charlick, Sheldon Gellar, Abdou Salam Fall, and Sémou Ndiaye for Management Systems International under a USAID contract.

2. Senegalese do not seem to consider local government as part of the state, although it clearly is in terms of the control mechanisms placed on its operation.

3. Lydia Polgreen and Marjorie Connelly. July 25, 2007. "Poll Shows Africans Wary, but Hopeful About Future," *New York Times*, A6. According to the Pew Global Attitudes/*New York Times* survey, Senegalese express the highest level of satisfaction of the 10 African countries polled "with the way democracy is working in (their) country," with 72% stating that they are "somewhat satisfied" or "very satisfied."

4. For public acceptance of corruption, see Cabinet ORGATECH. 2001. *Enquête sur les Manifestations de la Corruption au Sénégal: Enquête aux Prés des Entreprises.* Dakar: Forum Civil.

5. Our argument is not that Wolof or "Senegalese culture" is intrinsically more subject to corruption than others but that corruption flourishes in this and other cultures in the presence of extreme poverty and economic inequality where traditional norms can be manipulated and distorted for personal gain.

6. Ibrahima Thioub. 2007. "Les Mouvements de la Société Civile globale: Dynamiques des campagnes internationales et mise en œuvre locale: La Lutte contre la Corruption (Senegal)." Unpublished.

7. Cabinet ORGATECH 2001.

8. See Abdou Salam Fall and Babacar Gueye, editors. May 2005. *Gouvernance et Corruption dans le Systeme de Santé au Sénégal: Rapport Final.* Dakar: Forum Civil, and Centre de Recherches Pour le Developpement International.

9. Ibid.

10. For a detailed study of corruption in this sector, see Abdou-Salam Fall, editor. October 2006. *Gouvernance et Corruption dans le Domaine des Ressources Naturelles et de l'environnement au Sénégal, Rapport final.* Dakar: Forum Civil.

11. Cabinet ORGATECH 2001.

12. "Statuesque or Grotesque?" February 25, 2010. *The Economist,* http://www.economist .com/world/middle-east/displaystory.cfm?story_id=15581322.

13. Lawrence Delevingne. February 4, 2010. "The Joy of Doing Business in Africa: How Senegalese Politicians Tried to Shake Down Millicom for $200 Million," *Business Insider,* http:// www.businessinsider.com/business-in-africa-how-corrupt-senegalese-politicians-tried-to-shake-down-millicom-for-200-million-2010-2.

14. Ibid.

15. Sy Tidiane. November 16, 2009. "Senegal Colossus Proves Sore Point," BBC News, http://news.bbc.co.uk/2/hi/africa/8353624.stm.

16. "Statuesque or Grotesque?" 2010.

17. Millennium Challenge Corporation website: Senegal, http://www.mcc.gov/mcc/ countries/senegal/index.shtml.

18. Delevingne 2010.

19. USAID website: Senegal, Healthcare Policy and Financing, http://senegal.usaid.gov/ node/147.

20. USAID website: "USAID Supports Good Governance in Health," http://senegal.usaid .gov/node/147.

21. USAID website: Senegal, Healthcare Policy and Financing.

22. World Bank website: "Status of Projects in Execution, FY09," http://www.google.com/ url?sa=t&source=web&ct=res&cd=2&ved=0CBoQFjAB&url=http%3A%2F%2Fsiteresources .worldbank.org%2FEXTSOPE%2FResources%2F5929620-1254491038321%2F6460830 -1254525284835%2FSenegal.pdf&rct=j&q=world+bank+sope+senegal&ei=oBjyS8eYN 8L98Aaz1Y3pDQ&usg=AFQjCNF4tj9nWanu6Tabdd1ixHEMunODEg&sig2=-ubH0E1u ATFPDhaKzl7gzA.

23. Ibid.

24. Ibid.

25. USAID website: Senegal Overview, http://www.usaid.gov/locations/sub-saharan _africa/countries/senegal/.

26. USAID website: "New USAID Local Governance Project Targets Five Pilot Regions in Senegal," http://senegal.usaid.gov/en/node/161.

27. USAID website: Senegal, Supporting Democracy, Good Governance and National Reconciliation, http://senegal.usaid.gov/en/node/164.

28. France Diplomatie website: Senegal, http://www.diplomatie.gouv.fr/en/IMG/pdf/ANNEXE_2.pdf.

29. World Fishing & Aquaculture: "Senegal." June 1, 2009. http://www.worldfishing.net/features/new-horizons/senegal.

30. World Bank website: "Integrated Marine and Coastal Resources Management Project," http://web.worldbank.org/external/projects/main?menuPK=228424&theSitePK=40941&pagePK=64283627&piPK=73230&Projectid=P058367.

31. World Bank, "Status of Projects in Execution, FY09."

32. Ibid.

33. Ibid.

34. USAID website: "Agriculture and Natural Resources Management: USAID/Wula Nafaa," http://senegal.usaid.gov/en/node/137.

35. World Bank, "Status of Projects in Execution, FY09."

36. World Bank website: "Private Sector Adjustment Credit, Implementation Completion and Results Report, Vol. 1," http://www-wds.worldbank.org/external/default/WDSContentServer/WDSP/IB/2009/08/21/000333037_20090821013253/Rendered/PDF/ICR11030P080011C0disclosed081181091.pdf.

37. USAID website: Senegal, Economic Growth Project, http://senegal.usaid.gov/en/node/141.

9

Honduras (2008)

Corruption is deeply embedded in all levels of Honduran society.[1] It has permeated most government institutions, is associated with most public-private transactions, and is viewed by citizens as a normal feature of daily life. A 2008 survey revealed that 76.5% of Hondurans regarded corruption as highly prevalent in their country, and between 18.2% and 19.4% considered payment of bribes to be justified, given the otherwise poor services available.[2]

Although the country possesses a formal anticorruption architecture generally consistent with international norms, its effectiveness is hindered by widespread corruption at all levels, a profound incapacity of the legal and judicial sectors to reliably and consistently enforce the law, and a highly entrenched system of patronage.[3] Contributing to a growing sense of frustration is a nearly complete absence of will by the political elite to effectively implement the legal and institutional reforms embodied in this architecture. Even progressive initiatives have been repeatedly neutralized by what could be described as a process of "preemptive co-optation," where institutions with anticorruption mandates have been hijacked through the appointment of leadership beholden to economic and political forces intent on interfering with the implementation of anticorruption agendas. Prominent examples include the selection of magistrates of the Supreme Court and the Supreme Electoral Court and the commissioners of the national Public Information Access Institute (*Instituto de Acceso a la Información Pública*; Transparency Institute).

The crux of the corruption problem lies in the nearly total control of the state by a deeply rooted political and economic elite. Political party patronage and clientelism, embedded within the country's power structures, provide perceived and actual impunity to an entrenched ruling class. Among the country's two main political parties—the Nationals and the Liberals—personal ties rather than ideologies determine factional loyalties. The country's dominant elites tend to unite across political lines when protecting their economic interests. As these interests also include the resources of the state, elites are relentless in their attempts to thwart meaningful anticorruption reforms. Contributing to this problem is the general inefficiency of the Honduran government, which can be attributed to the country's poverty, low educational levels, and absence of a professional, nonpoliticized career civil service.

Legal-Institutional Analysis

Official statements of government policy strongly condemn corrupt practices, although the political will to provide meaningful support to effectuate anticorruption policies is scant. A National Anticorruption Plan under the jurisdiction of the National Anticorruption Council (*Consejo Nacional Anticorrupción*; CNA) was designed to go into effect in 2002, then again in 2006, but ultimately failed both times in implementation. Two years later, that plan was again being updated. In addition to the CNA plan, President Manuel Zelaya's administration put into effect an Executive Branch Anticorruption Plan (November 2007), which generated quarterly progress reports in February and May 2008 and was demonstrating modest results. The Zelaya plan and progress reports have been prompted by a threat from the US Millennium Challenge Corporation (MCC) to cut funding when Honduras failed to meet several benchmarks of progress, specifically on the anticorruption and rule of law indicators. The plan was accepted by the MCC as a remediation program, and it was reselected as an MCC compact country for another year.

The so-called Remediation Plan reflects a piecemeal approach to anticorruption planning that deals first with "easy" program components while deferring the more difficult, politically demanding issues. Compliance reports boast of the plan's achievements in many of its lesser activities, such as systems design, training, inter-entity coordination meetings, and the like.[4]

Institutional implementation flaws and other more serious shortcomings receive much less attention. The Remediation Plan offers some small hope, however, of bringing Empresa Hondurena de Telecomunicaciones (HONDUTEL) and Empresa Nacional de Energía Eléctrica (ENEE),[5] two highly corrupted institutions, under scrutiny by the supreme audit institution—the Superior Court of Accounts (*Tribunal Superior de Cuentas*; TSC)—and private audit firms.[6] The US government insisted on the addition of harsh conditions such as audits to measure progress. Other donors, including the European Union, imposed similar conditions on their continued assistance. As a consequence, these audits have been initiated.

The 1982 Constitution of Honduras begins by declaring the "state of law" to be fundamental to the existence of the Honduran Republic to ensure a democratic society conferring political, economic, and social justice on its citizens.[7] The constitution grants powers of constitutional interpretation and judicial review upon the Supreme Court, and in theory the court has the legal authority to act as a check on Congress and the Executive.[8] In practice, however, the Honduran Supreme Court suffers from politicization, a lack of independence, and alleged institutional corruption that constrains its ability and willingness to exercise credible authority over other branches. As a result, the judiciary is one of the least respected governmental institutions in Honduras.

The Honduran framework of anticorruption enforcement and prevention legislation, although indisputably open to modification and improvements, is basically sound. The Criminal Code contains provisions that punish corrupt practices, although there is no specific statute defining or sanctioning "corruption" per se. In addition, there are a number of laws and regulations that can be applied directly or indirectly to prevent, reveal, or sanction corrupt practices and a variety of citizen complaint mechanisms and internal disciplinary mechanisms within most governmental institutions, including the judicial branch. However, the disparity between legal theory and application in practice is striking.

Criminal anticorruption laws. The Criminal Code sanctions public administration crimes, including the misappropriation of public funds, bribery, fraud, illicit enrichment, breach of trust, and abuse of authority. These provisions are enforced by the Public Ministry through the Office of the Special Anticorruption Prosecutor and through the court system. However, under the attorney general (*fiscal general*) in office in 2008, powerful and wealthy individuals increasingly appear to be receiving immunity from corruption prosecutions. In addition, the Office of the Special Anticorruption Prosecutor is widely perceived as ineffectual and has negligible impact on corruption prosecutions. Although the caseloads of these prosecutors are extraordinarily low, a minimal number of cases are ever investigated and prosecuted, and only a handful of convictions have resulted in recent years—primarily in minor cases or against low-level officials.

Money laundering. The Special Law on Money Laundering is enforced by the Public Ministry in the criminal courts. The law has been used primarily in prosecutions involving allegations of narco-trafficking and organized crime, with mixed results. Such cases present many prosecutorial challenges and often result in corruption of the justice process through threats, intimidation, or inappropriate third-party payments.

Illicit enrichment. The Organic Law of the Superior Court of Accounts (TSC) authorizes it to investigate and impose administrative sanctions for cases of illicit enrichment of public servants or to report to and cooperate with either the solicitor general (*Procuraduría General de la República*) in civil cases or the Office of the Special Anticorruption Prosecutor in criminal cases. However, criminal prosecutions are often slow to be processed, are rarely tried on the merits, and almost never result in convictions.

The Superior Court of Accounts also audits and investigates projects funded under the Poverty Reduction Strategy Plan at the municipal level, as misappropriation occurs frequently as a result of municipal corruption, inefficiency, or incapacity. The Superior Court of Accounts possesses principal responsibility for corruption prevention mechanisms.

Forfeiture and asset recovery. The Superior Court of Accounts also has the authority to issue fines and seek administrative reimbursement of public funds in the case of illicit enrichment; criminal prosecutions often result in out-of-court settlements incorporating some measure of restitution. In cases involving organized crime, the Office of Forfeited Assets sometimes freezes assets pending conviction. The solicitor general has the power to impose civil forfeitures to recover public assets lost as a result of corrupt practices but has not exercised that power except in cases of minor-level officials or claims.

Laws on disclosure of assets. The Organic Law of the Superior Court of Accounts requires elected officials, civil servants, and the judiciary to file asset declarations with the TSC prior to taking office. These records are not made public, however. In cases of noncompliance, the TSC has the authority to withhold salaries and issue fines; it further has the legal authority to proceed with criminal actions, such as prosecution for disobedience, although this is not done in practice. The Supreme Court normally ensures strict compliance within the judicial branch of assets disclosures. However, some compliance problems have been encountered within other branches and with civil servants.

Public contracts and procurement. The State Contracting Law, through the Public Procurement Policy Office and internal offices within state entities, governs contracts for public works, the provision of goods and services, and consulting services in all branches. The Superior Court of Accounts exercises external control over the national procurement system. Procurement laws and regulations are often manipulated or bypassed, however, by tactics such as the issuance of decrees declaring "emergency situations" or "government secrecy needs" that allow for direct contracting.

Public hiring and appointments. The constitution provides that public employment be regulated by a civil service regime. The Civil Service Law and its regulations govern executive branch employees and purport to establish a system of merit selection, promotion, salary schedules, and security in public administration, enforced by the directorate general of the service. In practice, the law is widely disregarded, and public servants in many public institutions are routinely replaced with each new administration as a result of political party patronage, paybacks, nepotism, favoritism, and personal connections. Other institutions and public entities have similar detailed merit-based career laws and regulations, including the judicial branch, Public Ministry, and Superior Court of Accounts. These rules are likewise often ignored in favor of politics and patronage.

Professional codes of ethics. The Civil Service Code of Conduct was passed in late 2007 and contains administrative sanctions for violations. The law is supposed to be applied by internal units within governmental institutions, but regulations and training are still lacking, and the law is still in a "grace period" and unenforced. A Code of Ethics for Judicial Officials and Employees is applied through the Judicial Career Council of the Supreme Court.

Laws on conflict of interests. The concept of "conflict of interest" is not well developed or regulated in Honduran law and practice; it is left largely to discretion and thus commonly ignored. The Civil Service Code of Conduct imposes some restrictions on persons leaving public office, but it is not yet enforced. (In theory, the Superior Court of Accounts and Ethical Committees within each institution is responsible for its implementation.) The judicial Code of Ethics and the Criminal Code contains provisions that proscribe conflicts of interest, but they are applied very infrequently. Political will to sanction conflicts is very low.

Access to information. The Transparency and Access to Public Information Law (Transparency Law), a citizen initiative that gained support from the international donor community, went into effect in January 2007 with a one-year grace period for implementation. In theory and intent, this law is akin to the US Freedom of Information Act, although it is based on a Mexican model. The law regulates and guarantees access to public information and requires public institutions to publish certain categories of institutional information.

In a feat of legislative sleight of hand, however, a provision was tacked on in passage limiting the law's application only to information generated *after* its effective date; in other words, the Transparency Law provisions do not permit access to any public records or information produced *prior* to January 2007 and affirmatively prohibits retroactivity in public access to information.[9] This significantly undercuts the utility of the law and narrows the realm of discoverable public documents.

In addition, and despite initial reforms that were compelled by public outcry, several significant problems in the language of the legislation remain. For instance, the law permits certain types of information to be withheld if considered "reserved," "confidential," or "secret." These categories are overly broad, ill defined, internally inconsistent, and granted undue discretion in resisting disclosure.

The Public Information Access Institute was created to supervise and train public employees and users, and the CNA was charged with ensuring that the laws are correctly applied. However, the institute's recent approval of a number of "reservations" protecting state financial documents from disclosure—including budget information, public employee names, alcohol production, and even cigarette consumption—caused enormous public dissatisfaction.[10]

Political party funding. The Electoral and Political Institutions Law regulates political party funding and expenditures and requires political party asset disclosures. The Supreme Electoral Court is charged with the application of the law but in practice does not effectively or reliably enforce it.

Witness and whistleblower protection. No specific whistleblower protection is provided, but there is a Witness Protection Law under the Criminal Code and Procedural Code. In addition, regulations under the Organic Law of the Superior Court of Accounts provide, in theory, for the protection of persons making reports of public corruption. The Public Ministry is responsible for enforcement, and special police units are supposed to be created to work in witness protection. In practice, witness protection is provided primarily in cases of organized crime and rarely in corruption cases. Funds are limited, and the protection provided is usually very basic, such as concealing a witness's identity while testifying and sealing or expunging identifying file data. In real circumstances of threatened reprisal, protection is often inadequate, and the witness ultimately tends to flee the jurisdiction.

Sunshine laws and open hearings. A proposal has been recently submitted to Congress to permit open hearings for the selection of high officials, but public hearings are generally not required by law. The Municipal Law requires that meetings of municipal officials be held openly (apart from exceptional cases), allowing for public presence and participation, but compliance is mixed and enforcement absent. The Citizen Participation Law (*Ley de Participación Ciudadana*) enacted in February 2006 was supposed to create new routes and mechanisms for citizen participation and social auditing, although it mainly just consolidated existing legal rights. Even so, it has not had much impact; many people are largely unaware of the law and do not take advantage of its provisions.

Citizen complaint mechanisms. Citizens are able to file complaints for misconduct or suspected corruption with a number of entities, including the Superior Court of Accounts (through the Citizen Participation Directorate), the Public Ministry, the CNA, the National Human Rights Commission (Ombudsman), and the inspector general of courts. Those complaints are widely viewed to be ineffective, however, because of corruption and inefficiency within these institutions.

Anticorruption Stakeholders

The recent US Agency for International Development (USAID) Democracy and Governance (DG) Assessment explored and analyzed in depth key actor support and opposition to various categories of political and institutional change, including the establishment of a credible rule of law and reduction of corruption.[11] In those key areas, the assessment found "little demand, capacity, or meaningful support among key and/or prominent stakeholders for real reform or enduring systemic and institutional improvements."[12] Applying techniques of political mapping, the report found virtually no core domestic support for anticorruption activity among key government actors, and a political environment unlikely and unable to exert control, certainly at least through the end of the Zelaya administration. "Publicly, of course, all [national-level government actors] are against corruption, but the lack of interest or will to actually pursue and prosecute cases simply perpetuates anticorruption inertia. Unfortunately, since many of these institutions are allegedly mired in corrupt activities themselves, it is unlikely that many will risk putting themselves squarely in support, both by word and action, of more aggressive anticorruption methods, strategies, and prosecution."[13]

The institutions in charge of enforcement are largely unwilling or unable to apply anticorruption-related laws in an evenhanded, credible manner. Such institutions include the judicial branch, the Bar Association (*Colegio de Abogados*), law schools, the Public Ministry, the police, the Superior Court of Accounts, the Supreme Electoral Court, the Human Rights Ombudsman, the Transparency Institute, executive agencies, and the ultimate power broker: Congress. Corruption is alleged at every level of these institutions, from the lowest administrative positions to the highest controlling officials. True progress in anticorruption enforcement will depend on fundamental changes in the structure and operations of these chronically flawed institutions.

National Congress. Opaque and resistant to citizen scrutiny, the Congress implements unsavory deals arranged by the country's two major national parties and dilutes citizen initiatives intended to limit discretion and abuse of authority. Highly vulnerable to state capture, Congress's deputies often receive rewards for advancing the economic interests of powerful, wealthy families. Legislative language can be changed at the last moment, in violation of agreements reached with civil society or backroom deals cut to appoint officials for crucial anticorruption positions accountable to political patrons, not institutional mandates.

Deliberations on important matters are conducted in secret, and initiatives to promote transparency and accountability are routinely distorted. Recent electoral and procedural reforms to make Congress less vulnerable to unwarranted political pressures and its internal operations more open to the electorate have met with a modicum of success, but much remains to be done. Barring major congressional reforms, the unlikely election of a congressional majority committed to a reform agenda, or increasing citizen pressure for Congress to back effective anticorruption measures, the success of potential interventions is unlikely.

Superior Court of Accounts (TSC). The TSC is directed by three magistrates appointed by Congress and is principally responsible for serving as an external *a posteriori* auditor of government dependencies and for supervising and evaluating their internal control functions with the goal of ensuring the efficiency and accountability of the public sector. Among other duties, the TSC is responsible for gathering and examining asset declarations by public officials; assigning administrative, civil, and criminal responsibilities resulting from its audits; assisting with the government-wide implementation of ethical standards; receiving and channeling corruption allegations; providing follow-up to audit findings forwarded to the solicitor general and Public Ministry; and monitoring implementation of the Inter-American Convention Against Corruption.

When initially established, there was concern that the TSC would be as vulnerable to political meddling as other Honduran government institutions. Although some of these concerns remain, the TSC has proven to be somewhat more robust than other governmental control institutions, even though most of its top- and mid-level administrative positions are occupied by individuals with known political affiliations. Although its performance is improving, it continues to be subject to political pressures, difficulties controlling the expenditures of the Presidential Office, difficulties obtaining necessary follow-up to corruption findings forwarded to the Public Ministry and Supreme Court, inconsistent standards, and the lack of absolute operational and financial independence.[14] The TSC's oversight abilities are further hindered by the inadequacy of accounting and internal control standards in the public sector and by defective administrative procedures within the institution. This results in the poor and incomplete documentation of audit findings shared with other control institutions.[15] The implementation of an Integrated Financial Management System (*Sistema de Administración Financiera Integrada*) was supposed to have resolved accounting shortcomings, but its introduction has been plagued by poor administrative capacity and considerable technical problems. Plans are under way to reconstruct a new system, despite considerable additional cost.[16]

In early 2008, the National Congress approved the establishment of a specialized internal control entity, the National Office for the Comprehensive Development of Internal Control (*Oficina Nacional del Desarrollo Integral del Control Interno*; ONADIS). ONADIS is to be responsible for designing the National Control System for Public Resources (*Sistema Nacional de Control de los Recursos Públicos*) to introduce modern internal controls, in conjunction with the TSC, with the goal of implementing continuous management improvements across the country's government dependencies. With regard to the implementation of this system, Honduras is following the lead of countries such as Colombia and Mexico that were already doing so successfully.

In tandem with decentralization goals, the TSC completed the audit of all Honduran municipalities in 2008, with plans under way to repeat the cycle every three years, rather than over decades, as previously done. The audit program found irregularities in about 10% of municipalities, mostly resulting from poor management practices.[17] Evidence of fraud and corruption was documented in four municipalities. However, local administrators complained about the alleged inability of the TSC to apply consistent standards across municipalities and the time demands placed by the audits on local staff poorly trained in managing resources and record keeping. To correct some of these deficiencies, the TSC began conducting financial management training workshops for municipal officials in conjunction with the Ministry of Governance and Justice. USAID/Honduras supported this training.

Another recent indication of the increasing ability of the TSC to carry out its control mandate was the teachers' audit it submitted to the Executive in July 2008. The audit found that between 10,000 and 12,000 teachers (out of some 63,000 teachers) were collecting salaries and special stipends to which they may not have been entitled, confirming widely held assumptions.[18] This and other audits were made public—an important achievement considering that until a few years ago, audit results were viewed as privileged information.

The TSC has also made gains in securing asset declarations required of public officials. In 2007, declarations were submitted by 99% of public servants. Those failing to comply could be penalized by salary suspension and imposition of fines. The information collected is not made public, however, and critics of the asset declaration procedures decry this lack of transparency. In response, the TSC claimed that public officials' asset declarations were scrutinized when they left office, and sanctions were levied if irregularities were detected.

Since 2006, the TSC has established approximately 200 ethics committees in government entities at the central and departmental levels and disseminated information about the Transparency Law. A strategic alliance has also been created between the TSC and the CNA to promote a culture of transparency, public ethics (as defined in the 2007 Civil Service Code of Conduct), social auditing, and processing of corruption allegations.

Government Contracting and Purchasing Standards Office (Oficina Normativa de Contratación y Adquisiciones del Estado; ONCAE). ONCAE was established in 2001 with a major anticorruption role as a technical and consultative body responsible for improving the national public procurement system, a major font of corruption. ONCAE has jurisdiction over *Honducompras*, the Internet-based national electronic procurement system through which most government purchases at the central and municipal level will presumably have to pass. In 2007, 69% of all public procurements were announced through the system.[19] Between February and April 2008, this figure rose to 82.4%.[20] It is yet unclear whether this increased transparency in announcing public procurements will lead to better compliance practices and less corruption in awarding contracts.

Numerous irregularities still confront the Honduran public procurement system. Particularly vulnerable to corruption and collusive arrangements are the so-called private procurements (in contracts below a certain value), where only a few select bidders are invited to participate. It is also allegedly a common practice to break down larger procurements into smaller purchases so as to favor some vendors over others. Equally vulnerable are so-called emergency purchases, a major source of graft under grand corruption schemes, whereby standard competitive and transparency provisions can be legally bypassed. Recent instances of emergency procurements to the detriment of competitive bids include pharmaceutical purchases by the Ministry of Health (MOH) and a foiled attempt to correct safety issues at Tegucigalpa's airport through public work contracts. Another common corrupt procurement practice involves issuing contracts to firms surreptitiously controlled by politicians and high-level government officials. The practice is said to be particularly prevalent with changes of presidential administration and more so with the issuance of consulting contracts for the design of public projects.

National Anticorruption Council (Consejo Nacional Anticorrupción). First established in 2001 as a government–civil society forum to formulate the national anticorruption strategy, the original CNA achieved only very modest results. In 2002, it was restructured via an executive decree as an autonomous civil society entity with legal identity and partial funding from the National Congress. It is composed of 12 umbrella civil society organizations (CSO) representing some 1,000 affiliated organizations. These organizations act on behalf of the Catholic and Evangelical churches, businesses, labor and peasant sectors, municipal organizations, professional associations, university presidents, and good governance NGOs. The CNA mandate includes formulating preventive anticorruption policies, strategies, and action plans; conducting studies and issuing recommendations about alleged corruption acts; providing anticorruption technical assistance; gathering information and managing the processing of anticorruption allegations; submitting an annual report to Congress; informing the citizenry and responding to civil society demands; and, generally, promoting a culture of transparency. The CNA also has its own legal department, its investigative clout enhanced by the authority to compel public officials to testify before its governing assembly. Moreover, Article 30 of the Transparency Law declares that the CNA is responsible for ensuring that the law is correctly applied.

The restructuring of the CNA was enthusiastically received by civil society. In some respects, at least initially, the CNA fulfilled popular expectations. Of particular note were its studies and publications, professionally executed and often hard-hitting. These included designing a comprehensive national anticorruption strategic plan and releasing a series of analytical studies examining in detail the strengths and weaknesses of control agencies and other transparency-related topics, while issuing carefully thought out recommendations for improvements. Additional topics covered in these publications included the subject of state capture, the role of the media in combating corruption, problems affecting the judiciary, ethics in business, the donor community role in assisting Honduran anticorruption efforts, and the revised Criminal Procedures Code, among others.

Of particular significance was the ongoing public debate between the CNA and the Public Information Access Institute, the presumably autonomous body entrusted with promoting and facilitating citizen access to public information and regulating and supervising how the various government entities implemented the law. In early 2008, the CNA issued a harshly critical report about Transparency Institute regulations concerning information the Finance Ministry was allowed to define as "reserved," the length of time it could be held as such, and other matters.[21] In the CNA's judgment, the Transparency Institute overstepped its powers by emphasizing strictly formal criteria, while ignoring the spirit of the law, "strengthening the secretive nature of the Honduran state . . . eliminating the possibility of combating corruption through fiscal evasion, smuggling, and other crimes against the public treasury." The CNA report went further, noting that some of the regulatory provisions constituted backsliding that would allow classification of previously public information as reserved.[22] Regardless of the debate's legal merits, it was a rare healthy display of two high-profile, publicly funded Honduran entities engaging in public debate.

Like so many other Honduran organizations, the CNA has devoted a considerable amount of energy to the promotion of social auditing concepts, strategically linking its efforts in this area with the promotion of the Transparency Law. As part of these initiatives, the CNA collects, processes, and monitors the manner in which control agencies investigate and act on information requests stemming from social audit activities. Aside from its activities to promote transparent and accountable behavior among public officials, the CNA also runs programs designed to encourage youth to embrace ethical values.

The CNA achieved extensive publicity when, in 2007, it sponsored the March Against Corruption (*Marcha contra la corrupción*), a demonstration partly motivated by the low corruption score received by Honduras from the World Bank Institute in its governance indicators. An estimated 30,000 citizens participated, with accusations that political factions, particularly those associated with the Executive, attempted to take advantage of the event, even paying some participants to attend. Changes in the technical leadership of the institution had also been questioned, as had the appearance of nepotism and clientelism within the CNA itself. The CNA's generally positive image also suffered from the lackluster support some of its members offered striking anticorruption prosecutors. On balance, the CNA appeared to have performed its oversight and analytical functions relatively well, although in the final analysis it seemed to be susceptible to many of the same maladies affecting other Honduran institutions.

Public Information Access Institute (Transparency Institute). The enactment of the Transparency Law raised public hopes and expectations and generated congressional commitments. Unfortunately, Congress dashed much of that hope by appointing commissioners (in August 2007) of the governing Transparency Institute whose credibility and roles were highly suspect and whose appointments were conducted in violation of parliamentary procedures, that is, without debate.

The institute is charged with the supervision and training of public employees and information users, the publication of information required by the Transparency Law, and the ability to grant or deny petitions to withhold (reserve) specific information. Although it has an independent budget, the institute is still dependent on the Ministry of the President, reporting to both Congress and the president.

Controversy surrounding the institute increased with a recent spate of reservations it approved favoring the Finance Ministry, in addition to conflicts with the CNA. The institute maintained that the CNA did not possess the power of institutional oversight, and a very public sparring match ensued. Regardless of the merits of this controversy, the public lacked confidence in the institute, perceiving it as political, protective of the current administration, and more inclined to maintain secrecy than to promote openness and transparency.

Superior Court of Elections (Tribunal Supremo Electoral; TSE). Despite the abolition of voting on a party list basis, reform of the national electoral system in the early 2000s, and the creation of the current TSE, considerable concern remains about the integrity of national elections. The highly political structure of the TSE is preordained, as its leadership structure precludes citizen oversight. Problems managing the latest elections contribute to the unease: several thousand electoral urns disappeared, and there have been considerable procedural shortcomings in electoral registries.

Law enforcement institutions. The institutions charged with enforcing anticorruption laws are paradoxically perceived to be among the most corrupt of Honduran government institutions. Not only do these institutions fail to check burgeoning external corruption through the laws that they are supposed to enforce, but they are also themselves riddled internally with corrupt institutional practices. There is, according to the US State Department, a "widespread perception that the government's anticorruption institutions had not taken the steps necessary to combat corruption and were unwilling or lacked the professional capacity to investigate, arrest, and prosecute those involved in high-level corruption."[23] As stakeholders, these enforcement groups are, at best, either lacking political will and capacity to reform or, at worst, resistant to any change that would diminish the power they exercise. The institutions that are politicized are almost certain to vote in accordance with their political affiliations in the upcoming Nominating Commissions for the replacement of high officials of justice institutions.

The Supreme Court (*Corte Suprema de Justicia*) supervises the administration of the judicial sector, selects all lower-court judges, and also manages and administers the Office of the Public Defender as a Supreme Court dependency. Historically, the appointment and tenure of Supreme Court justices are linked to the national election cycle and heavily tied to political favoritism. Constitutional reforms in 2001, backed by USAID and Honduran civil society, separated those appointments from the election cycle, expanded the term of justices, and implemented a more transparent selection process. The goal was to foster increased judicial independence and decrease politicization, but the process became highly politicized, and the resulting Supreme Court bench empanelled in 2002 was thought to have been largely controlled by its National Party majority throughout its tenure.[24] Politicization, lack of independence, nepotism, favoritism, and a monopolistic bureaucratic structure placing excessive powers in the chief justice all contributed to an image of the courts as corrupt and of serving the interests of the powerful elite.

The Public Ministry (*Ministerio Público*) is an independent autonomous entity responsible for criminal investigations and prosecution. It is directed by the attorney general (*fiscal general*). The Public Ministry is divided into prosecutorial divisions, including one devoted to anticorruption, and has developed a strong reputation for the skills, training, and dedication of its young prosecutors.

The Office of the Special Anticorruption Prosecutor began to aggressively prosecute higher-level officials and high-profile cases, including claims against former officials such as ex-president Rafael Callejas. These prosecutions were highly controversial, and many were ultimately resolved or dismissed without convictions, often with the perceived or actual complicity of the institutional leadership and the courts.[25] A number of young prosecutors alleged corrupt practices within the Public Ministry and were thereupon dismissed or resigned (in 2003–2004). Many of the replacement prosecutors were said to have been selected based on political connections rather than on merit. Training requirements and programs were then drastically reduced.

Although many capable and conscientious prosecutors remain with the Public Ministry, in recent years, the ministry has become increasingly politicized, compromised, and institutionally weak; its failure or unwillingness to investigate and prosecute corruption cases is a point of increasing contention and publicity. Allegations made by prosecutors *within* the Public Ministry of institutional corruption, concealment of cases, and failure to prosecute powerful interests escalated in April–May 2008, when four prosecutors went on a hunger strike in the congressional square, alleging corruption and collusion by the attorney general and his deputy. They were joined by three other prosecutors, as well as a number of civil society representatives, in a hunger strike that lasted 38 days and sparked mass demonstrations and marches against corruption by tens of thousands of citizens.

The strike reflected a very public rupture within the institution and revealed important anticorruption forces and actors both within and outside the Public Ministry, who may be expected to maintain their pressure and position. The strike ultimately became politicized, ending without a negotiated agreement but with a compromise to investigate the allegations and a new law permitting future appointments of a special prosecutor under certain circumstances. In addition, a loosely organized, diverse anticorruption civil society movement—*Movimiento Amplio por la Dignidad y la Justicia*—emerged as a product of this strike.

The solicitor general (*procurador general*) represents the executive branch in criminal and civil matters and litigation, including state claims to property or assets and claims against the state. The solicitor general has principal legal responsibility to bring corruption cases against current or former state officials, but it has effectively ceded that authority to the Public Ministry, although it sometimes joins in cases in a secondary role. The solicitor general also has broad authority to represent the state in both civil and criminal cases stemming from corruption but tends to defer the criminal cases to the Public Ministry and has little presence or impact in civil causes of action. In addition, the solicitor general is responsible for following through with the Superior Court of Accounts' investigations and resulting claims. In general, the office has minimal presence, function, and effectiveness.

The mission of the National Human Rights Commission (Ombudsman) is to monitor and ensure respect for human rights and to guarantee rights and freedoms under the constitution and international treaties ratified by Honduras. The office is poorly funded and has no real legal power or jurisdiction, and the success of its efforts is highly dependent on the "moral authority" to investigate, publicize, and pressure prosecution. The office has been conducting social audits but has not taken any significant or confrontational role in fighting or preventing corruption.

The Ministry of Public Security is part of the executive branch. It operates the prison system and oversees Honduran police forces, which includes the Preventive Police, Transit Police, Border Police, Tourist Police, Prison Police, and Investigative Police (*Dirección General de Investigación Criminal*).

Investigative Police are responsible for investigating criminal complaints and collecting evidence but are inadequately trained and largely unwilling or unable to collaborate with prosecutors toward successful prosecutions. Corruption and impunity are serious problems within the security forces, with police allegedly involved in crimes such as kidnapping, extrajudicial killings, gangs, and narco-trafficking.[26] A new minister of security seems receptive to reform, and there is a new Organic Police Law reform, but it is too early to tell what its impact might be.

The mandatory Bar Association is highly politicized, is protective of the legal profession, and does not exercise any meaningful discipline over its own ranks. The law schools have a similar reputation of politicization and low quality. They both play roles in the appointment of high positions, including seats on the Nominating Commissions for both Supreme Court appointments and the attorney general and deputy attorney general.

Civil society. Honduran civil society is increasingly energized by the support it receives from the international donor community following Hurricane Mitch and increasingly aware of its rights and obligations in a democratic state. This kaleidoscope of civil society institutions has played a major role in the achievement of modest advances made in the country to thwart corruption. Because of these experiences, governance-oriented anticorruption NGOs have generally developed the acumen and strategic vision to demand more transparent and accountable government. Despite the opaque nature of Honduran society, civil society organizations laboriously gain ground from grudging political-economic elites intent on derailing reform efforts by any means. Prominent among these NGOs are the *Federación de Organizaciones para el Desarrollo de Honduras* (FOPRIDEH), the *Centro de Investigación de los Derechos Humanos*, the *Foro Nacional de Convergencia*, *Alianza por la Justicia*, the *Foro Social de la Deuda Exerna de Honduras* (FOSDEH), *Democracia sin Fronteras*, and the federation of organizations under the CNA umbrella. Often the NGO groupings include a wide array of religious, labor, professional, peasant, and business organizations, as well as civil society organizations with a particular sector focus.

While their program orientations vary considerably, Honduran civil society organizations can generally be classified according to those seeking to reform the macro-policy environment and those with a micro-level focus, generally at the local level. The former has led the charge for many successful reforms, such as the Citizen Participation Law and the more recent Transparency Law. These organizations often provide impetus for the design and implementation of numerous social auditing programs across Honduras, though actual implementation of these programs has fallen under the responsibility of local citizen organizations.

At the national level, for example, FOPRIDEH spearheaded a Justice Alliance (*Alianza por la Justicia*), consisting of 164 NGOs, to ensure a transparent and well-informed selection process for the Supreme Court justices to be appointed in 2009. It planned to do the same for the selection of the next attorney general and magistrates for the Supreme Electoral Court. Democracy Without Borders, meanwhile, maintains focus on enhancing the transparency of the National Congress, monitoring the voting patterns and behaviors of legislators while lobbying for approval of a Public Hearings Law to end the practice of congressional deputies conducting secretive deliberations.

The diversity of social auditing initiatives in Honduras is staggering.[27] They are highly valued in the institutional mandates of numerous NGOs and government entities, are promoted by religious organizations and government officials alike, and are major components of CNA strategy. These programs generally receive reliable donor funding, with sponsors including the European Union, the United Nations Development Programme (UNDP), and USAID, as well as the *Fondo Hondureño de Inversión Social* and the Ombudsman (*Comisionado Nacional por los Derechos Humanos*).

Most social auditing programs at the local level are driven by a desire to enhance the decentralization process and improve implementation of Poverty Reduction Strategy Plan (*Estrategia para la Reducción de la Pobreza*) resources. As a rule, they depend on local governance participation and oversight tools, such as open council sessions and town meetings (*cabildos abiertos*), Municipal Commissioners (*Comisionado Municipal*), local Transparency Committees (*Comisión de Transparencia*), and, whenever possible, citizen access to open meetings of Municipal Corporations. Citizen participation mechanisms are embedded in legal instruments such as the Law of Municipalities (*Ley de Municipalidades*), Participation Law (*Ley de Participación*), and, most recently, the Transparency Law.

The important point to be drawn from this diversity of experience, and failed attempts to implement a successful anticorruption architecture, is that the basic constituent elements for the mobilization of Honduran civil society to combat corruption are already firmly in place. This is the case not only at the macro-level, where relatively sophisticated organizations have openly confronted entrenched corrupt forces, but also increasingly at the municipal level, where a growing number of successful experiences are showing citizens how personal involvement in transparency promotion initiatives can bring about results.

The burning policy question thus becomes how to assist civic-minded social organizations in developing successful strategies to prevent the hijacking of reform measures by corrupt stakeholders favoring the status quo. From the donor community perspective, this entails encouraging civil society organizations to overcome institutional disagreements and occasional personality clashes and offering support to worthy organizations committed to reform and not established primarily as employment vehicles.

The business community. The major constraint on the development of a more competitive business environment in Honduras is the control exercised by a few families over most major businesses and, to a certain degree, the dominant political parties. While this is an environment ripe for state capture, it is also a restrictive investment milieu due to rising crime, widespread administrative corruption, and difficulties in enforcing contracts. Within such a setting, corrupt practices are regarded as business decisions, with potential gains to be balanced against potential costs.

Familiar business corruption practices come under many guises. These include tax evasion, falsification of merchandise value by importers, outright customs evasion (as when some 50 gasoline tankers were illicitly brought into the country to avoid paying custom duties—the so-called *gasolinazo* scandal), under-the-table payments for awards of government contracts, bribes in exchange for violations of environmental regulations, payments to expedite business transactions, and even the illegal export of national commodities through third countries to take advantage of foreign trade preferences. But the more costly corrupt transactions are associated with state capture, involving manipulation of the state's legal and regulatory powers for economic advantage. These practices are conducted not only by businesses but also by professional and labor groups determined to obtain for their membership (and leadership) an inordinate amount of government resources. The most notorious are the educational associations (*gremios*) that have exercised their political influence to gain unaffordable salary benefits, forcing the reallocation of debt forgiveness resources away from social development projects in favor of teacher salaries.

Although economic competition remains restricted, there are slight signs of progress. These are partly associated with increasing competition brought about by globalization and, more particularly, by preferential trade agreements, such as the Dominican Republic–Central America Free Trade Agreement (CAFTA-DR). This agreement requires Honduras to comply not only with certain environmental and labor requirements but also with transparency and anticorruption conditions such as open bidding practices.

In addition, growing *maquiladora* and agricultural exports are gradually empowering smaller producers as they acquire the characteristics of an entrepreneurial class. While still dependent on dominant local business conglomerates for processing and access to foreign markets, smaller businesses appear to be developing power bases of their own. Agro-exporters, for example, have established their own independent trade association. Policies more favorable to their development, including easier credit access, should assist with expansion of the small- and medium-sized business sector, particularly in agriculture where the potential for growth is more substantial.

Other indicators suggesting the emergence of a more competitive business environment are the simplification of business procedures, the introduction of "one stop" bureaucratic shops, and reforms leading to the privatization of most banking functions. Of particular promise is the establishment of the National Commission for the Defense and Promotion of Competition (*Comisión para la Defensa y Promoción de la Competencia*; CDPC), a requirement under chapter 4 of CAFTA-DR. Modeled after similar commissions in the post-Soviet Eastern European countries, CDPC has as its purpose to identify and challenge oligopolistic business practices. Created under the Law to Defend and Promote Competition (*Ley para la Defensa y Promoción de la Competencia*), it can fine firms for violating competitive practices and issue rulings regarding its own areas of responsibility.

Media. Although the written and electronic media play a major role in increasing public awareness about corruption, its approaches are generally sensationalist, partisan, or both. Many observers note that "corruption allegations are tried in newspapers rather than courts." Although the extensive influence of the media can be seen as a tribute to freedom of expression in Honduras, the national outlets are controlled by a few powerful business families with their own private commercial agendas. Extended corruption coverage can therefore be attributed often to the desire of these competing interests to implicate each other in wrongdoing.

Still, there is some cause for optimism in this area. The Transparency Law, although flawed, enhances the potential role of the media as an anti-corruption tool, seeking to bolster the independence and technical quality of reports. Another positive development is the creation of Press Uncensored (*Prensa sin Censura*), an agency established by independent journalists following the prosecutors' hunger strike. Press Uncensored seeks to distribute information through unbiased corruption reports found on the Internet. In addition, the steady growth in the number of media outlets, particularly radio and television stations, is increasing competition for audience share. This phenomenon, combined with the increasing reliance on local stations in support of social audit initiatives at the municipal level, has the potential to improve media coverage.

Political-Economic Analysis

Petty or low-level corruption in Honduras has its roots in a lack of economic opportunities, low salaries, widespread poverty, and a deeply engrained tradition of taking advantage of official spoils. Though there are continued rhetorical calls for the establishment of a career civil service and the creation of a legal framework to do so, appointments to the government bureaucracy (often obtained through political or personal connections) are generally viewed as an opportunity to improve one's financial standing.

Grand corruption responds to a different dynamic, as it is mostly the purview of the traditional wealthy and politically powerful elite. There are, however, growing indications that this elite is being forced to compete, or in some instances collude, with new economic interests associated with the illicit international narcotics market and related money-laundering operations. To deflect growing international and civil society pressures to curb their well-established corrupt practices, the elites, it is thought, have started adopting more creative subterfuges. Such practices include the manipulation of presumably transparent National Assembly selection procedures and schemes to elect officials through irregular means. In 2007, for example, the commissioners of the Public Information Access Institute were appointed in what has been described as a political ambush: the vote was taken in the middle of a disturbance caused by outside protests, and it was doubtful that the required congressional quorum was present.[28] Civil society, and members of two minority parties, bitterly complained about the selection procedures and qualifications of the candidates chosen.

Respect for the rule of law and a strong justice sector—typically the hub of anticorruption initiatives—have consistently scored in the low ends of surveys of public confidence in Honduras. Traditionally the object of political patronage and subjugation to other branches, the judiciary is perceived as serving principally the interests of influential economic and political elites. There are also alarming reports of increasing levels of influence and intimidation from organized crime and narco-traffickers.

In addition to this lack of independence and politicization, the justice system is handicapped by inefficient administrative practices and institutions. Despite a basically sound legal framework, the justice sector has proven incapable of confronting corruption, either by credibly investigating, prosecuting, and resolving corruption cases brought before it or by checking corrupt practices within its own ranks and personnel. The major factors that contribute to this fundamentally flawed system include the following.

Lack of political will. The most significant hurdles to fighting corruption through the justice system are the lack of political will and public demand for enduring justice sector reform. As true reform requires the presence and commitment of key stakeholders, meaningful and sustainable change in the justice sector has proven particularly difficult to implement.[29] A strong consensus has emerged over the years that the Honduran justice sector lacks the necessary political will for genuine reform, especially in the area of anticorruption.[30] Legal reform efforts with anticorruption components have been attempted for decades with international support but have been relatively unsuccessful, due largely to insufficient political will. Substantial investments in the justice sector have accomplished little in terms of productivity, systemic achievements, or a reduction in corruption and impunity. The recent DG Assessment observed that "Honduran legal culture and institutions have proven to be resistant to change and modernization without high and sustained levels of effort. Political will is low, and resistance to reform by important national actors and institutions vested in maintaining the status quo, is high."[31] In this scenario, working with civil society actors to create demand from the bottom upward seems to be the most promising and realistic of alternatives.

Failure to implement and enforce existing laws. Certain regulatory revisions are needed in the anticorruption legal framework, such as closing the loopholes for withholding information in the Transparency Law, strengthening the Procurement Code to restrict emergency contracting, and protecting whistleblowers. The consensus among experts, however, is that legal reforms are not as necessary as credible and consistent implementation of existing laws. The widespread acceptance of selective disregard for the law not only eviscerates the legal framework for preventing and combating corruption but also further feeds public perceptions of impunity and corruption in the justice sector.

As the DG Assessment noted, improving enforcement of existing laws would be a daunting task under the current configuration of interests and actors: "Although none of the actors . . . is completely opposed to improving the application of laws as a general matter, the important and necessary levels of support and strength to accomplish real and enduring change are not evident. At this point, no significant actor, including the President or the Supreme Court, appears both willing and able to provide solid and unwavering support for improving the application of laws."[32]

Politically driven interference and corruption. The judicial branch has been historically subjugated to other branches of government and suffers from a chronic lack of independence. In addition, the sector is the alleged target of political manipulation by wealthy and influential private and political actors, especially at the Supreme Court level and particularly in cases involving charges of corruption.

Political interference in the judicial branch manifests itself clearly in the manipulation of judicial selection and appointments. Appointments of Supreme Court justices are heavily tied to political favoritism and patronage, thereby lessening the court's inclination to rule objectively in cases alleging government corruption. The Supreme Court has been ruled by National Party interests throughout its tenure. In the political cases that the court has decided, most, if not all, decisions reflect an eight-to-seven split, exactly along party lines, with a National Party majority.[33] This partisan whitewashing contributes to the perception of political control at the highest level of the judiciary and further erodes the public trust.

Politics also greatly influences judicial appointments below the high court, affecting appellate courts, first instance courts, justices of the peace, and judicial personnel, among others. The Supreme Court possesses the constitutional authority to appoint lower-court judges, and in accordance with the Judicial Career Law of 1982, these decisions are to be based on merit and subject to the recommendation of the Judicial Career Council. Instead, however, the Supreme Court delegates its collective authority to make personnel decisions entirely to the (National Party) chief justice, who has made all decisions concerning judicial selection, assignments, transfers, and dismissals since shortly after assuming her position.

Systemic and structural corruption. Corruption in the Honduran justice sector also arises from systemic failures and structural inefficiencies that have created a climate conducive to corrupt practices, which can go largely undetected because of a lack of transparency and accountability. The productivity of the justice system and its key actors is reported to be remarkably low, with little or no incentive for improvement.

In addition, administrative functions are not separate from judicial functions in Honduras, which contribute to poor management practices. Often, the inefficiency of the judicial administration prompts illegal payments to facilitate the progress of cases. In this environment, a variety of corrupt practices thrive, including misplacement or concealment of files, alteration and theft of records, tampering with writs and document authorizations, manipulation of judicial case assignments, illegal fees and bribes (or "gifts"), improper seizure or return of assets and bank accounts, "loss" of material evidence, issuance of false summons and warrants, unjustified and repeated delays in judicial proceedings, and payments to clerks and process servers to obtain favorable or expedited treatment.[34]

The recent Criminal Procedures Code has changed the essential structure of institutional and individual responsibilities and relationships. This has increased transparency in some areas but has also generated conflicts and tensions that have led to new manifestations of corruption. For example, the Public Ministry now exercises primary control over the investigation of cases, which reportedly often leads to abuses of authority, such as the manipulation of prosecutors to influence particular cases. Cases also tend to be stalled in the Public Ministry instead of the courts or simply are never brought to prosecution.[35]

A significant element of institutional corruption is the top-down, monolithic power structure in key institutions, including the Supreme Court and the Public Ministry. This creates an environment highly conducive to arbitrary and corrupt practices with little chance of oversight or accountability. Moreover, any change in leadership under this structure can drastically transform the entire institution in one fell swoop, either for better or for worse. Support to institutions dependent on a single powerful protagonist at the top is therefore not realistically sustainable, since any gains achieved can be lost precipitously when the leadership changes. A stark example is the transformation of the Public Ministry in recent years, which resulted in substantial loss of trained personnel and prosecutorial practices built with the assistance of USAID.

Prosecutorial obstacles and influence of narco-trafficking and organized crime. The competence and motivation of the special anticorruption prosecutor and his office has been called into serious question. The number of cases actually investigated and prosecuted is minimal, delays are extraordinary, and the conviction rate is deplorable. Although statistics from that office are of uncertain reliability, it appears as though only two to four convictions have been made in the past two years in reportedly minor cases. Significant corruption cases have evaded prosecution altogether. Similar problems of incompetence, corruption, and abuse of authority affect the police. In general, these forces lack adequate education, training, salaries, equipment, vetting, internal controls, and oversight. A police reform is being planned with European Union funding but is still in preliminary stages.

In addition, the increasing influence of narco-traffickers and organized crime poses serious threats to the rule of law as corruption and criminal activities escalate. Threats and intimidation from these criminal groups are rising at alarming rates, especially in smaller municipalities and in rural areas used as drug corridors (primarily the northern and Atlantic zones). Gangs are becoming increasingly professionalized and making forays into lesser categories of organized crime, such as trafficking in small quantities, for example, *narco-menudéo*. Although narco-trafficking and organized crime are not characterized as the main causes of corruption, they are consistently cited as an increasing factor in the justice system's inability to control corruption in these trafficking areas, especially at the municipal and local levels.

Inadequate oversight and accountability mechanisms. Both internal disciplinary control methods and external control methods (via criminal proceedings) are poorly designed and effectuated in the justice sector. The Office of the Inspector General of Courts has the power to investigate complaints of judicial misconduct made by any source. If cause for discipline is found, the case proceeds to hearing before the director of the Judicial Career Office, which issues recommendations to the chief justice of the Supreme Court, who takes final action. Appeals can be pursued through the Judicial Career Council.

Overall, this political-economic analysis suggests that Honduras can be best described as a country where high-level figures collude to weaken political-economic competitors (see Type 2 syndrome in the typology described in table 5.1 in chapter 5). Honduras is a country dominated by extended networks of diverse elites (generally colluding to advance their economic interests) who share major benefits among themselves while staving off political and economic competitors. Furthermore, in Honduras, leaders of nominally competing political parties may share money and power, while corruption underwrites de facto political stability and policy predictability, thus compensating for institutions intentionally kept weak.

Proposed Strategic Directions

Despite considerable advances in developing a formal anticorruption infrastructure, much of its potential effectiveness has been hindered by political machinations and opaque deals and by the general incompetence of the state. Limited political and economic competition—and the near complete absence of political will within the controlling elite—consistently undermines meaningful implementation of anticorruption reform.

There is, however, near universal awareness about the deleterious consequences of corruption and a range of potential policy interventions to confront it. Many of the most promising are at the local level, which has the potential to develop the grassroots support that could eventually influence political will to attack corruption seriously. Several leading governance NGOs have begun preparing (if in a fragmented fashion) carefully calibrated initiatives to prevent additional efforts by the political and economic elite to weaken anticorruption institutions. Potential allies in this effort are the few true reformers within the political class; essentially marginalized from the country's main political parties, they nevertheless have the potential to join with civil society actors to advance the anticorruption agenda.

Given this state of affairs, and the considerable advances Honduras has made in developing a formal anticorruption architecture, the priority strategy requires support of NGOs seeking to increase the integrity and transparency of anticorruption institutions. The civil society community needs immediate and aggressive assistance to ensure a transparent, nonpoliticized selection of magistrates and top managers for key control institutions. With proper leadership and the enactment of relatively minor legal and regulatory reforms, the country's most important control institutions can, with relative ease, begin fulfilling their mandates to successfully confront the corrupt practices of the economic and political elite. Crucially, however, such success would require honest leadership with a commitment to an anticorruption agenda.

In particular, members of Congress seeking reelection need to be held accountable for their voting records when appointing officials for important anticorruption positions. Mid- to long-term complements to this strategic priority direction involve educating and mobilizing the public to demand accountable government, primarily through the promotion of citizen oversight programs (e.g., social auditing) at the local level and hard-hitting, electronic media–based public awareness campaigns. The latter would be aimed not at raising overall corruption awareness—public opinion surveys demonstrate that this is already quite high—but rather at how to energize the public to demand and monitor anticorruption initiatives at the central, local, and sector levels.

Analysis of Key Sectors

We focus on just three sectors in which the assessment team believes there to be opportunities to reduce corruption in Honduras—education, health, and economic growth. The full report also highlights potential reform programs in the judicial and local government areas.

Education Sector
The education sector in Honduras is plagued by administrative and grand corruption, including a rather peculiar variant of state capture. Through it, teachers

are appropriating a disproportionate share of state resources through pressures exerted on the Executive and agreements reached between labor unions (*gremios*) and politicians. Corruption in this sector, however, is far more widespread than that. It manifests itself in the purchase of school supplies (including in the construction of school facilities), in the appointment of teachers and administrators (with political and personal connections playing a major role), in the falsification or inflation of credentials, and in unexcused classroom absences. Corruption is also present in public universities, where bribes and fraud in examinations are frequent and unearned diplomas can be obtained for the right price.

In comparison to similarly educated professionals in the public sector, teachers are paid considerably more, while working five rather than eight hours a day, and receive 90 days of vacation as opposed to 12 in other sectors. The government's social security contributions for teachers are far more generous than those for other government employees, and teachers are entitled to salary bonuses that others are not. Teachers' unions have achieved these conditions through influence over politicians, who view teachers and certain union leaders as uniquely suited to mobilize voters during elections. According to a recent TSC audit, 10,000 of the 63,000 teachers in the country work in administrative positions, many at the Ministry of Education in Tegucigalpa, where some union leaders and their representatives purportedly wield enough political power to influence ministerial decision making. This political power is enhanced by the unions' ability to mobilize membership in public demonstrations and, if necessary, go on strike—even if it paralyzes the national school system (a frequent occurrence). As a concession negotiated between the unions and the Ministry of Education in resolution of one of the teachers' strikes, more than 12,000 teachers are allowed to receive educational premium pay intended to reward exceptional professional merit or advanced academic achievement without having to establish proof for those entitlements.

Corrupt officials, often influenced by union leaders, allegedly manipulate programs and funding allocations. The 2007–2008 TSC audit, conducted to verify the number of school facilities and to determine the status of teachers' credentials, seniority, special benefits, and workloads, uncovered evidence suggesting fraud, corruption, and malfeasance. Although the findings were only tentative, and were likely to change as the irregularities were investigated, the initial findings of this preliminary audit were troubling nonetheless. The TSC was reportedly unable to physically locate 4,323 school facilities, with a satellite search under way to determine if the missing schools actually existed. If not, it would mean that some such "schools" were never built, the construction funds were misappropriated, and operational expenditures of imaginary schools were being pocketed by corrupt officials. "Virtual," that is, nonexistent, teachers were suspected of collecting salaries, as were the relatives of deceased teachers or of teachers who had left the country. "Virtual" students may also have been created on paper to justify additional classrooms, teacher salaries, and perhaps subsidized school lunches.

The Environment for Reform

Addressing the corruption challenge in the education sector demands, among other tactics, confronting the powerful educational unions and working with reformist teachers' unions. The country also needs to determine how to manage future financial burdens in light of a projected inflated teacher salary bill. Since these outlays have already been codified, unions are certain to resist any attempts to curtail growth in teachers' salaries.

A clear opportunity to limit corruption in the sector will involve the improvement of educational authorities' record-keeping capacity. As the TSC audit revealed, the ministry was incapable of determining accurate numbers of schools, teachers, or students in the system. Poor management capacity facilitates corruption, allowing fraudulent deals, bribes, and other unscrupulous practices.

Another option, already being pursued by reform-minded education officials, with donor community support, is to gradually decentralize the educational system. Decentralized schools are thought likely to be more accountable and transparent, as they respond directly to the communities they serve. Implementing this strategy, however, requires a detailed plan for the nature of the decentralization process (e.g., administrative, financial, or both, and at what level—municipal, departmental) and the strengthening of public and civic oversight mechanisms. The TSC educational audit suggests possible future courses of action, as did many of the social auditing programs already operating in Honduras. The key lies in developing required standards and regulatory procedures and providing sufficient resources and training for professional and social auditors to perform their functions in a timely and conscientious manner.

Recommendations

- Support the Ministry of Education and/or the TSC in developing a computerized record-keeping system to facilitate accurate local data gathering that can be compiled at the central level, creating accurate tallies of schools, teachers, and students, including teachers' qualifications and whether they justify pay scales, salary premiums, and other benefits. Establish verifiable procedures to validate teachers' credential claims.

- Support the establishment of cooperative links between the CNA, Transparency Institute, and TSC to regularly disseminate educational audit results, including developing capacity to respond to citizen information requests.
- Develop and implement a GPS-based location system to keep track of school settings as part of the education sector master development plan.
- Provide financial and technical support to the TSC to allow it to conduct education sector audits on a timely and regular basis. The scope of such audits should be expanded as experience is gained and additional issues uncovered.
- Apply and publicize the results of education sector audits on a regular basis, providing results at the municipal level.
- Promote standardization of audit procedures to minimize complaints by municipal authorities that audits are not being consistently performed between localities.
- As part of the decentralization plan, and in light of audit results, continuously update the existing education sector master development plan.
- Develop appropriate manuals and materials to train social auditors.
- Articulate a well-defined strategy for educational sector audits in Transparency Committee manuals and training programs.
- Support reform-minded teachers' unions in developing a more nuanced sense of their mission in society as stewards of their country's future.
- Lobby for the inclusion of educational decentralization and local oversight as one of the issues in the new Municipalities Law.

Health Sector

Corruption is as widespread in the health sector as in the education sector. Low-level corruption ranges from health organizations charging excessively for workshop materials and other events, to dishonest billing for per diems by health personnel, to double-billing for purchases made. Official cars are often driven for personal reasons, while expensive diagnostic equipment is frequently stolen from public health posts and hospitals and transferred to private clinics.

Patients are sometimes steered to private clinics by public sector physicians or solicited for bribes in exchange for timely medical care. Clientelism and political interference dominate the appointment of physicians and other personnel to scarce and highly sought-after positions in the public health care system, while rural areas remain severely underserved. Employees are frequently absent or not on the job for the required number of hours at many health facilities.

These instances of petty corruption, while significant in the aggregate, pale in comparison with the grand corruption abuses committed with funds allocated for construction and maintenance of the public health infrastructure and, most of all, with the large-scale purchase of essential medicines by the MOH. In addition, in the private sector, instances of collusive practices to maintain high drug prices have been uncovered.

Health sector corruption is particularly deleterious for women and children in Honduras. Preventive medicine is not commonly practiced, and much of the sophisticated diagnostic equipment—especially to detect catastrophic diseases such as cancer—is not available in public health clinics. If purchased for public use, the equipment is often stolen and transferred to private fee-generating clinics. Consequently, when serious diseases in poor women and children are diagnosed, they tend to be at later stages and more difficult or impossible to treat.

In addition, women are most often responsible for providing or arranging medical care for the family, frequently waiting long hours at public health clinics for their children to be seen. Duties such as these interfere with women's abilities to hold jobs outside the home. Improved accountability in the health system would mean better treatment for these women and their families and more opportunities for them to participate in livelihood activities.

Vulnerabilities in the sector largely involve limited management capacities and an inability to meet programming priority guidelines. Management control systems, including those regulating expenditures, are inadequate or ineffective. In particular, medication purchases have been historically vulnerable to manipulation, to the point that the administration of President Maduro in 2002 decided to assign the responsibility to the UNDP. Upon assuming office, President Zelaya cancelled the arrangement, claiming implementation problems and that the fee (3.5% per transaction) levied by UNDP for handling medication procurements was onerous and could be better used directly for Honduras's public health needs.

One particularly egregious and costly corrupt practice is the purchase of large quantities of medications under emergency rules that allow the MOH to sidestep more transparent and competitive open bids. Inventories are intentionally allowed to decline to critically low levels, thus creating an "emergency." The emergency will then be "solved" by drastically accelerating the procurement cycle through solicitation of bids on a restricted and expedited basis from only a few firms. Such procedures open the door for collusive bidding and overcharges, often alleged to be in the millions of lempiras.

In 2008, Honduras experienced a notorious MOH emergency procurement scandal. The current minister, under pressure to approve a 470 million lempira medicine purchase by the Inter-institutional Medical Supplies Commission (*Commisión Interinstitucional de Medicamentos*; CIM), refused and agreed to approve only 170 million lempira worth of critically needed supplies on an emergency basis. The Executive was suspected of concocting the emergency in conjunction with some CIM officials by declaring an early open competitive bid null and void. (Ironically, the commission had been established precisely to prevent such abuses.) Afterward, the minister of health supposedly agreed to remain at her post contingent on future medication purchases being handled through ONCAE, and not the CIM, at least throughout her tenure. The CIM 2008 incident demonstrated yet again how authorities in Honduras often subvert the intent of organizations established ostensibly to prevent fraud and corruption.

The Environment for Reform

The main obstacles to reform are the inefficiencies characterizing the sector in general, in terms of both administration and service delivery and its vulnerabilities to political manipulation. The system is so flawed that many donors view decentralization of service delivery as one of the only options available to improve the situation.

Such a strategy would depend, in part, on funding third-party providers (including public decentralized health units and networks) to serve the needs of some of the most underserved rural populations, while strengthening the capacity of the MOH at the central and departmental levels to manage the decentralized system. The goal would be to ultimately separate functions, with the ministry responsible for financing, regulating, and quality assurance, and third parties and public decentralized health units responsible for service delivery. The CIM scandal and the attention it generated also present an opportunity to revisit the MOH medicine procurement procedures and encourage steps to prevent future fabricated emergencies in the purchase of medications.

A new service delivery strategy would take advantage of the social auditing experiences acquired in Honduras and systematize those lessons, with particular focus on applying best practices in the sector at the local level. This would include assessing experiences gained by governance NGOs working at the municipal level, specifically with regard to the support they have offered to transparency commissions and other community-based modes of social community oversight.

In Choluteca, for example, the departmental public health authorities are implementing a system to improve the transparency and accountability of the procurement of medications and other medical supplies. It established a Medical Purchases Commission, which was headed by the president of the municipal Transparency Commission and included representation from the sector's medical, nursing, technical, and labor union staff. Although only 8% of medical supplies were acquired locally, rather than provided by the MOH, a more transparent process could increase the sector's efficiency and give added confidence to the public that the common good was being protected.

Recommendations
- Support initiatives to make medical purchase procedures more transparent.
- Establish an Internet-based catalog of current medication prices.
- Tighten and better regulate conditions under which emergency purchases of medications are permissible.
- Include a corruption specialist in the health sector decentralization design team in order to anticipate and integrate fraud and corruption prevention interventions.
- Systematize knowledge gained in Honduras and elsewhere of best health sector social auditing practices.
- Provide health sector social auditing training to municipal transparency commissions as decentralization of the sector is rolled out.

Economic Growth Sector
Economic competition in Honduras is hindered by traditional elites' control over much of the nation's wealth and the private sector's close ties to corrupt politicians. Nevertheless, globalization and trade competition are gradually having an effect, as businesses are forced to adopt more ethical practices and operate according to international rules. Since the private sector plays such a large role in most corruption transactions, it therefore also represents a significant opportunity in the effort to reduce corruption in the economic sector.

The extreme concentration of economic wealth in the hands of a privileged few and their influence over the political levers of the state does not bode well, as shown by past experience, for the success of anticorruption reform policies over the short to medium term. A major surge in crime, the growing influence of drug trafficking cartels, and a deficient infrastructure, among other problems, make Honduras an unattractive prospect for foreign investment.

The Environment for Reform

To the extent that increasing economic competition can eventually contribute to a less corrupt environment, there are a few signs that Honduras is moving in the right direction. While the competitiveness of the national economy in the *maquila* sector is limited, due to the impact of exports from China and other low-cost-producing countries, Honduras enjoys substantial agro-export advantages as a result of its climate, geography, and location. These competitive advantages may help the country to continue growing as a supplier of agricultural commodities to the United States and other markets. In addition, supporting agro-exporters—particularly small- and medium-sized producers— is one way to contribute to economic growth while simultaneously diluting the highly concentrated economic power that obstructs the modernization of the country's political institutions. Although national elites would presumably resist the relinquishment of power, a rising economic tide could benefit the country at large.

Recommendations

- Support entities such as the CDPC to create a more competitive and fluid business environment.
- Increase the capacity of medium-sized and small enterprises to become more competitive and export oriented.
- Review national legislation to harmonize its content with international business practices.
- Monitor enforcement of CAFTA-DR competitive business rules.
- Promote ethical standards within the private sector in its dealings with government.

Epilogue

Governance problems in Honduras came to a head in June 2009 when President Manuel Zelaya was forcibly removed from power by the Honduran military on the day of a controversial poll on a potential constitutional referendum. Since his election in 2005, Zelaya had moved increasingly to the political left, allying himself with Venezuelan president Hugo Chavez and signing the socialist leader's Bolivarian Alternative for the Americas, an alternative trade agreement generally unpopular in Honduras. Before his ouster, Zelaya had advocated for a constitutional reform initiative that many perceived as a veiled attempt to extend presidential term limits. The June 28 poll had intended to gauge public support for constitutional reform, although the National Assembly opposed the poll, and the Supreme Court declared it unconstitutional.

Zelaya's overthrow incited outrage from the international community, and many development programs stalled as donor organizations halted or reevaluated their funding. In the immediate aftermath of the coup, USAID, the World Bank, the European Union, and the Inter-American Development Bank, among others, suspended several million dollars' worth of aid to the country. The MCC, which had signed a US$215 million compact with Honduras in 2005, partially terminated the agreement with one year left in its implementation.[36] Although development funding eventually resumed, at least in part, the political situation in Honduras remains tenuous.

Despite a November 2009 presidential election generally regarded as free and fair, the instigators of the Honduran coup have escaped accountability for their part in the destabilization of Honduras's democratic system. The current president, Porfirio Lobo of the conservative National Party, faces significant political and economic challenges, including reservations about his government's very legitimacy. The progress of reform in many key sectors is considerably reliant on the status of development programs in place before the coup. However, continuing reform efforts are hindered by a crippled economy (deeply shaken both by cuts in aid and investment and by the worldwide recession) and a significantly weakened democratic system.

Governance Reforms

The 2009 coup merely highlighted deep-seated and continuing governance problems in Honduras. In January 2010, the CNA released a report emphasizing that corruption had penetrated all levels of government and that confidence in oversight institutions was extremely low.[37] Ninety-five percent of Hondurans surveyed felt that the country was suffering from significant corruption problems and cited the issue as their third major cause of concern behind crime and unemployment.[38] In the MCC's 2010 scorecard, the categories in which Honduras ranked below the median in its income peer group were "control of corruption," "rule of law," and "fiscal policy."[39]

Donors have been all too aware of these ongoing corruption issues. A significant proportion of aid programming over the years has been directed toward decentralization and anticorruption efforts, and these are slated to continue in the postcoup political environment, though with more clouded prospects for success.

Several USAID programs focus on decentralization and empowerment of local government. These efforts aim at improving municipal capacity to manage and report public expenditures and involving local citizens in budget and policy meetings. USAID also provides support for the Superior Court of Accounts and its Transparency Law. As noted earlier, the court had proven surprisingly vigorous in its oversight role, completing audits of all the country's municipalities, teacher practices, major state-owned enterprises, and public officials. Nevertheless, it remains hamstrung by political pressures, budget constraints, and generally inadequate authority and independence. USAID efforts to strengthen the Transparency Law also face obstacles, from ineffective implementation measures to outright legislative efforts to weaken the bill.[40]

The World Bank has also initiated several programs aimed at governance reform. After freezing aid in the aftermath of the presidential coup, the World Bank restored US$270 million in loans in February 2010.[41] Many of them had demonstrated meaningful progress at the time they were assessed, before the 2009 coup. One such project focused strongly on central government administration reform, successfully establishing an Integrated Financial Management System, an internal control office (ONADIS), and a results-based management system at the national government level.[42] The justice sector, cited by Hondurans as the most corrupt branch of government, received millions of dollars in support for new information management systems, justice of the peace courts, "mobile" courts, and other means of improving the capacity and performance of the judiciary.[43] The World Bank is also attempting to address one of the most serious and growing concerns of Honduran citizens through an Urban Crime and Violence Prevention initiative, helping municipal officials cooperate with community leaders on strategies to reduce crime in their neighborhoods.[44]

Education Sector

The education system remains one of the most corrupt sectors in Honduras, largely because of the inordinate power of the teachers' unions. To this end, many reform projects emphasize standardization and accountability measures that decrease the potential for exploitation of the system. USAID is working with the national government to align certain academic disciplines with international standards and to implement national standardized testing in the elementary through high school levels. It is also supporting efforts to decentralize responsibility for education services from the central ministry. These initiatives seek to engender a sense of community ownership of education and provide benchmarks by which teachers and officials in the education sector can be held accountable for their performance.[45]

The World Bank initiated a five-year program in 2008 focused on improving accountability in the sector, while also strengthening education programs in disadvantaged communities. In its early stages, the program successfully conducted an Early Grade Reading Assessment and a training program for teachers in rural schools and helped to establish 309 new preschools that opened in February 2010. It also designed a human resources module for teachers at the Ministry of Education.[46]

Health Sector

Donor programs in this sector also tend to focus on decentralization to limit the potential for political manipulation and large-scale misappropriation of funding. While support is provided to the central MOH to monitor and regulate decentralized services, USAID's efforts center on developing partnerships and municipal capacity to provide localized delivery of health services, particularly with regard to medication and other supplies. The aim is not only to improve efficiency of health care delivery but also to avoid the systematic corruption of the procurement process that has occurred at the national level.[47]

The World Bank is currently focusing more exclusively on health care delivery and improvement, funding health services contracts in seven municipalities and increasing health care coverage to tens of thousands of Hondurans. Its main initiative in this sector began in 2002 and was scheduled for completion in the summer of 2009.[48]

Economic Growth Sector

The Honduran economy took a major hit after the 2009 political crisis. According to one estimate, 200,000 jobs were lost in the aftermath of the coup, and the unemployment rate rose to 36%, one-third higher than the rate of the previous two years.[49] The national economy shrunk by 2%, and though it was forecasted to recover in 2010, the 2% expected growth rate places Honduras among the poorest economic performers in Latin America.[50] The resumption of aid funding by major donors helped stave off further economic damage, though many ongoing projects suffered a loss of momentum. Significant existing investments in agro-industry development and financial reform nevertheless contain the promise of eventual recovery in this critical national sector.

A primary focus of economic development efforts in Honduras was the agricultural sector. USAID has channeled millions of dollars toward improving agricultural production and marketing: increasing productivity, shifting cultivation to value-added crops, creating linkages along the value chain, and so on. These projects also provide market information, technology transfer, and farmer extension services and access to credit—seeking to build a foundation on which producers can replicate best practices.[51] In 2008, the World Bank initiated a similar project, focusing on developing the productivity and competitiveness of small-scale producers in the agriculture, fishing, and forestry sectors in western Honduras. Worth approximately US$43 million and scheduled for completion in 2015, the project has disbursed just over 1% of funding as of summer 2009. The World Bank has also managed a forestry and rural productivity project since 2004 that promoted sustainable community forestry enterprises and benefited 17,860 families in its first three years. The project also assists 26 municipalities in preparing and executing plans for municipal development, land use, and zoning.[52]

Efforts are also under way to improve the trade and investment environment in Honduras. With traditional political elites dominating the economic system, the opening of the Honduran economy to increased competition and international regulation represents a potential check on corrupt practices. As its largest trading partner, the United States provides technical assistance to help Honduras meet its commitments under the CAFTA-DR. This includes support for increased market access, sanitary and phytosanitary inspection, protected intellectual property rights, and improved trade analysis. A large part of trade development efforts focus on policy reform, such as modernized trade and financial policies, antimonopoly measures, and streamlined procedures for opening a business.[53]

The World Bank is also contributing to this effort through a seven-year trade facilitation and productivity enhancement project started in 2003. Although progress has been difficult to measure, the project has made such strides as significantly decreasing the number of days it takes to open a business and obtain a construction license and establishing a competition agency and relevant national bodies for measuring and certifying product quality standards. The project has also trained nearly 400 small- and medium-sized enterprises in ways to enhance productivity, and it claims the creation of 6,000 new jobs as a result of initiatives promoting foreign investment.[54]

In addition, the World Bank is attempting to reform critical elements of the Honduran financial system, with an eight-year project to increase the institutional capacity of the *Comisión Nacional de Bancos y Seguros* (CNBS) and *Banco Central de Honduras* and modernize the payment system. After a slow start in 2003, the project has made progress and is currently working to increase transparency and oversight in this sector. It provides support to the Financial Sector Superintendence for improved financial monitoring practices, development of antimoney-laundering regulations, regulation of remittance companies, and introduction of risk-based supervision.[55]

Notes

1. This chapter is adapted from the assessment written by Sergio Diaz-Briquets and J. Michele Guttmann for Management Systems International under a USAID contract.

2. Kenneth M. Coleman and José René Argueta. March 2008. *Political Culture, Governance and Democracy in Honduras, 2008.* Vanderbilt University.

3. USAID/MSI. December 2007. *Honduras—Democracy and Governance Assessment,* vi (hereafter DG Assessment).

4. Secretaría de Estado del Despacho Presidencial. February 2008. *Avances en el cumplimiento del: Plan del Poder Ejecutivo contra la Corrupción.* Unidad de Apoyo Técnico; Secretaría de Estado del Despacho Presidencial. May 2008. *Avances en el cumplimiento del: Plan del Poder Ejecutivo contra la Corrupción.* II Informe de Avance. Unidad de Apoyo Técnico.

5. Foro Social de Deuda Externa y Desarrollo de Honduras (FOSDEH). 2008. *Apuntes sobre la corrupción en Honduras durante el 2007.* Tegucigalpa.

6. Secretaría de Estado. May. Avances, 9–10.

7. See Constitución De La República De Honduras (1982) (Preámbulo; Artículo 1), http://www.honduras.net/honduras_constitution.html.

8. This authority has, however, been the subject of conflict between the judicial and the legislative branches. In 2002, Congress attempted to pass an amendment granting it exclusive authority to interpret the constitution. The National Human Rights Ombudsman filed suit challenging the constitutionality of the amendment. The Constitutional Chamber of the Supreme Court ruled in favor of the Ombudsman, defending its power of constitutional review against the congressional incursion.

9. Transparency Law, Article 32. According to a well-recognized expert in the field of transparency laws, this restriction is unheard of. FOSDEH, *Apuntes sobre la corrupción en Honduras durante el 2007,* 21, citing Ernesto Villanueva. The prohibition arguably contravenes the constitution and the Inter-American Convention Against Corruption and other international treaties. Article 32(A) was later added to prohibit the *destruction or alteration* of prior records, although still precluding their *production.*

10. El Heraldo, *Gobierno Rechaza la Transparencia.* July 1, 2008.

11. DG Assessment, n. 2.

12. Ibid., vi.

13. Ibid., 61.

14. Federación de Organizaciones para el Desarrollo de Honduras (FOPRIDEH). February 2007. *El Tribunal Superior de Cuentas: Un diagnóstico desde la perspective de sociedad civil.* Tegucigalpa.

15. Consejo Nacional Anticorrupción. 2007. *Informe Nacional de Transparencia: Hacia un sistema nacional de integridad.* Tegucigalpa, 69.

16. Consejo Nacional Anticorrupción. 2007. *Evaluación social al Tribunal Superior de Cuentas.* Programa de Cara a la Cuidadanía. Tegucigalpa.

17. Ibid., 61.

18. See, among others, Alessandra Fontana. May 2008. "Teachers and Taxis: Corruption in the Education Sector in Honduras," *U4 Brief,* Anticorruption Resource Centre, CHR, Michelsen Institute, 16.

19. Secretaría de Estado. February. Avances, 3.

20. Secretaría de Estado. May. Avances, 1.

21. Consejo Nacional Anticorrupción. 2008. *Las resoluciones de clasificación de reserva de información hechas por el IAIP: La DEI y la Secretaría de Finanzas.* Programa de cara a la ciudadanía, Number 8. Tegucigalpa.

22. Ibid., 21–22.

23. US State Department. 2008. *Honduras: Country Reports on Human Rights Practices— 2007,* 14.

24. See discussion of upcoming Supreme Court selection process in Section 3(C)(3).

25. See description of Callejas proceedings at n. 32.

26. *Honduras: Country Reports on Human Rights Practices—2007,* 7.

27. For a representative sampling of the literature on social audit in Honduras, see, among many others, USAID and AMHON. Undated. *Experiencias exitosas en gestión descentralizada de municipios.* Programa de Gobernabilidad y Transparencia. Tegucigalpa; USAID, AMHON, and FOPRIDEH. Undated. *Experiencias exitosas en Transparencia, gobernabiliada y participación ciudadana en el municipio.* Programa de Gobernabilidad y Transparencia. Tegucigalpa; and UNDP. Undated. *Herramientas para las Comisiones de Transparencia.* Tegucigalpa.

28. FOSDEH, *Apuntes sobre la corrupción en Honduras,* 19.

29. "A quarter of a century of support for the judiciary in Latin America has demonstrated some of the limits of institutional assistance absent the political will by . . . powerful domestic forces to implement a true rule of law. . . . Absent political will to implement a rule of law, donor assistance to its institutions has had disappointing results." *Conducting a DG Assessment: A Framework for Strategy Development* (USAID, November 2000): 40.

30. FOPRIDEH, *II Informe Sobre el Estado de los Casos de Corrupción en Honduras 2006,* 62. See also DG Assessment.

31. DG Assessment, 55.

32. Ibid., 57.

33. The court was heavily criticized for its decision affirming dismissals of a series of cases against ex-president Rafael Callejas involving allegations of abuse of authority and misappropriation of government funds. Then–attorney general Ovidio Navarro—who had formerly represented Callejas—moved to have all pending criminal corruption cases against him dismissed when he took control of the Public Ministry. Several prosecutors objected and resisted abandoning the Callejas cases; they were transferred or fired, allegedly in contravention of the Public Ministry Career Law. The Supreme Court thereafter cleared Callejas of all criminal liability. The US Embassy then revoked Callejas's visa on the basis of corruption.

34. For a more extensive laundry list of corrupt systemic practices in Honduras, see *Evaluation of Judicial Corruption in Central America and Panama and the Mechanisms to Combat It* (Due Process of Law Foundation, 2007), 38–39, and *Controles y descontroles de la corrupción judicial* (Due Process of Law Foundation, 2007), *Informe Nacional Honduras* (Rigoberto Ochoa), 271–338.

35. FOPRIDEH, *II Informe sobre el estado de los casos de corrupción en Honduras 2006*, 61.

36. Millennium Challenge Corporation, Honduras page, http://www.mcc.gov/mcc/countries/honduras/index.shtml.

37. Thelma Mejia. January 4, 2010. "Entrenched Corruption Stymies Hope," InterPress Service News Agency, http://ipsnews.net/news.asp?idnews=49882.

38. Ibid.

39. Millennium Challenge Corporation 2010 country scorecard, Honduras, http://www.mcc.gov/mcc/bm.doc/score-fy10-honduras.pdf.

40. USAID Honduras website: Governance, http://www.usaid.gov/hn/governance.html.

41. Cecilia Farfan Mendez. June 28, 2010. "Honduras One Year Later: The Costs of a Coup," Americas Society website, http://www.as-coa.org/article.php?id=2487.

42. World Bank website: "Status of Projects in Execution, FY09," http://www.google.com/url?sa=t&source=web&ct=res&cd=2&ved=0CBoQFjAB&url=http%3A%2F%2Fsiteresources.worldbank.org%2FEXTSOPE%2FResources%2F5929620-1254491038321%2F6460830-1254525284835%2FSenegal.pdf&rct=j&q=world+bank+sope+senegal&ei=oBjyS8eYN8L98Aaz1Y3pDQ&usg=AFQjCNF4tj9nWanu6Tabdd1ixHEMunODEg&sig2=-ubH0E1uATFPDhaKzl7gzA.

43. Ibid. Also Mejia 2010.

44. World Bank, "Status of Projects in Execution, FY09."

45. USAID Honduras website: Education, http://www.usaid.gov/hn/reforms.html.

46. World Bank, "Status of Projects in Execution, FY09."

47. USAID Honduras website: Health, http://www.usaid.gov/hn/healthreform.html.

48. World Bank, "Status of Projects in Execution, FY09."

49. Farfan Mendez 2010.

50. Ibid.

51. USAID Honduras website: Economic Growth, http://www.usaid.gov/hn/agriculture.html.

52. World Bank, "Status of Projects in Execution, FY09."

53. USAID Honduras website: Economic Growth.

54. World Bank, "Status of Projects in Execution, FY09."

55. Ibid.

10

Timor Leste (2009)

As one of the world's newest nations, Timor Leste is engaged in a struggle to ensure that its young democracy can succeed. Not unexpectedly, for a nation that has seen foreign powers come and go, the Timorese are suspicious of outside assistance but accept that it will be needed well into the future to get a handle on pressing social, political, and economic problems. Memories of the country's recent violent past are still fresh, and Timor Leste's legal and administrative structures remain a work in progress.[1]

Many of these troubles stem from a brutal and exploitative history. Portuguese rule had been repressive and primarily extractive, focusing on the export of sandalwood and coffee with few investments in infrastructure, health, or education. This gave rise to the earliest forms of a resistance movement that would gain in numbers and force and carry on into modern times. After World War II and until the 1975 Indonesian invasion, a small number of *mestizos* and individuals from traditional ruling families were able to receive an education in the colony's few schools. This small, educated elite would later command the resistance and become the country's leaders. This group's influence is still felt today in government and in the country's limited private economy.

In 1975, without Portuguese resistance, Indonesia invaded Timor Leste, using the pretext of fighting communism for what would become a cruel and repressive occupation. The pervasive and systemic corruption found all over Indonesia would be incorporated into the administration of what was now Indonesia's 27th province. After the fall of Indonesian president Soeharto in 1998, and in the face of increasing violence from anti-independence activists and resistance forces in Timor Leste, Indonesian president Habibe set the stage for a UN-organized referendum in 1999. Seventy-eight percent of the Timorese electorate voted for independence. Shortly thereafter, violence erupted as pro-Indonesia militias launched a scorched earth campaign that left little of the country's already limited infrastructure in place and more than 100,000 dead.

In October 1999, the UN Transitional Administration in East Timor (UNTAET) was established, and the difficult process of nation-building was begun. Thousands of UN troops and advisers, along with a large number of international donors, flooded the capital of Dili and surrounding districts, bringing with them the promise of security and democratic governance. In 2002, a Constituent Assembly approved Timor Leste's first constitution, which was followed by the election of former guerrilla fighter and independence leader Xanana Gusmao as the country's first president. In May 2002, Timor Leste became a fully independent nation, and the UN Mission of Support in East Timor (UNMISET) was established as a successor to UNTAET, its mandate to provide assistance to core administrative structures critical to Timor Leste's political stability.

Because the senior ranks of the bureaucracy in Indonesian times did not include Timorese officials and because public infrastructure was almost entirely destroyed, the United Nations had the daunting task of building the country's administration from the ground up rather than working from an already existing base. A silver lining here may have been that the inefficiencies and corruption of Indonesian administration were not part of the mold from which the United Nations would work, although the legacy of corruption remains strong to this day.

An outbreak of violence in 2006, initially triggered by the dismissal of 594 soldiers but also fueled by weak and politicized governance, poverty, and unemployment, prompted the United Nations to set up a new peacekeeping force known as the UN Integrated Mission in Timor Leste (UNMIT), which remains in force today.

Parliamentary and presidential elections were held in 2007, notably representing the country's first successful nonviolent transfer of power. Jose Ramos Horta was elected president, and Xanana Gusmao became prime minister and head of government. An Alliance for Parliamentary Majority (AMP) ruled over a fragile coalition that did not include Fretilin, the nation's largest political party and the one most closely associated with the resistance movement. This added tension to the political situation and increased the possibility of recurrent violence.

Adding to an already combustible mix is the frequent use of presidential pardons, which have been unpopular among the country's human rights community, civil society organizations, and the general population, who are increasingly troubled by what they see as impunity. Pardons have been provided for a number of prisoners who were former members of anti-independence groups and those blamed for directing the violence of 2006. The use of pardons threatens the credibility of the judiciary and other oversight institutions.

Although Timor Leste suffers from high illiteracy, poor health, unemployment, and insecurity, it was able to establish a Petroleum Fund to ensure that revenues from its vast offshore oil and gas fields would be used in perpetuity for the benefit of the population. The fund appears to be well managed and serves as an example of transparent and accountable governance in an environment where these qualities are often lacking.

Legal-Institutional Analysis

The constitution of the new Democratic Republic of Timor Leste was adopted by a Constituent Assembly on March 22, 2002. The constitution provides for a "democratic state . . . based on rule of law" and separation of powers. It includes a number of important protections relating to anticorruption, including freedom of speech and information, freedom of the press and mass media, freedom to assemble and demonstrate, freedom of association, a right to political participation, habeas corpus, access to courts, and universal suffrage. It also explicitly provides for a legislative supervisory power, as well as a number of key oversight bodies, including the Ombudsman (Provedor), a Supreme Audit Institution (High Administrative, Tax, and Audit Court [HATAC]), and disciplinary bodies for judges and prosecutors (Superior Councils).

The Ombudsman is defined by the constitution as "an independent organ in charge of examining and seeking to settle citizens' complaints against public bodies, certifying the conformity of the acts with the law, preventing and initiating the whole process to remedy injustice." The Ombudsman is also given the power to challenge the constitutionality of laws. This capacity was expanded by an implementing law that created the Office of the Provedor for Human Rights and Justice. The law established the Provedor as an independent body charged "to combat corruption and influence peddling, prevent maladministration and protect and promote human rights and fundamental freedoms of natural and legal persons throughout the national territory."[2] The law set out the following definitions[3]:

> "*Corruption*" refers to the act of offering, giving, receiving, or soliciting anything of value with the aim of deviating the legal procedures of a public service meanwhile influencing the action of a public official for satisfaction of one's private interests, including

those of friends and family members; corruption presents itself in different forms such as bribery, conspiracy, nepotism, extortion, embezzlement, fraud and favouritism;

"*Maladministration*" means acts and omissions outside the powers conferred, made on the basis of irrelevant considerations, mistake of facts and law or lack of due process, and which disrupt or undermine the effective and proper functioning of the Public Administration;

"*Influence Peddling*" refers to the practice of soliciting, demanding, charging or accepting, for one's benefit or that of a third person, by oneself or through an intermediary, and with one's consent or endorsement, an advantage or promise of advantage, in the form or property or otherwise, to abuse one's influence, real or presumed, with the aim of illegally obtaining from any public entity an order, competitive bid award, contract, job, allowance, subsidy, benefit or any other favourable decision.[4]

The law tasked the Provedor with anticorruption education, prevention, and investigation. The Provedor was permitted to investigate cases and forward them to the prosecutor general but not to prosecute cases directly.

In 2009, parliament adopted the Creating the Anticorruption Commission law that repealed key portions of the law on the Provedor and transferred competence for corruption issues to a newly created commission. A principal (if unconvincing) argument for establishing the new body was that because the Provedor was charged with both human rights protection and investigation of corruption, he or she could face a conflict in a case in which investigators violated a suspect's human rights.[5]

The new Anticorruption Commission (ACC) is intended "to provide the State with a specialized and independent criminal police body, the authority of which was guided only by legality and objectivity criteria, in articulation with the competent authorities, as is indispensable for its credibility while [providing a] mechanism for fighting corruption."

The ACC has powers similar to those of the Provedor, but with expanded police authority, including (with appropriate judicial approval) arrest, search, seizure of assets, surveillance, and wiretapping. As with the Provedor, the ACC can forward cases to the prosecutor general but cannot directly prosecute a case.

The law provided additional definitions relevant to corruption, including the following.

Passive corruption for illicit act means, under article 292 of the Penal Code, an officer who, by himself or through a third party, with his consent or ratification, requests or accepts, for himself or for a third party, an undue patrimonial or non-patrimonial advantage, or the promise thereof, against any act or omission contrary to the duties of their position, even if prior to that request or acceptance;

Passive corruption for licit act means, under article 293 of the Penal Code, an officer who, by himself or through a third party, with his consent or ratification, requests or accepts, for himself or for a third party, an undue patrimonial or non-patrimonial advantage, or the promise thereof, against any act or omission that is not contrary to the duties of his position, even if prior to that request or acceptance; and an officer who, by himself or through a third party, with his consent or ratification, requests or accepts, for himself or for a third party, an undue patrimonial or non-patrimonial advantage from a person that has had, has or will have any claim depending from the exercise of his public functions;

Active corruption means, under article 294 of the Penal Code, a person who, by himself or through a third party, with his consent or ratification, gives or promises to give an officer or a third party with the officer's knowledge, an undue patrimonial or non-patrimonial advantage with the purpose indicated in article 292 or article 293 of the Penal Code;

Embezzlement means, under article 295 of the Penal Code, an officer who unduly seizes for himself or for a third party money or a movable asset, whether public or private, that is in his possession or available to him by way of his functions;

Illegitimate use means, under article 296 of the Penal Code, an officer who uses or allows another person to use, for purposes other than those for which they are meant, vehicles or other movable assets of significant value that are delivered to him, in his possession or accessible to him by way of his functions, in order to obtain an illegitimate benefit for himself or for a third person, or to cause damage to someone;

Abuse of power means, under article 297 of the Penal Code, an officer who abuses powers or breaches duties inherent to his functions, in order to obtain an illegitimate benefit for himself or for a third person, or to cause damage to someone.[6]

The commissioner of the ACC is to be appointed by parliament on proposal by the government, and he or she would then appoint three deputy commissioners. The criteria for selection of the commissioner are relatively strict and include experience as a judge, prosecutor, lawyer, police officer, or investigator. In the interim period between publication of the ACC law and establishment of the commission, there would be a gap in anticorruption authority—temporarily filled by the Office of the Prosecutor General. It was widely expected that choice of the commissioner would be extremely difficult.

The ACC was tasked with developing a comprehensive anticorruption strategy.[7] While drafts of such a strategy did exist, they were at a very early stage and needed substantial elaboration to be of use.

As noted, the constitution endowed parliament with legislative supervisory power, though there were indications that this was not well understood by members of parliament (MPs). Parliament did hold legislative hearings, which were attended by government actors, but there did not appear to be a regular "question time" or interpellation process.

The Supreme Court was also supposed to fill the role of Supreme Audit Institution until the HATAC could be established. However, the Supreme Court itself has yet to be formed, and its duties are being performed by the Court of Appeals.

A decree law of 2009 confirmed the Office of the Inspector General (first established in 2000 under UNTAET) as an internal audit body reporting to the prime minister.[8] It did not have authority over internal audit bodies created within line ministries, but such a role is under consideration.

A 2009 law transformed the Directorate for Public Service,[9] under the Ministry for State Administration, into a more autonomous Civil Service Commission (CSC).[10] The commission is "responsible for ensuring a politically neutral, impartial, merit based Public Sector, holding a high standard of professionalism with the purpose of providing quality services to the State and to the people of Timor Leste." The CSC has administrative, financial, and technical autonomy under the oversight of the prime minister.[11] Limited civil service training is available through the National Institute of Public Administration (INAP), though this appears to be a very weak body. Because of a prior limit on the size of the civil service, the government is still heavily reliant on national consultants—hired outside the civil service system—and often highly paid.

A law on political party financing was adopted in 2008 and appears to be respected. The law requires annual reporting of party assets to the National Electoral Commission, with sanctions for nonsubmission. All parties appear to have submitted fairly timely information in the first round of reporting.

The Timorese government is highly centralized, with virtually all authority at the national level. There are plans to gradually decentralize to a system of municipalities (replacing the current districts) that would have a mix of devolved and delegated powers, starting with those ministries that are most deconcentrated. While decentralization can encourage greater involvement by citizens, it also offers more avenues for corruption. Timor Leste has very little capacity to responsibly staff new local governments. While it appears that the decision to decentralize has already been made, the process envisioned is highly unclear.

On an international level, Timor Leste signed the UN Convention Against Corruption (UNCAC) in 2003 but did not ratify the convention until early 2009.[12]

Despite this progress on an anticorruption framework, the Timor Leste legal structure does not include several important anticorruption elements, including the following:

- *Freedom of information.* While the constitution provides for freedom of information, there is no implementing law. This key omission means that there is no practical provision for public access to government-held information.
- *Asset disclosure.* While a few laws provide for disclosure of assets by key officials (e.g., laws concerning ACC and the Provedor), there is no overall system for asset disclosure by high government officials. What few disclosures have been made (some required by law, some voluntary by ministers in the AMP government) are not updated regularly and are not available to the public for review.
- *Conflicts of interest.* There are effectively no regulations on conflicts of interest.[13] This may be in large part because the concept is not well understood. Even individuals with authority over recruitment or procurement do not appear to understand how favoritism toward family members can interfere with a strictly merit-based approach and that the latter method is superior.
- *Code of ethics.* There is effectively no code of ethics for civil servants.[14] There has been some discussion of establishing an ethics

information-training program,[15] but it is not clear what standards would be used in this program.

- *Whistleblower protection.* The Provedor and ACC are charged with protecting the confidentiality of complainants and witnesses up to the time of indictment. The Provedor can accept anonymous complaints, and the ACC can request police protection for witnesses. Although witness protection legislation does exist,[16] there appears to be no other provision for whistleblower protection.

- *Public participation.* There is no systematic provision for public participation in government decision making, although parliament does hold public hearings and invite witnesses. The government has made public consultation a priority, though there have been few visible attempts at implementation.

- *Freedom of the press.* There is no regulation of the press of any sort, though several somewhat restrictive draft laws are being considered.

Anticorruption Stakeholders

The following stakeholder analysis identifies and analyzes important groups that have demonstrated either a commitment or an opposition to reform. In particular, the analysis looks for anticorruption champions, groups that can be nurtured, those ready to advocate for reform, those already advocating for reform, and those with vested interests in maintaining currently corrupt systems.

Oversight institutions. Timor Leste's oversight institutions suffer from severe human resource constraints and inefficiencies stemming from overlapping functions.

- *The Office of the Provedor.* Until recently, this office had responsibility for investigating corruption cases in addition to its roles investigating human rights abuses and maladministration. However, the ACC is scheduled to take over most of the Provedor's anticorruption role, diminishing its significance as an oversight institution.

- *The Office of the Prosecutor General.* With a severe case backlog, this office is widely considered to be a major bottleneck in the pursuit of state corruptors. Because it has not prosecuted any high-level corruption cases, it is often viewed with suspicion and as a source of frustration among other oversight institutions, the media, and civil society. This office rates low in terms of capacity and moderate in terms of political will.

- *The Office of the Inspector General.* This office has very limited capacity to carry out financial inspections and audits of other government bodies. Its leadership, however, appears committed to reform. The OIG ranks low in terms of capacity and moderate in terms of political will to fight corruption.
- *The Anticorruption Commission.* The ACC is favored by the coalition government and may have a promising future, although it is still too early to know for sure. Much will depend on the selection of a highly qualified commissioner and the ACC's ability to work with the Office of the Prosecutor General.
- *The new Civil Service Commission.* The CSC holds promise in terms of its ability to bring order to recruitment, promotion, and appointment processes—areas in which conflicts of interest and susceptibility to other corrupt practices are traditionally high. It is still too early to determine the level of political will the CSC will bring to the drive against corruption. As with other oversight bodies, its capacity will presumably remain low for the foreseeable future.
- *The Ministry of Finance.* The ministry has limited resources to carry out its audit function or provide comprehensive review and control of state budgets. Its political will to provide oversight appears moderate.
- *The judiciary.* Timor Leste's judicial branch remains mostly untested in terms of its anticorruption mandate. In noncorruption cases, there have been complaints about the quality of decisions rendered, although no allegations of corruption have been made within the judiciary itself. While inexperienced, its judges can eventually prove to be effective in the fight against corruption. The judiciary can therefore be considered moderately capable of fighting corruption.

Parliament. Parliament is a potential player in the movement to combat corruption in Timor Leste but has shown relatively little interest to date. Many of its MPs come from the resistance movement and have taken up the anticorruption mantle as an extension of previous activities to ensure the strength and independence of their country. Fretilin functions as a strong opposition, and it is often behind corruption allegations directed at the government. The AMP coalition government has adopted a tough stance against corruption as well. The activity of Committee C on Economy, Finance, and Anticorruption, with a subcommittee devoted to the corruption issue, is a promising development, as is parliament's recent decision to ratify UNCAC.

In spite of these positive developments, it remains to be seen how parliament will function if faced with a high-level corruption case. Some members are from powerful families with ties to business and important parts of government. Furthermore, members have limited capacity to do research and to draft anticorruption legislation. Overall, parliament exhibits moderate capacity and political will to fight corruption.

Civil society. Timorese civil society is broad and diverse, especially for a country of its size. There are at least (and perhaps *only*) three NGOs devoted wholly or partially to anticorruption issues, and for the most part their work is of high quality. These groups are La'o Hamutuk, LABEH, and Luta Hamutuk.[17] They are often able to provide the substance and credibility that is mostly lacking among the media community: conducting investigations, writing reports, and disseminating information to policymakers and others with an interest in their work. In addition, Forum Ong Timor Leste (FONGTIL), an umbrella NGO group with strong links to government, has a 10-member working group on transparency and accountability, but it appears not to be very active.

In an environment where access to government information is limited, the NGO community can play an important role in disseminating information. In general, the NGO community tends to display antigovernment biases, which can be balanced only if the government commits to providing the public with adequate access to information. While the three NGOs named above can be seen as the nucleus of a strong civil society, it is essential that other strong NGOs (in any field) also develop if civil society is to become a truly significant force in Timor Leste.

Private sector. In terms of anticorruption tendencies, the Timorese business community is often in conflict with itself. Power is vested in a few controlling families with links to government, and other business owners are mostly small and willing to pay bribes for contracts. Members of the local business community complain about corruption but are willing to engage in corrupt practices to ensure their own success.

While business associations do exist, they appear weak and unstructured. Given the role of prominent families and pressing needs among small businesses to compete, it is unlikely that Timor Leste's small and insular business community will become a vocal advocate for reform in the near term. Their political will and capacity to battle corruption are simply too low. In fact, certain controlling families engaged in business represent a likely *opposition group* to reform efforts.

Media. While print and broadcast media in Timor Leste are generally free to report on corruption, their capacity is minimal. Because of low literacy levels, many people rely on radio or on state-controlled television for news. Threats from the government to news outlets for reporting on corruption appear minimal, and there are no recent confirmed cases of journalists having been harmed. In addition, the decriminalization of defamation removes a disincentive for journalists to report on corruption. The Timor Leste press does report frequently on alleged corruption at the highest levels, but most of this reporting is not supported by solid investigation and often amounts to nothing more than rumor. This presents the risk that the government can decide in the future to tighten its grip over the media in an attempt to rein in spurious and unprofessional reporting.

The media in Timor Leste therefore represents a strong potential advocate for anticorruption reform, but deficient reporting skills are a severe impediment to that goal. As a group, the media can be nurtured and developed over the short to medium term.

International donors. The donor community plays a vital role in monitoring and providing support for anticorruption initiatives in civil society, the media, and government. The Australian Agency for International Development (AusAID), the UN Development Programme (UNDP), the US Agency for International Development (USAID), and the World Bank appear to be the major international players in the anticorruption arena. Without their support, Timorese efforts to combat corruption would be greatly diminished. Ironically, some of these same players have been singled out for failure to effectively monitor how their funds are spent, thus contributing to the corruption perception problem. The United Nations in particular is often cited for lacking strong internal controls over the way its own contracts are awarded, although these claims are difficult to verify. Moreover, there appears to be little coordinated oversight of the many donor-funded international advisers, who, because of their great influence, also present a corruption risk. Overall, the donor community rates high in political will and capacity to deal with corruption issues.

Political-Economic Analysis

Little hard information about corruption in Timor Leste is available, but perception surveys suggest a gradual increase in corruption. While the country has established some important corruption safeguards, many institutions are very new, and much remains to be done. Petty corruption is widespread, if perhaps not yet systemic, and though there are frequent allegations of grand corruption, they are difficult to substantiate.

The country does have in its favor a steady flow of recent anticorruption legislation, a free media environment, and a strong opposition party. A recent turnover of power following a hotly contested election indicates a commitment to the democratic process. While still strongly divided on key leadership issues, the government and opposition have shown a willingness to work together on anticorruption efforts. A recent example of this collaboration is the establishment of the ACC with strong investigative powers.[18] The nearly unanimous vote to pass the ACC law suggests that parliamentarians understand the need to be seen as acting against corruption.

The business environment is widely considered noncompetitive, and a real private sector is mostly absent. Human resource constraints plague government operations and extend to the country's few businesses, civil society organizations, and media, where the skills to investigate and analyze the complex problems of corruption and economic development remain deficient.

A key overarching weakness is the country's pervasive low capacity. Only about half the population is literate, and even fewer are numerate. In the Ministry of Finance, the average employee possesses only a third-grade education, and the ministry recently conducted a training workshop for staff on how to calculate simple percentages. A 2007 numeracy assessment of the ministry found very high error rates and noted that "errors were made all day, every day, by everybody."

This is not solely a problem at the Ministry of Finance or even confined to government institutions. Nationwide, most organizations lack adequate staff—not primarily because of low salaries but because there are simply not enough qualified people available to hire. This small pool of human capital has a limiting effect on virtually all anticorruption actors. Because the problem is so widespread, it is not amenable to rapid change. In the long term, the Government of Timor Leste needs to invest heavily in basic education that can, with time, produce a much larger pool of citizens with basic literacy and numeracy skills. From an anticorruption perspective, a literate and numerate civil service is necessary to carry out audit functions and adopt other sophisticated processes. Moreover, civil society and the media will be able to better oversee and challenge government actions.

The following factors are seen as inhibiting corruptive tendencies.

- *Legislation.* While many gaps remain, Timor Leste has adopted a number of important anticorruption laws in recent years, including the creation of a CSC and the ACC, a law on political party financing, and codes of ethics related to elections.
- *Government turnover.* The simple fact that there was a turnover of power between political factions in 2007 is in itself a check on corruption, as it helps to prevent any one group or individual from becoming politically entrenched. It also encourages review of current processes and past actions.
- *Strong opposition party.* The existence of Fretilin as a large and strong opposition bloc helps provide a significant check on executive power. While the legislative branch has thus far not exerted its oversight powers strongly, parliament can eventually grow into this role.
- *Free media.* Timorese media, while extremely weak, does enjoy substantial freedom. While the quality of reporting is generally low, the media has used its freedom to comment extensively on alleged corruption in government.
- *Strong NGOs.* Timor Leste has a few strong NGOs that perform excellent oversight work.
- *Petroleum Fund.* As noted earlier, the Timor Leste Petroleum Fund, conceivably quite susceptible to corruption, is in fact well structured and transparent.

On the other hand, several factors are viewed as facilitating corruption.

- *Lack of a sustained high-level anticorruption effort.* Broad public perception of widespread corruption, sinking indicator scores, and high-profile corruption allegations point to the need for government to undertake a visible and sustained anticorruption effort. It not only needs to acknowledge that corruption exists and should be fought but also has to commit to immediate action to prevent corruption from becoming systemic. This would require serious commitment to broad reforms.

The creation of the new ACC was a positive step, but corruption in Timor Leste has the potential to grow substantially. As noted about the vice prime minister tasked with anticorruption efforts, "The majority of measures he has undertaken to date have met with silence, disinterest and passivity. Most of the sixty-seven memos written to Ministries and Secretaries of State have received no response. One of the greatest challenges he has encountered has been the tendency to seek protection from the hierarchy to protect personal interests."[19] This passivity has to be replaced with aggressive action if corruption is to be stemmed.

- *Family linkages in a small society.* Timor Leste is a small country, and the educated ruling elite is an even smaller group. Timorese culture places high value on family connections, even those that are quite distant. This results both in complications (in a small society, conflicts of interest are more likely) and in opportunities for corruption (a tendency to first consider who could help to get a favor done). These inevitable close connections suggest an urgent need for definition and regulation of transactions involving family.
- *Weak oversight institutions.* Essential accountability institutions in government do exist, but they suffer from low capacity, overlapping roles, and the absence of an established track record of prosecutions.
- *Lack of citizen access to reliable information.* Official language constraints, the absence of laws ensuring citizens' access to information, and poor journalistic standards have created an information void that contributes to a culture of suspicion. Public officials and citizens have a poor grasp of fundamental anticorruption concepts. Because the basics are not understood, anticorruption laws and their enforcement are often lacking.

The corruption literature suggests that analyzing the political-economic dynamics in a country can point to potential vulnerabilities and risks for corrupt practices, as well as effective and targeted remedies that address corruption's underlying causes rather than just its symptoms.[20] In brief, the drivers of politics and economics in Timor Leste are strongly characterized by powerful competing patronage networks countered only by very weak governance institutions and regulatory structures. The concentration of power in these networks revolves around their access to, and distribution of, state resources related largely to government jobs and public procurements. Unclear boundaries between an underdeveloped business sector and the ruling elite have led to abuses, while patronage in filling government positions contributes to a highly politicized and captured bureaucracy. With weak loyalty to the state but strong social bonds to rival patronage networks, political legitimacy and stability of government are precarious, especially given the continuing potential for violence as a means of problem resolution.

Overall, the ruling elite can act with a sense of impunity, given an environment of limited accountability. According to the typology described in table 5.1 in chapter 5, this description of political-economic dynamics places Timor Leste somewhere between two corruption syndromes (Type 3: "Oligarchs contend in a setting of pervasive insecurity," and Type 4: "A dominant inner circle acts with impunity"). Characteristic of Type 3 countries is Timor Leste's transitional politics and economy, very weak institutions, pervasive insecurity, and very strong political elites who appear able to interfere with legitimate political processes. As is characteristic of Type 4 countries, there are few checks on political elites who make use of their positions to benefit themselves or their families and face little accountability for their actions. Moreover, personally controlled state power appears to intrude into the national economy.

Proposed Strategic Directions

Based on this analysis, several hypotheses about the underlying causes of corruption can be formulated and an associated strategic framework developed that point toward appropriate objectives for future anticorruption programs.

- *Oversight institutions are weak.* Essential accountability institutions in government do exist, but they suffer from low capacity, overlapping roles, and the absence of an established track record of prosecutions.
- *Citizens do not have access to reliable information.* Official language constraints, the absence of laws ensuring citizens' access to information, and poor journalistic standards create an information void that contributes to a culture of suspicion.
- *Human resources are limited.* Low capacity in government means that essential anticorruption functions are not effectively carried out.

- *Public officials and citizens have a poor grasp of fundamental anti-corruption concepts.* Because the basics are not understood, anti-corruption laws and their enforcement are often lacking.

These dynamics suggest anticorruption programming recommendations that may be able to address these particular underlying causes. These include weakening patronage networks by strengthening the effectiveness of the government's delivery of public services, strengthening the institutional underpinnings for future anticorruption programs (laws, agencies, procedures), and establishing stronger accountability mechanisms (both inside and outside government) to reduce impunity and make corruption a high-risk activity.

Analysis of Key Sectors

No one sector emerged as the primary focus of corruption. Anecdotal evidence of widespread petty corruption is strong, and there are frequent allegations of high-level corruption, but hard evidence is lacking. Corruption in public works and customs receives significant mention,[21] as does the government procurement process as a whole, but generally it appears that corruption is reasonably uniform across government functions and sectors. This lack of good information is reflected in a recommendation to conduct corruption experience surveys on a regular basis in the future.

Because no one sector emerges for special attention, our analysis focuses on the most evident structural weakness—the lack of oversight—and capacity strengthening for two essential sources of external monitoring and control—civil society and the mass media. Other sectors discussed in the full assessment report include the judicial sector and the private sector.

Oversight Agencies
While there has been steady recent progress toward improved government oversight within and among branches, significant gaps remain. Many of these have been noted in earlier discussions of the legal framework but are presented here, along with specific recommendations for action.

Provedor
Because most anticorruption responsibilities had been transferred from the Provedor to the ACC, specific anticorruption support to the Provedor appears to be unnecessary, although the office could continue to require assistance on issues of human rights and justice. In general, the Provedor appears to be well

respected, and the public seems comfortable submitting complaints with the expectation that action will be taken.

Civil Service Commission

The CSC, while newly established, is built on a relatively strong predecessor body. The CSC can logically play a role in issues including conflicts of interest, codes of ethics, civil service training, and asset disclosure. Its civil service training institute (INAP), however, is weak, limiting the development of Timorese professionals in this sector. The CSC possesses a plethora of international advisers, so additional support does not appear to be warranted.

Recommendations

International donors should coordinate their strategies for the CSC and ensure that support is provided for development of appropriate conflict of interest standards and training. Background support should include analytical information on international models and their application in Timor Leste.

Anticorruption Commission

The ACC, like the CSC, is a brand-new entity, although it was not developed from an existing body. It was designed to be the central anticorruption actor in the government, and although it took on some of the functions of the Provedor, there appears to be no sense of territoriality within the Provedor, OIG, or CSC that would impede the ACC's main function.

As previously noted, the ACC faces certain challenges. Choosing a commissioner promised to be extremely difficult, in terms of both politics and meeting legal criteria. Opposition party Fretilin appeared willing to use its influence to prevent a quorum and thus slow down the selection process.[22] While it seemed likely that the process could be deadlocked for months, the commissioner was selected in February 2010.

Because the ACC was in formation, some existing bodies already ceased taking on new corruption cases. While the law appeared to transfer authority only once the new commission was active,[23] the practical result was a significant gap in anticorruption authority and investigations.

Finally, the ACC is expected to face the same bottleneck in prosecution that the Provedor had experienced. No matter how well the commission functions, it has to rely on the prosecutor general to move corruption cases forward.[24] Several solutions for this have been proposed, including long-term secondment of prosecutors to the ACC and the establishment of a special corruption unit within the Office of the Prosecutor General. Secondment would offer greater control of the prosecution process by the ACC, but it results in complicated loyalties for prosecutors working with the ACC while expecting careers in the Office of the Prosecutor General. The prosecutor general does not appear to support this option. Another option is a special prosecution unit, which would avoid the previous problem but limit ACC influence on prosecutions. The prosecutor general has indicated that formation of a special prosecution unit for economic crimes (including corruption and money laundering) is already under way.

Recommendations

A few donors already have shown a strong interest in the ACC, with AusAID and USAID the lead candidates for support. All the following recommendations require close donor coordination in terms of both strategy and financial assistance.

The ACC will be a completely new body and will be in need of considerable support. Needs will likely include materials (office space, furniture, equipment) and, more important, development of appropriate processes. Donors should offer medium-term capacity-building support to the office in the form of materials and one or more advisers (keeping in mind the need for mentoring rather than direct action).

One of the ACC's tasks will be to develop a comprehensive anticorruption strategy. Donors should help the ACC work with a broad range of stakeholders to develop a realistic but wide-reaching strategy, consistent with UNCAC, to address corruption in Timor Leste in the long term. Such a strategy should include completion of the legal framework, appropriate media regulation, administrative procedures, strong oversight bodies, and long-term capacity building.

The ACC will need to work closely with prosecutors, whether seconded or from the prosecutor general. Both options offer benefits, but creation of a special prosecutor general unit may be simpler, keep reporting and loyalties clear, and make it easier to establish accountability if prosecution of corruption cases continues to lag. Because the Office of the Prosecutor General is already forming a special economic crimes unit, donors should focus support on that option.

Donor support can be utilized to help the ACC develop and widely publicize simple, reliable, and confidential reporting mechanisms that the public can use to report acts or suspicions of corruption. Such whistleblower and complaint registration techniques are important approaches to generate public trust in the ACC and develop a ready channel for reporting grievances.

It is often noted that one reason for the success and credibility of the Hong Kong Independent Commission Against Corruption is that its work is reviewed by no fewer than four independent committees and a complaints committee. While this multiple oversight is too much to expect from Timor Leste's limited resources, it is important that the ACC be welcoming of external oversight—both by government (especially parliament) and by civil society. Donors should work with the ACC to design avenues for such oversight.

Timor Leste is currently not part of the Asian Development Bank–Organisation for Economic Co-operation and Development Anti-corruption Initiative. This network joins together about 27 countries in the Asia-Pacific region for peer review and cooperation. Its recently adopted action plan includes developing effective and transparent systems of public service, strengthening antibribery actions, promoting integrity in business operations, and supporting active public involvement. The initiative is among the most active regional corruption networks and would be well worth consideration by the government of Timor Leste. Study tours could be organized or special experts could be brought to Timor Leste from Singapore and Hong Kong where effective anticorruption commissions exist.

Note that the Association of Southeast Asian Nations also has an action plan that emphasizes attention to corruption, and the Asia-Pacific Economic Cooperation has an expert group on corruption. The Pacific Plan also has a focus on anticorruption agencies and auditors general. Timor Leste may not have the resources to join all these bodies, but they could be useful assets as the country develops its plans. Regional cooperation on anticorruption is a priority of the vice prime minister tasked with anticorruption work.

High Administrative, Tax, and Audit Court

At the time of the assessment, there was *no* domestic external audit of government finances.[25] This constitutes a major gap in the legal framework and a serious corruption vulnerability. While the HATAC was established by the constitution as a Supreme Audit Institution, there appears to have been no progress in actually establishing the body.

There was some suggestion that a forthcoming law might (with planned Portuguese assistance) establish a partial HATAC focusing on audits, and this would be an important first step. However, there seems to be little sense of urgency on this issue and no indication that action would come during the next several months. Such prolonged inaction (since the adoption of the constitution in 2002) is beginning to suggest a lack of political will to address the problem. While it is true that human resources are limited, the creation of a functioning HATAC needs to be given high priority. An independent, external audit facility is crucial to building the government's credibility.

Recommendations
Diplomatic efforts should be used to encourage the establishment of the HATAC. Donors should work with Portuguese assistance to offer technical support in designing the institution and drafting the law.

Office of the Inspector General
Internal audit responsibilities are spread among the OIG, the Ministry of Finance, and line ministries, with little coordination between actors and no consistency in structures or approach. While in a larger country this might be acceptable, Timor Leste does not have the human resources to successfully staff so many disparate bodies. This lack of coordination in internal auditing means that limited resources are used ineffectively, audits can be inconsistent (and of varying availability), and oversight of the audit bodies is limited. The OIG has also recently lost its only external adviser. But the OIG is already established, has the largest staff, and offers the greatest independence from the line ministries. It has the authority to forward cases directly to the prosecutor general rather than await prime ministerial approval.

Recommendations
Centralization of internal audit responsibilities under the OIG should be encouraged. Specific line ministry IGs can be solely responsible to the OIG. This centralized approach would increase independence of auditors, increase consistency, and simplify public access to audit results. Donors should offer technical assistance to the OIG in the form of one or more long-term mentors—conceivably one to advise the OIG on appropriate structure and procedures and one to provide on-the-job training for the OIG staff.

Parliament
Parliamentary elections in 2007 led to a handover of power from the Fretilin party to a coalition of smaller parties (the AMP). The dispute between the two was resolved only when the president asked the AMP to form the government. Since then, Fretilin has held a very strong opposition position in parliament and a (waning) feeling of grievance that it had not been selected.[26]

The current coalition government and the Fretilin opposition have highlighted corruption issues but not made any formal parliamentary inquiries on the subject. Committee C on Economy, Finance, and Anticorruption has established a subcommittee to deal specifically with corruption. However, over-all understanding of essential anticorruption concepts appears lacking among many parliamentarians. Without such an understanding, the parliament cannot be effective in establishing anticorruption measures. It remains to be seen whether parliament has the will or the capacity to provide oversight on anti-corruption matters.

In recent years, the quality of parliamentary debate, particularly on bud-get matters, appears to have improved, which partially can be a function of access to budget information and analysis. The Parliamentary Research Center provides some policy analysis and attempts to respond to requests from legisla-tors, while the UNDP provides international advisory support. The president of the National Parliament heads an administrative structure that consists of a powerful Council of Ministers and the Office of the Secretary General, which is undergoing reorganization but continues to emphasize administration, ple-nary assistance, and research and information technology. Providing support to 65 MPs, the secretariat employs 66 civil servants.

No MP has been prosecuted for corruption, although allegations of cor-rupt behavior surface from time to time in the press and elsewhere. MPs are protected from arrest relating to official duties, but protection is felt to extend beyond official duties in practice. The insular nature of Timorese society and the web of interlinked political and economic interests create a corruption vulnerability among MPs, which is exacerbated by the lack of laws mandating asset disclosure or clearly defining conflicts of interest.

Recommendations

Parliament already receives assistance from a number of UNDP advisers. However, a 2008 UNDP evaluation suggests that anticorruption training could be an area better served by another donor, thus providing a window for possible USAID or other support.[27] MPs, staff, and especially members of Committee C would benefit from training programs and activities specifically devoted to anticorruption. Modules could be developed and trainings deliv-ered that are specific to the circumstances of Timor Leste and that provide detailed information on essential concepts such as conflict of interest, asset disclosure, contracts and bids, access to state information, and investigative procedures. Note that this same material could be provided to INAP as the basis of a new civil service course. In addition, MPs could learn from par-ticipation in the Global Organization of Parliamentarians Against Corrup-tion (GOPAC) activities, including the Southeast Asia chapter of GOPAC (SEAPAC).

Civil Society

Timor Leste's civil society is remarkably broad and deep. FONGTIL has registered more than 500 local NGOs and 100 international NGOs that are engaged in advocacy, capacity building, the provision of essential services, and information dissemination. Civil society organizations appear to operate in nearly every developmental sector, with LABEH, La'o Hamutuk, and Luta Hamutuk comprising the principal actors on anticorruption activities.

The active civil society organizations in Timor Leste demonstrate a high degree of political will to fight corruption and appear to have the capacity to do so. Because Timorese civil society is bolstered by a resistance mentality and is firmly rooted in the country's independence movement, it commands respect in government circles and among the population.

There is one major corruption vulnerability that is particular to Timorese civil society. This relates to the large amounts of donor funding directed to civil society groups and the pressures that are often present to spend money quickly in an environment where absorptive capacity is very low. This presents a problem for two reasons. First, systems of financial control in local NGOs are often weak, providing opportunities for corruption for individuals in the organization and at an institutional level. Although it is difficult to verify how widespread these practices are, it seems likely that they are extensive, given the amounts of money available, weak controls, and pressures to spend. The next problem relates to perceptions that NGOs hold of the donor community. When the amounts of money budgeted for NGO programs exceed what is truly needed, NGO leaders are the first to notice. This leads to a widely held perception that international donors are an "easy target."

No civil society groups appear to have been blacklisted by the current or previous government, and there does not seem to have been serious threats posed to NGO leaders. However, ministries often do not comply with requests for information from NGOs, which these groups often view as a form of passive resistance, although it can also be the result of disorganization and poor record keeping.

A decree law on Associations and Foundations in Timor Leste is under discussion.[28] Article 11 of the draft legislation provides for significant state oversight, which can present problems in the future for civil society groups that monitor the government. Article 11 reads as follows:

> Associations and foundations administering funds allocated by
> the State, benefiting from any form of assistance from the State

or receiving funds from development partners for the purpose of implementing any activities included in the National Development Plan, are subject to direct oversight by the Ministry of Planning and Finance.

The meaning of *direct oversight* is not clearly defined and is subject to broad interpretation.

Recommendations

Civil society in Timor Leste has demonstrated the will and the capacity to fight corruption, and some of its leaders are considered champions of reform. Because the will and capacity are mostly absent within government, civil society represents a major entry point for anticorruption programming, with the possibility of creating reform momentum among citizens and inside the government. Creating this momentum would require solid information on the nature and extent of the corruption problem, the monitoring of government performance, and advocacy campaigns that are fact based, well targeted, and sustained.

Diagnostic corruption surveys, pioneered by the World Bank Institute and now used in various forms by other international organizations,[29] can provide detailed, experiential information on the nature and extent of corruption, primarily at the administrative level. Such surveys could be conducted by civil society groups on a continuing basis (annually) to monitor corruption trends and assess whether various initiatives are having their intended effects. Effectively conducted and used, the survey can unbundle corruption (administrative, state capture, bidding, theft of public resources, purchase of licenses, etc.); pinpoint weak and strong institutions; examine processes, sectors, and functions in depth; assess the costs of corruption to different stakeholders; and identify concrete and measurable ways to reduce those costs through targeted reforms. Given the absence of hard information on corruption in Timor Leste, a survey like this could be extremely beneficial in pinpointing important sources of corruption and in providing donors and the government of Timor Leste with an effective starting point for anticorruption programming.

Public service delivery report cards were pioneered in Bangalore, India, in 1993 and have been applied by civil society groups in many countries since.[30] Just as the private sector uses customer satisfaction information to adjust business practices based on demand, report cards enable citizens and policymakers to register their opinions on the quality, efficiency, effectiveness, and cost of services delivered by government authorities. The report card is a sample survey of service users that provides a rating of public agencies to determine satisfaction with different dimensions of their services. Information gleaned from the surveys can be used to quantify the extent of corruption and its overall costs to the consumer. Once complete, the survey information can be placed in a report card format that rates various agencies in terms of customer satisfaction, with an important determinant of overall satisfaction being the levels of corruption experienced at different divisions within a given agency. Civil society and government may use these report cards and periodic follow-up surveys to determine how well a public service provider is doing, what types of interventions are called for, and whether improvements have been made over time. The result is that citizens are given a means for challenging their government to become more efficient, and government is provided with a tool that should enable it to perform at increasingly high levels over time.

Public expenditure tracking surveys (PETS) have been used by NGOs with success in many parts of the world.[31] The objective is to track whether budget funds allocated are actually used for their intended purpose, by following the money trail from the budget itself to the government agency where the funds were expended. Surveys of this kind, often carried out by NGOs, can help communities to determine whether they are getting the full value of support anticipated or why they are not. Because donors may wish to target services within a particular sector that they already support and on a sector where services are especially deconcentrated, health and education appear to be attractive candidates.

Well-run advocacy campaigns provide an opportunity for civil society to mobilize the public against corruption. These campaigns can inform citizens about the corruption problem at different levels and solicit ideas for doing something about it. Advocacy campaigns provide an effective means for disseminating detailed information about local corruption gathered from surveys, the media, and other sources. The campaigns can also highlight best practices to fight corruption gleaned from other parts of the world. In Timor Leste, the most appropriate media for advocacy campaigns is radio, followed by television and newspapers. Given the overall security environment in Dili and district centers, public rallies are not advised. Another part of corruption awareness building can be the posting in government offices of simple notice boards showing the official fees charged for basic procedures. While these will certainly not eliminate corruption, they can discourage particularly brazen unofficial requests.

Mass Media

The number of daily and weekly newspapers in Timor Leste continually fluctuates. (At the time of the assessment, there were five dailies and two weeklies.) Papers are often created under idealistic leadership and then cease operations in the absence of sufficient capital or advertising revenue. There are 19 commercial and community radio stations, including RTK, which is run by the Catholic Church. RTL is the state-owned television station. Suara Timor Leste is currently experimenting with a private TV station in Dili, but because it is able to broadcast with only a limited UHF signal, few people are aware of the station's existence.

The Timorese media report frequently on high-level government corruption cases, but the low quality of this reporting renders most of it of little value and, in some cases, possibly detrimental to anticorruption efforts.[32] When reporters cannot be trusted to present factual information or check their sources, corruption claims will eventually be dismissed by the public, even in those instances where real corruption may exist. As things stand, suboptimal reporting on corruption adds to a culture of suspicion in which the public assumes—without a nuanced appreciation of the phenomenon—that corruption is the norm rather than the exception and that government at all levels is simply bad. This type of cynicism can, over time, undermine the democratic process.

It does not appear that reporters or editors engage in "envelope journalism," a common practice in Indonesia and elsewhere in Southeast Asia, whereby journalists or editors are paid to write or place stories that are favorable to the paying party. Certain media outlets and two of the country's four printing presses are tied to leaders in government, and journalists can potentially be swayed by the opinions of powerful figures. However, this does not constitute outright corruption, and the absence of envelope journalism in Timor Leste is a bright spot for the profession, which needs to be guarded through continuous monitoring and self-regulation.

Five draft media laws have been prepared, with UNDP assistance, for consideration by the Timor Leste government. Article 19, an international freedom of information advocacy group, and members of the Timorese community of journalists and civil society have conducted a thorough analysis of these laws and drew the following conclusions:

> The draft laws are unnecessarily complex and, taken together, they are potentially confusing and contradictory. This should be avoided in any legal system, but it is of particular concern in Timor Leste,

a small country with few legal resources. It would be better if the media laws were simplified and integrated into one law, and there should be a separate law for freedom of information. There are many problems with each of the draft laws, but the main dangers to journalists are in the draft law establishing a *Media Council,* and in the draft *Journalists Statute.* Adoption of these laws would seriously damage the ability of Timor Leste's citizens to obtain information of public interest.[33]

As a result of the Article 19 analysis and civil society advocacy against the draft laws, policymakers appear willing to reconsider major portions of the drafts.

The current government has for the most part allowed the Timorese press to report without any significant restrictions. However, in the face of so much poor reporting on corruption, it is possible the government could begin rolling back media freedoms. The Timorese press would be well advised to begin a regime of self-regulation, sustainable business practices, and training for journalists to upgrade reporting skills. Some of this work is already under way with support from USAID and other donors, and a working group of several journalists' associations appears to be working toward this end. Given vulnerabilities within the Timorese press, these efforts should be redoubled and infused with a greater sense of urgency.

Recommendations

Learning and applying sustainable business practices will be central to ensuring the future of the media in Timor Leste. Papers and radio stations that rely on idealism and community support alone will often fail. The market for dailies and weeklies in Timor Leste is probably not large enough to sustain more than a couple of publications. But those that succeed will be able to provide better pay and support for their reporters, thus upgrading the quality of news that is available. Short-term courses on sustainable business practices for the media could be offered through an existing Timorese institution or a contractor. These courses would likely be small—given the size of the community—and well targeted to those with serious interests in creating viable media businesses. Coursework would ideally be complemented by one-on-one mentoring, in which a seasoned international media operator (possibly someone already in retirement) would provide daily assistance to aspiring media businesses.

Continued emphasis on the journalism program at the National University of Timor Leste is recommended. This is a new program, receiving support through the International Center for Journalists, which merits future attention in terms of curriculum development and mentoring of the most promising students.

Through one of the existing associations of journalists or a prominent civil society organization, an awards program for excellence in journalism could be established. A panel of respected judges could provide annual awards for the best examples of investigative journalism and financial journalism, along with other areas such as sports and political cartoons that help in sustaining a vibrant press.

In tandem with other efforts to expand access to information, reporters could be challenged through the various journalists' associations to "test" repositories of public documents and to report back on how easy or difficult it was for them to obtain what they were looking for. This could be a valuable exercise to highlight in the press and as a means to encourage the government to increase access to records and reinforce more systematic record keeping. Once a freedom of information law is in place, this strategy could be augmented by lawsuits to enforce the law, though this may stretch legal resources more than is wise in early years.

Journalists' associations in Timor Leste are weak, unstructured, and divided among rivaling interests in the community. Efforts should be made to create one strong, broadly representative press council. A respected and authoritative press council can provide self-regulation and the moral force that is needed to develop a more responsible press. An independent press council is always a better alternative than government regulation, which can represent a slippery slope toward censorship.

Good investigative journalism requires learning and practicing research and interview techniques, doing evidence-based data analysis, and offering clear writing. The investigative journalist must know how to make balanced political judgments, possess basic skills in economics, and be numerate. There is no way around the fact that Timor Leste's journalists will need training if they are to fulfill their essential role of providing the public with the information it needs to understand and participate fully in the affairs of the nation. While some investigative journalism training has been provided in recent years with the support of AusAID and USAID, continued training is still needed. Training should be provided to reporters, editors, and publishers who are working for publications and media outlets that appear ready to make themselves into viable, long-term business enterprises. Courses can be designed specifically for the Timorese context and build on what the World Bank, USAID, and others have offered in other developing country contexts. On-the-job training and mentoring can be provided, along with a flexible schedule of coursework to accommodate the on-call demands of a normal journalist. Training could include information on the structure and function of the justice system and anticorruption bodies so that journalists better understand the legal framework.

Epilogue

Timor Leste is now enjoying one of the longest periods of stability in its history. It experienced a brief recurrence of political turmoil in February 2008, when President Ramos-Horta and Prime Minister Gusmao were the victims of thwarted assassination attempts. While Gusmao escaped unharmed, Ramos-Horta required two months of medical treatment in Australia for gunshot wounds, during which emergency measures were temporarily imposed in Timor Leste as security forces hunted for the culprits. Calm was restored toward the end of April when the last antigovernment rebels surrendered to authorities.

In February 2010, the Timor Leste National Parliament finally confirmed an anticorruption commissioner. The process had taken almost two years, involving dialogue with civil society groups and the development of the commission's legal framework. Under the new laws, the ACC is independent from the national government and reports directly to parliament. In addition to instigating and conducting investigations into corruption offenses, the ACC is mandated to conduct public education and outreach and to identify and implement preventive anticorruption measures. The 2010 ACC budget was just over US$1 million and included funding for 38 staff members.[34]

The newly established commission faces significant challenges. The ombudsman for human rights, who previously handled corruption cases, reported that he had turned over 28 corruption cases in his first term to the prosecutor general's office, but not a single one had yet come to trial. There had also been several corruption scandals the previous year. The justice minister was accused of influencing government contracts, the finance minister was charged with improperly awarding jobs to her friends, and one of the deputy prime ministers allegedly abused his power by giving his wife a high-paying job with the United Nations.[35]

A scandal also erupted about the expenditure of US$70 million that Prime Minister Gusmao distributed to 774 small infrastructure projects around the country, using funds left over from an oil project. The funding was distributed—with no tenders—through a body created by Julio Alvaro, head of the Business Forum of East Timor. Some of the contractors receiving the money were partly owned by Alvaro, and there were allegations of shoddy work and a financial discrepancy of US$3 million. Although the government defended its actions as simply poorly managed attempts to create business for small enterprises, it did open an investigation into the quality of work provided and the missing money.[36]

Timor Leste will get some assistance in the anticorruption fight with a US Millennium Challenge Corporation (MCC) grant of US$10.5 million over three years, announced in May 2010. As part of the threshold program to help Timor Leste become eligible for MCC compact assistance, this funding will be used largely to strengthen the capacity of anticorruption institutions, streamline their processes, and improve their coordination.[37]

Government Oversight Bodies

Many oversight entities have benefited from a strong donor focus on building the capacity of the national Timor Leste government. The UNDP is currently implementing a four-year, US$3 million training program aimed at improving the human rights knowledge and management capacity of the Provedor office. This includes support for strategic planning and budgeting skills and an overhaul of the case management and knowledge management systems. Another major project focuses on the judiciary, with US$34 million over five years to train legal actors such as magistrates, lawyers, and clerks and support decentralization of the judicial system through capacity building at the district level. In addition, the funding will help establish a modern information technology infrastructure for all the judicial institutions.[38]

Other efforts to bolster the young government's capacity will eventually have the effect of improving the transparency and accountability of its financial and operational practices. Both the World Bank and the UNDP are implementing programs to help the government improve its budgeting, planning, and human resource systems, with projects of about US$10 million each. The World Bank program is set to close in 2011, with results thus far including an increase in budget execution, the computerization of records, and the regular publication of public finance reports. The Ministry of Finance also implemented a major organizational reform, which included the establishment of merit-based appointments. In addition, the national government updated its revenue and customs laws.[39]

USAID has also been active in capacity-building efforts, focusing on strengthening elections systems, improving the government's capacity to manage the voter registration process and database, and assisting the independent electoral commission.[40]

Parliament

In June 2010, the National Parliament established a local chapter of the GOPAC, an international anticorruption group. This followed an anticorruption conference held in April, where several MPs pledged to fight corruption in Timor Leste through legislation, institutional building, and preventive efforts.[41]

Donor support in this area, as in many other sectors, focuses on building capacity and thereby laying the foundation for efficient and transparent processes. The UNDP has dedicated almost US$11 million over three years to strengthen the National Parliament, advising its leadership, training legal drafters, and helping to analyze legislation and organize public hearings. It is also providing extensive assistance in parliament's preparation of the national budget and has trained budget analysts and sectoral analysts. In particular, the UNDP works with the Committee on Economy, Finance, and Anticorruption (Committee C) to monitor government expenditures. Public outreach is achieved through the Democratic Representation, Transparency, and Accessibility Project, which relays information about parliament's activities through press releases and television, interactive radio debates on legislation, and coverage of important deliberations such as that of the national budget. Other outreach efforts focus on civic education and parliamentary engagement with the public, which has included the development of the parliament's website.[42]

Civil Society and Media

While significant funding and effort is invested in building capacity at the governmental level, many programs are also working to strengthen Timor Leste's nascent civil society and media organizations. One World Bank program is focused on empowering youth groups to participate in community development initiatives and USAID is helping build the conflict prevention capabilities of local NGOs.[43]

The UNDP worked with the National Parliament in 2008 and 2009 to develop, disseminate, and implement media laws. It also supported community radio stations in the development of their technical and managerial expertise. Under this program, employees received training in market research, among other topics, helping them determine how best to engage their audiences. In addition, eight stations completed business management plans and received assistance in their implementation. In addition, in recognition of the dearth of serious investigative reporting in Timor Leste, print and radio journalists received training in investigative journalism and media laws (and, where applicable, radio program formats and production). The UNDP also supported efforts to establish a national institute of journalism.[44]

USAID has also been active in developing media capacity, implementing a Strengthening Independent Media program through the International Center for Journalists. In addition to expanding the quality and reach of the public broadcast service, the program conducts extensive training programs for journalists.[45]

Notes

1. This chapter is adapted from the assessment written by Benjamin Allen and Edward Anderson for Management Systems International under a USAID contract.

2. Act no. 7/2004 of May 26, Approving the Statute for the Provedor for Human Rights and Justice, Article 5.3.

3. While the Provedor is no longer tasked with corruption issues, the above definitions remain in the law and should provide guidance to the new ACC.

4. Act no. 7/2004 of May 26, Approving the Statute for the Provedor for Human Rights and Justice, Article 1.

5. It is not clear why it is so widely assumed that a legal investigation would necessarily violate human rights.

6. Law Creating the Anticorruption Commission, Article 2.

7. This was also a priority of the vice prime minister charged with anticorruption work.

8. Laws in Timor Leste were of three major types: laws (statutes) adopted by parliament, decree laws adopted by the Council of Ministers, and decrees adopted by individual ministers. Decree laws were adopted under Constitutional Section 115.3, which gave the government the power to regulate its own activities. However, they are used with sufficient frequency as to cause concern, since they often cover important topics, but do not allow for a parliamentary legislative review.

9. Law on Creation of the Civil Service Commission.

10. In some cases referred to as the Public Service Commission.

11. Somewhat worryingly, the English translation of the law describes the CSC as being "under the tutelage and oversight of the Prime Minister," though it is not clear what "tutelage" is intended to convey.

12. Dates according to records of the UN Office on Drugs and Crime (UNODC) (http://www.unodc.org/unodc/en/treaties/CAC/signatories.html). UNODC is the "custodian" of UNCAC.

13. There are conflict of interest provisions in Article 10 of Law 8/2004 on the Civil Service. However, they do not appear to be implemented, and there was little awareness of their effect.

14. There are several codes of ethics related to elections but none of general applicability. There are broad provisions in the Law on the Civil Service.

15. Draft April 28, 2009, meeting minutes of the NP6 working group on national priorities.

16. ACC law, Article 22, and Law on Protection of Witnesses 2-2009.

17. While the team's search for plausible anticorruption champions produced little result, these three NGOs were the most frequently mentioned candidates.

18. Some argue that the original concept of the ACC did not survive the parliamentary process unscathed but instead emerged much weaker than intended. However, the commission does in fact have important powers and could play a strong role in anticorruption efforts if it gains its feet quickly and is allowed to work unhindered.

19. Government of Timor Leste (2009), VPM five-month summary report.

20. Peter Blunt. 2009. "The Political Economy of Accountability in Timor Leste: Implications for Public Policy." *Public Administration and Development* 29:89–100; Michael Johnston. 2005. *Syndromes of Corruption.* New York: Cambridge University Press; Management Systems International. 2009. *Corruption Assessment Handbook.* Washington, DC: MSI; Debbie Warrener. November 2004. *The Drivers of Change Approach.* London: Overseas Development Institute.

21. Note the recent establishment of an Inter-Ministerial Committee on Infrastructure charged with monitoring infrastructure procurement actions.

22. Article 7 of the ACC law requires that three-quarters of the total working MPs be present.

23. Article 32 of the ACC law suggests that current bodies will turn over cases and authority only once the new commission is active. Interlocutors, however, interpreted the law to mean that they can continue current investigations but not open new cases.

24. Note that this is generally, but not universally, true of most anticorruption commissions in the region, the clear exception being Indonesia, where the Corruption Eradication Commission has broad powers of both investigation and prosecution and a Special Corruption Court has been established to try cases expediently and without the judicial biases found in the regular Indonesian court system. The Philippines Ombudsman Office also has investigative and prosecutorial powers.

25. Discounting international firms hired for specific purposes—at present, Deloitte, which appears to have won *all* the 2009 government audit contracts.

26. Fretilin generally refers to the current administration as the "de facto" government.

27. 2008 Mid-Term Evaluation of the UNDP Timor Leste Parliamentary Project.

28. Law 5/2005.

29. See www.worldbank.org/wbi/governance.

30. "Citizens' Report Cards on Public Services: Bangalore, India," n.d., accessed August 2010, http://siteresources.worldbank.org/INTEMPOWERMENT/Resources/14832_Bangalore -web.pdf.

31. See http://web.worldbank.org/WBSITE/EXTERNAL/TOPICS/EXTPUBLICSEC TORANDGOVERNANCE/EXTPUBLICFINANCE/0,,contentMDK:20235447~pagePK:1 48956~piPK:216618~theSitePK:1339564,00.html.

32. Also of note is the poor quality of the Tetum to English translation. In one instance the assessment team found reference in a corruption article to the Ministry of Public Works,

while the Tetum version of the paper referred to the Office of the Prosecutor General in the same place.

33. From Article 19's short summary of TL Media Laws.

34. East Timor Law and Justice Bulletin, "Timor Leste Independent Anticorruption Commission Under Way," February 10, 2010.

35. Matt Crook. April 18, 2010. "Analysis: Tough Task to Tackle Corruption in East Timor." *Global Post.*

36. Ibid.

37. MCC website: "MCC Approves $10.5 Million Grant for Timor Leste to Improve Childhood Immunization, Curb Corruption," May 28, 2010, http://www.mcc.gov/pages/press/release/release-052810-timorleste.

38. UNDP Fact Sheet: "Democratic Governance: Human Rights Capacity Building on the PDHJ," http://mdtf.undp.org/factsheet/fund/JTP00.

39. World Bank: Status of Projects in Execution, Timor Leste, http://siteresources.world bank.org/INTSOPE/Resources/5929468-1286307702807/7453146-1286503789398/Timor LesteFinal.pdf.

40. USAID website: Timor Leste (Democracy and Governance), http://timor-leste.usaid .gov/.

41. Asia Foundation website: "National Parliament of Timor Leste Launches Local Chapter of International Anticorruption Organization," June 15, 2010, http://asiafoundation.org/news/2010/06/national-parliament-of-timor-leste-launches-local-chapter-of-international-anti -corruption-organization/.

42. UNDP Fact Sheet: "Democratic Governance: Human Rights Capacity Building on the PDHJ," http://mdtf.undp.org/factsheet/fund/JTP00.

43. World Bank: Status of Projects in Execution, Timor Leste; USAID website: Timor Leste (Democracy and Governance), http://siteresources.worldbank.org/INTSOPE/Resources/5929468-1286307702807/7453146-1286503789398/TimorLesteFinal.pdf; http://timor-leste .usaid.gov.

44. UNDP Fact Sheet: "Democratic Governance: Independent Media Development Project," http://www.undp.east-timor.org/undp/focus_areas/democratic_governance.html.

45. USAID website: Timor Leste (Democracy and Governance), http://timor-leste.usaid .gov.

11

Toward Accountable Solutions

Corruption is an inherently difficult phenomenon to detect, measure, and assess. It typically thrives on secrecy and informality. So, unfortunately, most serious attempts to uncover and evaluate the state of corruption in a country or in particular government sectors or functions are bound up in subjective judgment about the existence and levels of corrupt practices. There have been many efforts focused on developing broad country indices of corruption, but each one suffers from methodological inadequacies.[1] No measurement construct provides a clear and definitive indication of corruption levels in a country, and no index provides enough practical information to point the way to minimize the corruption risks identified.

The assessment method described in chapter 5 embraces a different approach. It does not produce a single measurement of corruption for a country but rather directs teams of corruption detectives to assess, analyze, and evaluate sets of potential corruption vulnerabilities in key government sectors and functions. If these vulnerabilities are identified—if there are evident cracks in the system—then the assessment team should be able to uncover more detail on these gaps and deficiencies that will suggest associated practical solutions and reforms.

Assessing Corruption: Variations on a Theme

As one might imagine in discussing countries as different as Ukraine, Senegal, Honduras, and Timor Leste, a comparative analysis of the four corruption assessments presented in this volume is likely to produce vastly diverging results. But the common assessment approach used to analyze each facilitates comparisons. While many differences do appear, there are many similarities as well—variations on a theme.

Contexts

The political situations within which the assessments were conducted were as different as could be. Ukraine was just one year into its Orange Revolution, a populist and hoped-for transformative political experience. In Senegal, the assessment was completed seven years after a major regime change that resulted in increasing centralization of power of the president. The assessment in Honduras was conducted amid brewing internal unrest and one year before a military coup that unseated the president. And in Timor Leste, the assessment was conducted shortly following a period of political violence in 2006 and an attempted assassination plot in 2008.

These situations suggest very different and unstable contexts that can strongly influence the state and the practice of corruption. In Ukraine, there were great expectations among the population and international donors that change was imminent. In Senegal, the progressive and personalistic concentration of power helped to perpetuate high levels of corruption, despite other reforms. In Honduras and Timor Leste, significant conflict and violence levels presaged a slowdown in reforms and a further retrenchment into corrupt practices.

Legal Frameworks

The legal frameworks to deal with corruption in all four cases were fairly robust, despite an acknowledged need for improvements. Each country had a substantial body of laws relating to corrupt acts that were in basic compliance and consistent with international norms and standards. Each of these countries had received technical assistance from a variety of bilateral and multilateral donors to develop their corruption-related laws, and if nothing else they were motivated to adopt these laws to appease these donors and international organizations. That is not to say that there were no deficiencies or gaps in their legal structure—especially in the corruption prevention area. The major problem in all of these countries was the minimal enforcement of anticorruption laws. The laws existed on paper but were only infrequently implemented and enforced.

Institutional Capacity

The institutional capacity to address corruption varied significantly by country. Ukraine's anticorruption-related institutions, while hampered by the lack of a coordinating agency, had made some useful progress. An active parliamentary committee promoted new policies and initiated needed legislation, the Accounts Chamber cooperated with the Prosecutor's Office, and the Customs Service, Tax Administration, and Department of Civil Service all actively initiated institutional reforms to reduce the opportunity for corrupt practices.

Moreover, civil society groups and the media possessed the basic motivation to serve as public watchdogs and keep anticorruption issues high on the public agenda.

In Senegal, while there is strong support for reform from such agencies as the National Commission Against Non-transparency, Collusion and Corruption; the National Program for Good Governance; and government control institutions, they do not wield very much influence over policymaking. That control is concentrated in the president's office, and most enforcement and oversight agencies lack sufficient autonomy to act. At the same time, civil society groups are generally well organized as a potential force for making demands on government for reform.

In Honduras, government enforcement and oversight institutions were generally unable or unwilling to apply the laws as intended. They were plagued by incapacities and inefficiencies and generally lacked the resources to do their jobs. Despite political statements in favor of fighting corruption, the leadership of most agencies lacked the political will to pursue and prosecute alleged corruption cases. In fact, many of these government institutions were suspected of engaging in extensive corruption themselves. The best of them were able to achieve only modest results, such as the National Anticorruption Council and the Superior Court of Accounts. As a counterforce to government, civil society organizations in Honduras are generally strong and have good experience in social auditing initiatives. If properly motivated, they can promote an anticorruption agenda and place demands on government to make necessary reforms and to enforce and apply the law.

Timor Leste is still a country in the making. Its oversight institutions exhibit severe human resource and capacity constraints. Parliament is unprepared to monitor the executive branch. There is no supreme audit institution or Supreme Court. The Office of the Prosecutor General is a significant bottleneck with a major case backlog. The Office of the Inspector General has limited capacity for financial investigations or audits. And the Anticorruption Commission is just getting under way. Moreover, civil society groups and the mass media are extremely limited in their advocacy and public information capacities.

Political-Economic Analysis

There were also a variety of "corruption syndromes" displayed by these countries based on their political-economic dynamics. Ukraine is seen as a Type 2 country (see table 5.1 in chapter 5)—as an "elite cartel"—where top political and business figures collude behind a façade of political competition and colonize both the state apparatus and the economic sector. They use their political power to acquire and privatize key economic resources of the state for their own purposes. It is viewed as an exercise of *state and regulatory capture.*

Senegal is more typified as a Type 4 country, where a dominant inner circle acts with impunity. Its highly centralized executive controls politics and the economy for the purpose of personal and familial enrichment. Hierarchical decision making controls and dominates all government agencies and limits independent oversight of government.

In Honduras, a deeply rooted political-economic elite controls based on personal loyalties and patronage. There is minimal respect for the rule of law and the justice system. The assessment team viewed Honduras as closest to a Type 2 country where high-level elites and their networks collude to weaken political-economic competition. It is a country typified by power chasing wealth.

Timor Leste is viewed a little differently from these other countries— somewhere between Type 3 ("Oligarchs contend in a setting of pervasive insecurity") and Type 4 ("A dominant inner circle acts with impunity"). The country operates within a new and transitional political and economic structure, has very weak institutions, is plagued by insecurity and violence, and has very strong political elites who have the power to interfere with legitimate political processes. Timor Leste is also characterized as having few checks on its political elites who use the state to benefit themselves and their families, especially to gain economic power and wealth.

Strategic Implications for Action

These analyses of legal-institutional and political-economic dynamics led the assessment teams to varying conclusions as to strategic directions that need to be followed and priority sectors or functions where opportunities exist to deal with particularly sensitive vulnerabilities. The corruption syndromes, especially, suggested particular implications for future action. For Honduras, the assessment team was drawn toward supporting civil society organizations so that they could serve as effective watchdogs and advocates, monitoring corruption and anticorruption initiatives, generating greater public awareness of the corruption problem, and energizing the public to demand reforms. The team in Honduras also saw the need to strengthen government anticorruption institutions by supporting champions of reform—those officials who demonstrated the political will to initiate new programs.

In Ukraine, the assessment team recommended similar directions but additional ones too. Capacity building for civil society to generate demand-side pressure on government and support for government institutions that showed their political will and readiness to act were both at the top of the list for future actions. But the assessment also recommended goals for Ukraine of completing the prerequisites for effective anticorruption programs—ensuring a solid legal framework against corruption and adequate training, resources, and funding for its oversight and enforcement institutions. In addition, the team recommended that anticorruption initiatives be incorporated into new programs in all sectors—that is, mainstreaming anticorruption throughout government.

Senegal's assessment team also saw the need to further support civil society groups in publicly demanding anticorruption reforms. In addition, it emphasized the need to deal with inadequate controls on executive decision making, problems with accountability mechanisms across government operations, and the lack of a service orientation toward the public when providing government services.

Timor Leste's assessment team focused on the need to generate greater public awareness and understanding of the corruption problem and its consequences and to mobilize the public and get it more engaged in the fight against corruption. Other priority directions include building the capacity of newly formed government oversight institutions, ensuring public access to government information, and, over the longer term, strengthening the human capacity to address oversight and enforcement issues.

The context and assessment of problems in each country differed, and the assessment teams recommended strategies for future action that took these differences into account. While practitioners often want to know about "international best practices" in fighting corruption, and there have been several attempts at developing "toolkits" to address corruption, the problem cannot be approached in a cookie-cutter fashion with the assumption that corruption is the same in all countries. The underlying problems in each country vary based on many factors—context, legal-institutional frameworks, and political-economic dynamics—which are addressed in our assessment methodology. The implications derived from understanding these root causes of corruption can lead the assessment team to recommend alternate paths to minimizing their impacts.

Sectoral Diagnostics and Recommendations

The application of this assessment method also leads the team to quickly home in on priority government sectors and functions where corrupting influences have had major consequences. As a result, it gets the team to address detailed vulnerabilities to corruption—where corruption hurts most—and identify targeted and customized recommendations for ameliorative reforms that can reduce the corruption impacts. This is especially important in countries where the basic prerequisites for anticorruption programs have already been established and there is a need to design and implement initiatives that will have a real and visible impact on the problem.

The sector-by-sector, function-by-function diagnostic questions contained in the assessment methodology helps the team pinpoint and analyze the areas of potential vulnerability. Culled from the corruption and sectoral research literature, these questions help to identify the high-risk procedures and transactions where corrupt practices can intercede into each sector or function. By examining the situation regarding these potential vulnerabilities in the subject country, the team can assess where the greatest risks are and what needs to be fixed. These vulnerabilities are the major corruption culprits—the *corrupting influences* in each sector or function—that, if eliminated, could make a major contribution to cutting down informal transaction costs, improving services provided, raising efficiency, reducing the incidence of nepotism and favoritism, and keeping public funds targeted on providing public services and not going into the pockets of corrupt officials. The use of these targeted questions especially supports generalist assessment teams that must be ready for any and all types of corruption across all sectors and functions and may not include particular specialists in each and every sector or function.

Follow-through

These assessments were meant to have concrete implications. The practical utility of these corruption assessments can be demonstrated by how they were used to design and push forward an agenda for anticorruption programs. Each of the assessments presented earlier were commissioned by US Agency for International Development (USAID) missions in each country, specifically to help them better understand the specific context, the corruption problems, and the best ways to tackle them. The assessments were made public immediately upon acceptance by USAID so that the government, civil society, and media could also begin a dialogue on next steps. As the epilogues in the case chapters indicate, there typically was rather quick follow-through on the assessments' recommendations—by the countries and donors alike.

Lessons Learned

The assessment methodology has been pilot tested in more than 10 countries and revised several times as a result of these experiences. Important lessons have been learned.

One of the most important features of this assessment process is attempting to understand the root or underlying causes of corruption in a country. The methodology does this by addressing the problem in a multidimensional way—examining legal, institutional, political, and economic frameworks and dynamics. Context can make a big difference in the capacity of countries, as well as their motivation, to seriously address corruption problems.

Based on this analysis, the factors that gave birth to corruption in a country and that facilitate and inhibit its practice can be detected and unearthed. These factors can provide direct implications for action. For example, countries where corruption is strongly related to highly concentrated and personalistic power might not be very amenable to initiatives aimed at reducing that power. So, under these circumstances, one of the goals should be to strengthen civil society and the press gradually so they can become an effective source of demand and pressure on government for accountability and transparency. Without the multidimensional perspective on how and why corruption thrives in a country, practical efforts to find solutions will not be sufficiently focused or customized to achieve real and visible results.

Another key feature of this assessment approach is its emphasis on drilling down to multiple sectors, functions, and institutions where corruption hurts the most and designing comprehensive action plans. For example, a typical complaint in countries where anticorruption programs have been implemented is that attention is paid to address corruption in only one domain, say the public procurement system, but that only serves to push rampant corruption to other domains, such as budget implementation or tax administration. Without a comprehensive plan of action that is implemented in a rigorous way, corrupt practices always seem to find their way to the weak and vulnerable points in the system. The sectoral diagnoses uncover very specific vulnerabilities that need to be addressed, reformed, reengineered, and revitalized—making these sectors more efficient and goal oriented and removing the informal, abusive, wasteful, and costly appendages of corruption.

Overall, this assessment approach shows great potential for combating the problem in a practical and realistic way—leading to implementable anticorruption initiatives and programs. As well, by offering a methodology that can be applied in any country, it provides the basis for developing comparable analyses that can benefit the policy and research communities in better understanding which reform programs work and which do not under differing circumstances.

A New Generation of Assessments

Moving beyond aggregate indicators of corruption is a first step to implementing practical assessment tools that can help policymakers understand the nature of corruption and what to do about it. While such indicators as the Corruption Perception Index (Transparency International), the Control of Corruption Index (World Bank Institute), and the Global Integrity Index (Global Integrity) are very useful in understanding broad trends and making comparisons across nations, they do not provide sufficient in-depth information to design meaningful programs. The assessment method described in this book offers a reasonable and tested approach to examine the depth, texture, and breadth of the corruption problem so that practical programs can be designed and implemented that attack the most important vulnerabilities. The self-assessment version (chapter 4) is perhaps the simplest approach, but it has some inherent limitations. The more comprehensive version in chapter 5 yields more substantial findings but requires the application of more time and resources.

This new generation of corruption assessment approaches addresses additional issues that further refine resulting insights and outputs. These include *resiliency, readiness,* and *performance and effectiveness* in fighting corruption.

Resiliency

Human resiliency is a powerful phenomenon that enables people to bounce back from adverse conditions. Psychologists have studied the conditions that facilitate and promote resiliency to help people overcome difficult life situations.[2] As well, political scientists have examined resiliency in the behavior of countries and societies—their capacity to extricate themselves from stalemates and deadlocks under crisis situations so that they can achieve their national interests and political stability.[3] The phenomenon of resilience needs to be examined further, this time related to a country's capacity to bounce back successfully from high levels of corruption and the conditions that helped to promote the turnaround. By understanding what those conditions are, policymakers can replicate them in other countries to promote future successful anticorruption initiatives. What makes some countries resilient and able to overcome high levels of corruption while others remain static or get worse despite extensive interventions by governments and donors? Why are some countries with high levels of corruption able to bounce back, improve their governance systems, reduce bureaucratic abuses, and allow public funds to benefit needy citizens while others are not?

Our hypothesis is that "anticorruption resiliency" is strongly influenced by a set of unique preconditions that makes countries ripe and ready for anticorruption initiatives. Without these preconditions, anticorruption initiatives, even those that are seen as best practice interventions, may not take hold or be sustainable. But if these preconditions for anticorruption resiliency can be replicated in the more intransigent corrupt societies, they will be better primed to successfully implement, adopt, and sustain anticorruption initiatives.

There are many examples of donor-supported anticorruption efforts that fail to achieve long-term improvements. Our hypothesis suggests that the preconditions for successful anticorruption resiliency may not have been present in these situations. These prerequisites can be identified and strategies can be designed and implemented to strengthen a country's profile and establish these basic conditions—thereby making these countries "resilient ready." If this is accomplished, subsequent anticorruption initiatives will more likely succeed and be long lasting.

A first step would be to conduct a quantitative empirical analysis of all countries, grouping them into three categories: resilient, intransigent, and status quo in relation to their corruption history (defined by the percent change in their corruption indices over the past 10 years). This analysis would identify the combination of conditions (profiles) that allowed some countries to be resilient (to bounce back from corruption) and others to be intransigent (to become more corrupt) or remain the same. These conditions can include, for example, trust in government, political stability, degree of political participation, degree of effective governance, the extent to which the rule of law is well established, and so forth. Once the combination of preconditions or profiles is identified empirically, it can be analyzed, and specific practical approaches can be designed to improve country conditions, and thus anticorruption resiliencies, so that future anticorruption initiatives can be more successful and their impacts can be more sustainable.

Readiness
Similar to the concept of military readiness, which emphasizes both the willingness and the capacity to act or respond in armed conflict situations, the

readiness of a country to address corruption is a function of two factors—motivation and capacity. Both factors are strategically linked and must be present for parties to decide to deal effectively with corruption issues.

Readiness indicators measure both the political will (stated commitments to turn words into deeds) and the institutional capacity of all sectors of society to deal with the problem of corruption (the physical ability to turn words into deeds). Observable indicators that are rated by country analysts can measure these elements. First, *political will* can be measured by *recognition indicators* that acknowledge that corruption exists and causes harm to the community. Second, political will can be measured by demonstration through various types of activities that profess interest in fighting corruption and have been backed up by concrete deeds. Some specific examples of these indicators are presented in table 11.1.

Institutional capacity can be measured by analyzing institutions, processes, resources, and cooperative arrangements that exist or have been established to implement anticorruption programs. Some indicators that can be monitored are presented in table 11.2.

Performance and Effectiveness

One way to overcome the difficulties of measuring corruption—an inherently secretive and informal set of behaviors—is to measure the other side of the coin: government performance and effectiveness, which are much more visible and measurable.[4] An implication of improved government performance and effectiveness is that corruption has been reduced or suppressed. Certainly, there can be other reasons for better performance—improvements in efficiency, greater professionalism, and increased funding and resources. But if these factors can be held constant, at least analytically, then reduced corruption can emerge as the important driver of improved performance.

Most of these performance and effectiveness indices are likely to reflect on administrative corruption, such as improved processing for permits and licenses (fewer steps, shorter time, fewer regulations), improved pricing obtained in competitive procurements, increased quantity of public services provided (patients served, students educated, pensioners paid, citizens getting electric service, etc.), more detailed audits of state institutions, and improved consistency in budget expenditure tracking, among others. Some of these are already monitored on a regular basis, such as in the World Bank's *Doing Business* and the UNDP's *Human Development Report* surveys. The benefits of these performance measures are that they are objective rather than perceptual and tend to monitor positive improvements in governance.

Table 11.1

Political Will Indicators

Indicator	Definition
Governmental Entities	
Recognition	
Public announcements or declarations against corruption	Announcements and/or declarations against corruption have been made publicly that recognize that the problem exists, that it imposes a major cost on society, or that solutions are required.
Requests for assistance or receptivity to assistance to fight corruption	There are public requests for assistance to fight corruption, or there is publicly demonstrated receptivity to outside assistance to fight corruption.
Demonstrated Will	
Legal and regulatory reforms enacted	Institutional and/or procedural changes and reforms have been enacted and implemented to enhance transparency, accountability, and integrity. These reforms can occur in the following categories:
	• Changes to laws and regulatory frameworks
Judicial reforms and law enforcement strengthening enacted	• Changes to the court system or strengthening of law enforcement activities
Economic and financial reforms enacted	• Changes to economic and/or financial systems
Administrative reforms enacted	• Changes to administrative procedures concerning government operations and the delivery of public services
International standards adopted and/or international anticorruption agreements adopted	• Adoption of international agreements and standards that result in changes to domestic laws, procedures, and institutions
Long-term strategy, plan, or program developed	A long-term planning document has been developed that outlines the policy and/or activities envisioned to fight corruption.

(continues)

Table 11.1

(continued)

Indicator	Definition
Nongovernmental Entities	
Recognition	
Public announcements or declarations against corruption	Announcements and/or declarations against corruption have been made publicly that recognize that the problem exists, that it imposes a major cost on society, or that solutions are required.
Requests for assistance or receptivity to assistance to fight corruption	There are public requests for assistance to fight corruption, or there is publicly demonstrated receptivity to outside assistance to fight corruption.
Popular support for reforms exists	There is popular support in favor of anticorruption reforms.
Demonstrated Will	
Research or monitoring conducted and assessments or reports written	Institutional changes and/or activities have been conducted to enhance transparency, accountability, and integrity. These include the following categories:
	• Research, monitoring, assessments, or reports concerning corruption
Public education and citizen awareness programs conducted	• Campaigns or programs to educate the public on the causes and costs of corruption or on the rights of citizens
Advocacy or lobbying conducted	• Campaigns or programs conducted to advocate or lobby government entities on behalf of particular reforms or changes
Recommendations for reform made public	Specific recommendations for reform are made and publicized.
Long-term strategy, plan, or program developed	A long-term planning document has been developed that outlines the policy and/or activities envisioned to fight corruption.

Table 11.2
Institutional Capacity Indicators

Indicator	Definition
Financial resources available	There are sufficient budgets, equipment, and materials allocated to anticorruption units and groups.
Human resources available	There are a sufficient number of staff and adequate training for anticorruption units and groups.
Cooperation exists within own sector	There is demonstrated cooperation and coordination of activities between governmental groups and units or between nongovernmental groups.
Cooperation exists across different sectors	There is demonstrated cooperation and coordination of activities across governmental and nongovernmental groups and units.

*   *   *

Ultimately, refinements to detection and assessment approaches will assist policymakers and donor organizations to produce improved and better targeted anticorruption programs that are more feasible, practical, focused on the underlying causes of the problem, and framed within the abilities and resource limitations of host countries. It is hoped they will also have near-term measurable and visible impacts on their country's corruption problems, having beneficial consequences as well for improved democratic participation and economic growth.

If left unattended, corrupting influences can wreak havoc on a society. It is well documented that corruption hurts, while our abilities to detect and assess corruption vulnerabilities, reengineer governance processes, and minimize corruption's impact are a developing art. The growing inventory of national efforts to detect and analyze corruption and implement tailored strategies to address the problem is providing analysts and policymakers with practical tools. It is worth the effort to do a good job of assessing this all-too-common problem and reducing its effects to reap the rewards of improved economic, political, and social development, country by country, step by step.

Notes

1. See annex A and also UN Development Programme and Global Integrity. 2008. *A Users' Guide to Measuring Corruption.* Oslo, Norway: UNDP.

2. Linda Liebenberg and Michael Ungar, editors. 2009. *Researching Resilience.* Toronto, Ontario, Canada: University of Toronto Press.

3. Bertram I. Spector. 2006. "Resiliency in Negotiation: Bouncing Back From Impasse." *International Negotiation* 11 (2): 273–86.

4. Michael Johnston. 2010. "Assessing Vulnerabilities to Corruption: Indicators and Benchmarks of Government Performance." *Public Integrity* 12 (2): 125–42.

Annex A:
Anticorruption Resource Links

Additional resources on corruption and corruption assessments in developing countries can be found at the following websites:

- **Anti-corruption Portal of the Americas** (http://www.oas.org/juridico/english/fightcur.html): An initiative of the Organization of American States, this site provides information on anticorruption efforts, news, and technical cooperation in the member states.

- **Anti-corruption Resource Centre** (www.u4.no): This site is a research-based portal that contains corruption assessments in the context of academic and practitioner papers and resources.

- **Council of Europe/Group of States Against Corruption** (GRECO) (http://www.coe.int/t/dghl/monitoring/greco/): This website provides news and information about anticorruption initiatives in the 49 member countries and also includes periodic evaluation and compliance reports on corruption in the member countries.

- **Crinis** (http://www.transparency.org/regional_pages/americas/crinis): This is a joint project of Transparency International and the Carter Center that assesses political financing transparency in Latin American countries.

- **Freedom House**
  - *Nations in Transit* **Reports** (http://freedomhouse.org/template.cfm?page=17): These are annual democratization assessments of 29 countries in the Baltics, Central Europe, and Central Asia.
  - *Countries at the Crossroads* **Surveys** (http://freedomhouse.org/template.cfm?page=139&edition=9): These are annual surveys of government performance in 70 countries at critical points in their political development.

- **Global Integrity Report** (http://report.globalintegrity.org): This site offers a narrative description of corruption by country, broken down by component area, and a quantitative index. These assessments are based on the work of several in-country researchers and journalists and include more than 300 indicators on corruption and governance.

- **Information Portal on Corruption and Governance in Africa** (www.ipocafrica.org): This is an online information center on corruption issues in Africa, providing relevant publications and case studies.

- **OECD Network of Governance (GOVNET)** (http://www.oecd.org): This site publishes a sourcebook on donor approaches to governance assessments.

- **Organisation for Economic Co-operation and Development**
  - **OECD and Asian Development Bank Anti-corruption Initiative for Asia and the Pacific** (http://www.oecd.org/pages/0,,en_34982156_34982385_1_1_1_1_1,00&&en-USS_01DBC.html): This site provides publications and resources regarding anticorruption policy dialogue and analysis for 28 members countries in the Asia–Pacific region.
  - **OECD Anti-corruption Network for Eastern Europe and Central Asia** (http://www.oecd.org/pages/0,,en_36595778_36595861_1_1_1_1_1,00&&en-USS_01DBC.html): This is a regional forum for 20 member countries, civil society, business, and international organizations.

- **Regional Anti-corruption Initiatives** (http://www.oecd.org/infobycountry/0,3380,en_2649_34857_1_1_1_1_1,00.html): This site provides publications, documents, and news on anticorruption issues in several countries.

- **Respondanet** (www.respondanet.com): A project of "Accountability 21," this site provides news, studies, and articles on worldwide corruption.

- **Southeast European Legal Development Initiative**
  - **Corruption Indices** (http://www.seldi.net/seldi_e.htm): These report on the findings of regional corruption monitoring conducted in seven southeastern European countries, officially launching the Regional Corruption Monitoring System of SELDI.
  - **Country Reports** (http://www.seldi.net/country_reports1.htm): These report on the status and scope of corruption in six different countries using information from local experts.

- **Stability Pact for South Eastern Europe, Regional Anti-corruption Initiative** (http://www.stabilitypact.org/anticorruption/): This site provides information and news about the organization's work to reduce corruption in southeastern Europe.

- **Transparency International**
  - **Corruption Perceptions Index** (www.transparency.org): TI publishes this annual index based on several expert and business surveys assessing the perceived level of public sector corruption around the world. Countries' TI "scores" are frequently cited in the media and in academic work.
  - **National Integrity Studies** (www.transparency.org): These provide detailed analyses of corruption and anticorruption efforts in many countries.

- **UN Office on Drugs and Crime** (http://www.unodc.org/unodc/en/corruption/index.html?ref=menuside): This site provides tools, manuals, publications, and other information on anticorruption issues.

- **The World Bank**
  - **Control of Corruption Indicators** (http://info.worldbank
    .org/governance/wgi/index.asp): These corruption assessments
    are one component of the World Bank's Worldwide Gover-
    nance Indicators project, which provides various governance
    indicators for 212 countries and territories from 1996 to the
    present. They are the aggregate result of several surveys of en-
    terprises, citizens, and experts.
  - **Governance and Anti-corruption Resource Center** (http://
    go.worldbank.org/KUDGZ5E6P0): This center provides re-
    search, news, data, and event information about worldwide
    governance and corruption issues.

- **The World Bank and European Bank for Reconstruction and
  Development's Business Environment and Enterprise Performance Survey (BEEPS)** (http://web.worldbank.org/WBSITE/
  EXTERNAL/COUNTRIES/ECAEXT/EXTECAREGTOPA
  NTCOR/0,,contentMDK:20720934~pagePK:34004173~pi
  PK:34003707~theSitePK:704666,00.html): This site provides
  reports on the business environment and firm performance using firm-level data in European and Central Asian countries. It
  also includes Country Profiles and Cross Country Reports that
  provide enterprise indicators in several areas over time.

Annex B:
Self-Assessment Checklist

PART 1. LEGAL ENVIRONMENT			
1. Criminal Code			
a. Does the criminal code explicitly define corruption as illegal?	Yes ☐	No ☐	
b. Does it specify actions considered to be corrupt?	Yes ☐	No ☐	
c. Does it indicate punishments for corruption?	Yes ☐	No ☐	
2. Conflict of Interest			
a. Is there a national law that defines conflicts of interest for public officials?	Yes ☐	No ☐	
b. Do government agencies have clear conflict of interest policies?	Yes ☐	No ☐	
c. If yes, are the policies widely understood by officials working in the agencies?	1 ☐ 2 ☐ 3 ☐ 4 ☐ 5 ☐ *Not understood* *Well understood*		
3. Public Hiring/Appointments			
a. Are laws in place that require public hiring to be based on merit rather than nepotism, connections, and bribery?	Yes ☐	No ☐	
b. Are public hiring decisions actually made on merit?	1 ☐ 2 ☐ 3 ☐ 4 ☐ 5 ☐ *Rarely* *Sometimes* *Always*		
c. Generally, are senior-level appointments given to qualified persons or to political supporters and friends of the top leaders?	☐ ☐ *Qualified person* *Supporters/friends*		

4. Freedom of Information	
a. Are freedom of information laws in place that allow citizens to access public documents related to government decision making?	Yes ☐ No ☐
b. If yes, are citizens actually able to obtain public records in practice?	1 ☐ 2 ☐ 3 ☐ 4 ☐ 5 ☐ *Never* *Always*
5. Sunshine Law	
a. Is a national "sunshine law" in place requiring that meetings of boards or commissions must be open to the public?	Yes ☐ No ☐
If yes	
b. Is reasonable notice of meetings given?	1 ☐ 2 ☐ 3 ☐ 4 ☐ 5 ☐ *Never* *Always*
c. Are minutes of the meeting published in a place accessible to the public?	1 ☐ 2 ☐ 3 ☐ 4 ☐ 5 ☐ *Never* *Always*
6. Asset Disclosure	
a. Are government officials required by law to disclose their assets?	Yes ☐ No ☐
If yes	
b. Does the law require public disclosure?	Yes ☐ No ☐
c. In practice, do public officials provide the information required by law?	1 ☐ 2 ☐ 3 ☐ 4 ☐ 5 ☐ *Never* *Always*
d. Is such information readily available to the public?	1 ☐ 2 ☐ 3 ☐ 4 ☐ 5 ☐ *Never* *Always*
e. Are asset disclosures verified by an independent body?	Yes ☐ No ☐
7. Codes of Conduct	
a. Are public institutions legally required to have a code of conduct?	Yes ☐ No ☐
If yes	
b. Do public institutions actually have codes of conduct in place with legally binding sanctions?	1 ☐ 2 ☐ 3 ☐ 4 ☐ 5 ☐ *None* *Some* *All*
c. Do public institutions provide ethics training?	1 ☐ 2 ☐ 3 ☐ 4 ☐ 5 ☐ *None* *Some* *All*
d. Generally, are public employees aware of the code?	1 ☐ 2 ☐ 3 ☐ 4 ☐ 5 ☐ *None* *Some* *All*

8. Whistleblower Protection	
a. Are whistleblower laws in place to provide protection for people who report cases of corruption?	Yes ☐ No ☐
b. If yes, are people who report cases of corruption actually protected from retribution?	1 ☐ 2 ☐ 3 ☐ 4 ☐ 5 ☐ *Never* *Always*
9. International Conventions	
a. Has the government ratified the UN Convention Against Corruption?	Yes ☐ No ☐
b. Has the government ratified the AU Convention on Combating Corruption?	Yes ☐ No ☐
c. For SADC countries, has the government ratified the SADC Protocol Against Corruption?	Yes ☐ No ☐

PART 2. ENFORCEMENT AND PROSECUTION	
10. Enforcement	
a. Has the government undertaken any corruption-related investigations in the last year?	Yes ☐ No ☐
If yes	
b. Have investigations avoided current members of the government?	Yes ☐ No ☐
c. Have any public officials been removed from their jobs, fined, or put in prison for corruption in the last year?	Yes ☐ No ☐
11. Judiciary	
a. Have any corruption cases been brought to trial in the court system during the last year?	Yes ☐ No ☐
If yes	
b. Have any cases resulted in convictions?	Yes ☐ No ☐
c. Have sentences been executed?	Yes ☐ No ☐
d. Is the judiciary sufficiently independent of political influence to be able to issue verdicts against members of the ruling party?	Yes ☐ No ☐
e. Do specialized criminal courts exist for corruption cases?	Yes ☐ No ☐

12. Money Laundering	
a. Are laws in place prohibiting money laundering (the process through which money derived from illegal activities is given the appearance of originating from a legitimate source)?	Yes ☐ No ☐
b. Has a special money laundering investigative unit been established?	Yes ☐ No ☐
c. In practice, do any agencies carry out investigations related to the movement of money derived from criminal activity?	1 ☐ 2 ☐ 3 ☐ 4 ☐ 5 ☐ *Never* *Frequently*
d. If yes, have any investigations led to convictions?	Yes ☐ No ☐
e. If convictions have been reached, have sentences been enforced?	Yes ☐ No ☐
13. Asset Recovery	
a. Has an asset recovery unit been created?	Yes ☐ No ☐
If yes	
b. Does the unit have sufficient capacity (people, training, funds) to carry out its mission?	1 ☐ 2 ☐ 3 ☐ 4 ☐ 5 ☐ *Insufficient capacity Sufficient capacity*
c. Have there been any cases in which public assets have been recovered (either domestically or from abroad)?	Yes ☐ No ☐
14. Witness Protection	
a. Are legal protections in place for witnesses in corruption cases?	Yes ☐ No ☐
15. Police	
a. Are efforts under way to monitor and curtail corruption within the police?	Yes ☐ No ☐
b. Have any police members been reprimanded or dismissed for corruption in recent memory?	Yes ☐ No ☐

PART 3. GOVERNMENT OVERSIGHT INSTITUTIONS	
16. Anticorruption Agency	
a. Has the government created a special anticorruption agency or commission?	Yes ☐ No ☐
If yes	
b. Does it have the power to investigate all branches of government?	Yes ☐ No ☐

c. Do investigations lead to referrals to the justice system?	Yes ☐ No ☐
d. Do investigations lead to prosecution by the justice system?	Yes ☐ No ☐
e. Does it have sufficient capacity (staff, training, funds) to carry out its mission?	1 ☐ 2 ☐ 3 ☐ 4 ☐ 5 ☐ *Insufficient capacity* *Sufficient capacity*
f. Is the agency/commission sufficiently independent to investigate members of the ruling party?	Yes ☐ No ☐
g. Is it generally seen as being credible?	1 ☐ 2 ☐ 3 ☐ 4 ☐ 5 ☐ *Not credible* *Very credible*
17. Ombudsman (Public Complaints Unit)	
a. Does an ombudsman exist to investigate claims of public corruption?	Yes ☐ No ☐
If yes	
b. Does it have sufficient capacity (staff, training, funds) to carry out its mission?	1 ☐ 2 ☐ 3 ☐ 4 ☐ 5 ☐ *Insufficient capacity* *Sufficient capacity*
c. Is it sufficiently independent of political influence to be able to issue accurate findings?	1 ☐ 2 ☐ 3 ☐ 4 ☐ 5 ☐ *Not independent* *Very independent*
d. Is the public aware of its existence?	1 ☐ 2 ☐ 3 ☐ 4 ☐ 5 ☐ *Not aware* *Very aware*
e. Is it generally seen as being credible?	1 ☐ 2 ☐ 3 ☐ 4 ☐ 5 ☐ *Not credible* *Very credible*
f. Do hotlines or other mechanisms exist for citizens to report cases of corruption?	Yes ☐ No ☐
18. National Strategy	
a. Does the government have a national anticorruption strategy?	Yes ☐ No ☐
If yes	
b. Has the government taken action to implement the strategy?	1 ☐ 2 ☐ 3 ☐ 4 ☐ 5 ☐ *No action* *Significant action*
c. Has the government created mechanisms for monitoring the implementation of its anticorruption strategy?	Yes ☐ No ☐
d. Does the government report regularly on its progress in combating corruption?	Yes ☐ No ☐
e. Has the government carried out an assessment of the causes and consequences of corruption?	Yes ☐ No ☐

f. Are there any senior government officials within the ruling party who have emerged as "champions" for anticorruption reform?	Yes ☐ No ☐
g. Do opposition parties call for corruption probes of the government?	1 ☐ 2 ☐ 3 ☐ 4 ☐ 5 ☐ *Never* *Frequently*
h. Does the country have viable opposition parties that could unseat the ruling party in the next election?	Yes ☐ No ☐
19. Parliament	
a. Is the parliament engaged in efforts to combat corruption?	1 ☐ 2 ☐ 3 ☐ 4 ☐ 5 ☐ *Not at all* *Significantly*
b. To what extent is the parliament able to act as a counterbalance to the executive branch?	1 ☐ 2 ☐ 3 ☐ 4 ☐ 5 ☐ *Not at all* *Significantly*
c. How frequently do concerns about corruption enter into debates within the parliament?	1 ☐ 2 ☐ 3 ☐ 4 ☐ 5 ☐ *Never* *Frequently*
d. Has the parliament initiated any investigations into corrupt practices within the last year?	Yes ☐ No ☐
20. Municipal/Regional Level	
a. Do municipalities or regional governments have anticorruption strategies?	Yes ☐ No ☐
b. If yes, have municipal/regional government units taken action to implement the strategy?	1 ☐ 2 ☐ 3 ☐ 4 ☐ 5 ☐ *No action* *Significant action*
21. Corruption in Public Services	
a. Are there functional mechanisms within the government to monitor the performance of public service agencies (health, education, etc.)?	Yes ☐ No ☐
b. Do civil society groups monitor the performance of public services?	Yes ☐ No ☐
c. Do citizens have recourse in cases where service delivery fails?	1 ☐ 2 ☐ 3 ☐ 4 ☐ 5 ☐ *Never* *Usually*

PART 4. BUDGET AND PUBLIC EXPENDITURE PROCESS

22. Financial Management System	
a. Is there an integrated national financial management system?	Yes ☐ No ☐
If yes	
b. Does that system provide reliable information for public decision making?	Yes ☐ No ☐

c. Does the system provide routine financial reports for legislative and parliamentary oversight committees?	Yes ☐ No ☐
d. If yes, are these reports made available in a timely manner?	1 ☐ 2 ☐ 3 ☐ 4 ☐ 5 ☐ *Never* *Always*
e. Are financial reports made available to the public?	1 ☐ 2 ☐ 3 ☐ 4 ☐ 5 ☐ *Never* *Always*
f. If yes, are these reports made available in a timely manner?	1 ☐ 2 ☐ 3 ☐ 4 ☐ 5 ☐ *Never* *Always*
23. Audits	
a. Is a law in place requiring periodic audit of public accounts?	Yes ☐ No ☐
If yes	
b. In practice, are audits conducted regularly?	1 ☐ 2 ☐ 3 ☐ 4 ☐ 5 ☐ *Never* *Always*
c. Are audit reports provided to parliament?	Yes ☐ No ☐
d. Are audit reports open to the public?	1 ☐ 2 ☐ 3 ☐ 4 ☐ 5 ☐ *Never* *Always*
e. Are the recommendations in audit reports implemented?	1 ☐ 2 ☐ 3 ☐ 4 ☐ 5 ☐ *Never* *Always*
f. If yes, are recommendations implemented in a timely manner?	1 ☐ 2 ☐ 3 ☐ 4 ☐ 5 ☐ *Never* *Always*
g. How would you rate the capacity of the supreme audit institution (staff, training, funds) to carry out its mission?	1 ☐ 2 ☐ 3 ☐ 4 ☐ 5 ☐ *Low capacity* *High capacity*
h. Are its findings heavily influenced by political actors?	1 ☐ 2 ☐ 3 ☐ 4 ☐ 5 ☐ *Never* *Frequently*
i. Are auditors required to follow international auditing standards?	Yes ☐ No ☐
j. Do national auditors associations exist that sanction corrupt auditors?	Yes ☐ No ☐
24. Parliamentary Oversight of Budget	
a. Does parliament have oversight power over budgets and expenditures?	Yes ☐ No ☐
b. If yes, does it in practice ensure that public funds are used for the intended purposes?	1 ☐ 2 ☐ 3 ☐ 4 ☐ 5 ☐ *Not at all* *Routinely*
c. Are open budget hearings held?	Yes ☐ No ☐

d. How often does parliament investigate executive fiscal practices?	1 ☐ 2 ☐ 3 ☐ 4 ☐ 5 ☐ *Never* *Frequently*
25. Procurement	
a. Are multiple bids required for major procurements?	Yes ☐ No ☐
b. Are invitations to bid advertised so that they are known by all interested parties?	1 ☐ 2 ☐ 3 ☐ 4 ☐ 5 ☐ *Never* *Always*
c. Are procurement decisions made public?	1 ☐ 2 ☐ 3 ☐ 4 ☐ 5 ☐ *Never* *Always*
d. In practice, are procurements made without following required procedures?	1 ☐ 2 ☐ 3 ☐ 4 ☐ 5 ☐ *Never* *Frequently*

PART 5. CIVIL SOCIETY, MEDIA, AND BUSINESS	
26. Civil Society	
a. Do civil society organizations exist that claim anticorruption as part of their mandate?	Yes ☐ No ☐
b. If yes, have these organizations initiated actions that have had an impact on government policy?	1 ☐ 2 ☐ 3 ☐ 4 ☐ 5 ☐ *No impact* *Significant impact*
c. Is the government receptive to civil society anticorruption oversight?	1 ☐ 2 ☐ 3 ☐ 4 ☐ 5 ☐ *Not at all* *Very*
27. Media	
a. Is the media considered to be independent of political influence?	1 ☐ 2 ☐ 3 ☐ 4 ☐ 5 ☐ *Not independent* *Very independent*
b. Are laws in place that *protect* the media's right to investigate cases of corruption?	Yes ☐ No ☐
c. Are laws in place that *inhibit* the media's ability to investigate cases of corruption (for example, libel laws)?	Yes ☐ No ☐
d. In practice, does the media report on corruption cases?	1 ☐ 2 ☐ 3 ☐ 4 ☐ 5 ☐ *Never* *Frequently*
e. Does media reporting ever lead to government investigations of alleged cases of corruption?	1 ☐ 2 ☐ 3 ☐ 4 ☐ 5 ☐ *Never* *Frequently*
f. Are any of the major media outlets privately owned?	Yes ☐ No ☐
g. Do "gag laws" exist that restrict media reporting on corruption?	Yes ☐ No ☐

28. Corruption Surveys	
a. Have public opinion surveys of corruption been carried out within the last three years?	Yes ☐ No ☐
b. If yes, have they succeeded in elevating the issue of corruption in national debates?	1 ☐ 2 ☐ 3 ☐ 4 ☐ 5 ☐ *Not at all* *Significantly*
29. Public Awareness Campaigns	
a. Have anticorruption public awareness campaigns been carried out in the last three years?	Yes ☐ No ☐
b. If yes, have they succeeded in elevating the issue of corruption in national debates?	1 ☐ 2 ☐ 3 ☐ 4 ☐ 5 ☐ *Not at all* *Significantly*
30. Business	
a. Have any professional groups formed associations to promote ethical practices?	Yes ☐ No ☐
b. Do any independent watchdog organizations exist to monitor business practices?	Yes ☐ No ☐
c. To what extent are local businesses engaged in and benefiting from government corruption?	1 ☐ 2 ☐ 3 ☐ 4 ☐ 5 ☐ *Not at all* *Extensively*
31. International Dimensions	
a. Have external actors (donors and/or foreign governments) pressured the government to implement anticorruption activities through conditional aid or other mechanisms?	Yes ☐ No ☐
b. Does the impetus to combat corruption come primarily from external actors, the government, or both?	☐ ☐ ☐ *External* *Government* *Both*
c. Overall, how would you rate the government's commitment to controlling corruption?	1 ☐ 2 ☐ 3 ☐ 4 ☐ 5 ☐ *None* *Significant*
d. Do multinational corporations in the country follow international ethical standards of good business conduct?	1 ☐ 2 ☐ 3 ☐ 4 ☐ 5 ☐ *Rarely* *Usually*
e. How would you rate the transparency/accountability of multinational corporations active in this country?	1 ☐ 2 ☐ 3 ☐ 4 ☐ 5 ☐ *Poor* *Acceptable*
f. To what extent are foreigners and multinational corporations engaged in and benefiting from government corruption?	1 ☐ 2 ☐ 3 ☐ 4 ☐ 5 ☐ *Not at all* *Extensively*

Bibliography

Anderson, James, and Cheryl Gray. 2006. *Anticorruption in Transition 3: Who Is Succeeding and Why?* Washington, DC: World Bank.

Barro, Robert J. 1996. "Determinants of Economic Growth: A Cross-Country Empirical Study." National Bureau of Economic Research Working Paper 5698.

Blunt, Peter. 2009. "The Political Economy of Accountability in Timor Leste: Implications for Public Policy." *Public Administration and Development* 29:89–100.

Bolongaita, Emil. 2005. "Controlling Corruption in Post-Conflict Countries." Kroc Institute Occasional Paper #26:OP:2, University of Notre Dame.

Brinkerhoff, Derick, and Benjamin Crosby. 2002. *Managing Policy Reform: Concepts and Tools for Decision-Makers in Developing and Transitioning Countries.* Bloomfield, CT: Kumarian Press.

Buscaglia, Edgardo. 2000. "Judicial Corruption in Developing Countries: Its Causes and Economic Consequences." Hoover Institution, Essays in Public Policy.

Cabinet ORGATECH. 2001. *Enquête sur les Manifestations de la Corruption au Sénégal: Enquête aux Prés des Entreprises.* Dakar: Forum Civil.

Campos, J. Edgardo, and Sanjay Pradhan, eds. 2007. *The Many Faces of Corruption: Tracking Vulnerabilities at the Sector Level.* Washington, DC: World Bank.

Cartier-Bresson, Jean. n.d. "Economics of Corruption." *OECD Observer.* Accessed January 16, 2011, http://www.oecdobserver.org/news/fullstory.php/aid/239.

Counterpart Creative Center. 2004. *Civil Society Organizations in Ukraine: The State and Dynamics (2002–2003).* Kyiv: Counterpart Creative Center.

Crook, Matt. 2010. "Analysis: Tough Task to Tackle Corruption in East Timor." *Global Post,* April 18.

Delevingne, Lawrence. n.d. "The Joy of Doing Business in Africa: How Senegalese Politicians Tried to Shake Down Millicom for $200 Million." *Business Insider.* Accessed February 4, 2010, http://www.businessinsider.com/business-in-africa-how-corrupt-senegalese-politicians-tried-to-shake-down-millicom-for-200-million-2010-2.

Dininio, Phyllis. 2005. "The Risks of Recorruption." In *Fighting Corruption in Developing Countries: Strategies and Analysis,* edited by Bertram I. Spector. Bloomfield, CT: Kumarian Press.

Dollar, David, and Aart Kraay. 2002. "Growth Is Good for the Poor." *Journal of Economic Growth* 7 (3): 195–225.

Easterly, William. 2001. *The Elusive Quest for Growth: Economists' Adventures and Misadventures in the Tropics*. Cambridge, MA: MIT Press.

Fall, Abdou Salam, ed. 2006, October. *Gouvernance et Corruption dans le Domaine des Ressources Naturelles et de l'environnement au Sénégal, Rapport final*. Dakar: Forum Civil.

Fall, Abdou Salam, and Babacar Gueye, eds. 2005, May. *Gouvernance et Corruption dans le Systeme de Santé au Sénégal: Rapport final*. Dakar: Forum Civil, and Centre de Recherches Pour le Developpement International.

Feldman, Tine Rossing, and Susan Assaf. 1999. "Social Capital: Conceptual Frameworks and Empirical Evidence: An Annotated Bibliography." World Bank Social Capital Initiative, Working Paper No. 5.

Goudie, Andrew, and David Stasavage. 1997. "Corruption: The Issues." OECD Development Center Technical Papers No. 122.

Gray, Cheryl W., and Daniel Kaufmann. 1998. "Corruption and Development." *Finance and Development* 35 (1): 6–10.

Gupta, Sanjeev, Hamid Davoodi, and Rosa Alonso-Terme. 1998. "Does Corruption Affect Income Equality and Poverty?" IMF Working Paper 98/76.

Gupta, Sanjeev, Hamid Davoodi, and Erwin Tiongson. 2000. "Corruption and the Provision of Health Care and Education Services." IMF Working Paper 00/116.

Guttmann, Michelle. 2003. "USAID's Approach to Poverty Reduction: The Case of Honduras." USAID, Evaluation Brief No. 5, PN-ACR-351, Washington, DC.

Heidenheimer, Arnold J., and Michael Johnston, eds. 2002. *Political Corruption: Concepts and Contexts*, 3rd ed. New Brunswick, NJ: Transaction.

Heineman, Ben W., and Fritz Heimann. 2006. "The Long War Against Corruption." *Foreign Affairs* 8 (3): 75–86.

Huntington, Samuel. 1968. *Political Order in Changing Societies*. New Haven, CT: Yale University Press.

Johnston, Michael. 2000a. "Corruption and Democracy: Threats to Development, Opportunities for Reform." Paper prepared for Department of Political Science, Colgate University.

———. 2000b. "The New Corruption Rankings: Implications for Analysis and Reform." Paper presented at the International Political Science Association, World Congress, Quebec City, Canada.

———. 2005. *Syndromes of Corruption*. New York: Cambridge University Press.

———. 2010. "Assessing Vulnerabilities to Corruption: Indicators and Benchmarks of Government Performance." *Public Integrity* 12 (2): 125–42.

Johnston, Michael, and Sahr Kpundeh. 2002. "The Measurement Problem: A Focus on Governance." Unpublished, January.

Karstedt, Susan. 2000. "The Culture of Inequality and Corruption: A Cross-National Study of Corruption." Paper presented at the ASC Conference, Department of Criminology, Keele University, San Francisco.

Kaufmann, Daniel. 2002. "Governance Empirics." Paper presented at State Department, April 19.

———. 2003. "Rethinking Governance: Empirical Lessons Challenge Orthodoxy." March 11. http://papers.ssrn.com/sol3/papers.cfm?abstract_id=386904.

Kaufmann, Daniel, and Aart Kraay. 2002. "Growth Without Governance." *Economia* 3.1, Fall.

Kaufmann, Daniel, Aart Kraay, and Pablo Zoido-Lobaton. 1999. "Governance Matters." World Bank Policy Research Working Paper No. 2196.

———. 2000. "Governance Matters: From Measurement to Action." *Finance and Development* 37 (2).

———. 2002. "Governance Matters II: Updated Indicators for 2000/01." World Bank Policy Research Working Paper No. 2772.

Kaufmann, Daniel, Gil Mehrez, and Tugrul Gurgur. 2002. "Voice or Public Sector Management: An Empirical Investigation of Determinants of Public Sector Performance Based on a Survey of Public Officials." World Bank Research Working Paper.

Klitgaard, Robert E., Ronald MacLean Abaroa, and H. Lindsey Parris. 2000. *Corrupt Cities: A Practical Guide to Cure and Prevention.* Oakland, CA: ICS Press.

Knack, Stephen. 1999. "Governance and Employment." ILO Employment and Training Papers 45.

———. 2002a. "Governance and Growth: Measurement and Evidence." IRIS Center, Forum Series on the Role of Institutions in Promoting Growth.

———. 2002b. "Social Capital, Growth and Poverty: A Survey of Cross-Country Evidence." In *The Role of Social Capital in Development: An Empirical Assessment,* edited by Christiaan Grootaert and Thierry van Bastelaer. Cambridge, UK: Cambridge University Press.

Knack, Stephen, and Philip Keefer. 1997. "Does Social Capital Have an Economic Payoff? A Cross-Country Investigation." *Quarterly Journal of Economics* 112:1251–88.

Krueger, Anne O. 1974. "The Political Economy of the Rent-Seeking Society." *American Economic Review* 64:291–303.

Kuzio, Taras. 2010. "Judges Mock Justice With Their Useless or Corrupt Rulings." *Kyiv Post.* April 8. http://www.kyivpost.com/news/opinion/op_ed/detail/63477/print/.

Lambsdorff, Johann Graf. 1999. "Corruption in Empirical Research: A Review." Transparency International Working Paper.

———. 2001. "How Corruption in Government Affects Public Welfare: A Review of Theories." Paper prepared for the Center for Globalization and Europeanization of the Economy, Gottingen, Germany.

———. 2003. "How Corruption Affects Persistent Capital Flows." *Economics of Governance* 4 (3): 229–44.

Le Billon, P. 2005. "Overcoming Corruption in the Wake of Conflict." In *Global Corruption Report 2005.* Berlin: Transparency International.

Lewis, James. 2005. "Earthquake Destruction: Corruption on the Fault Line?" In *Global Corruption Report 2005.* Berlin: Transparency International.

Liebenberg, Linda, and Michael Ungar, eds. 2009. *Researching Resilience.* Toronto, Ontario, Canada: University of Toronto Press.

Lieberson, Joseph, and Jonathan Sleeper. 2000. "Poverty: A CDIE Experience Review." USAID, PPC/CDIE/POA.

Management Systems International. 2000, August. *Ukraine Anticorruption Support Project, Final Report.* Washington, DC: MSI.

———. 2002a. *Handbook on Using Corruption Assessments.* Washington, DC: MSI.

———. 2002b. *Handbook on Using Existing Corruption Indices.* Washington, DC: MSI.

———. 2005, February. *A Rapid Anticorruption Assessment Technique for USAID/Africa: Developing a Practical Checklist for USAID Missions in Africa.* Washington, DC: MSI.

———. 2007, August. *Corruption Assessment: Senegal.* Washington, DC: MSI.

———. 2008a, July. *Assessment of Corruption: Paraguay.* Washington, DC: MSI.

———. 2008b, October. *Honduras Corruption Assessment Report.* Washington, DC: MSI.

———. 2009a, February. *Corruption Assessment Handbook.* Washington, DC: MSI.

————. 2009b, June. *Corruption in Ukraine: Comparative Analysis of National Surveys: 2007–2009.* Washington, DC: MSI.

————. 2010, February. *Promoting Citizen Engagement in Combating Corruption in Ukraine: Final Report.* Washington, DC: MSI.

Mauro, Paulo. 2002. "The Effects of Corruption on Growth and Public Expenditure." In *Political Corruption: Concepts and Contexts*, 3rd ed., edited by Arnold J. Heidenheimer and Michael Johnston. New Brunswick, NJ: Transaction.

Mietzner, Marcus. 1998. "Corruption: Causes, Consequences, and Agenda for Further Research." *Finance and Development*, March, 11–14.

————. 2010. "Funding Pilkada: Illegal Campaign Financing in Indonesia's Local Elections." In *Illegality and the State in Indonesia*, edited by Edward Aspinall and Gerry van Klinken. Leiden: KITLV Press.

Murphy, Kevin M., Andrei Shleifer, and Robert W. Vishny. 1993. "Why Is Rent-Seeking So Costly to Growth?" *American Economic Review* 83 (2): 409–14.

Nanivska, Vera. 2001. *NGO Development in Ukraine.* Kyiv: International Center for Policy Studies.

North, Douglass C. 1990. *Institutions, Institutional Change and Economic Performance.* Cambridge, UK: Cambridge University Press.

Organisation for Economic Co-operation and Development. 2005. "Paris Declaration on Aid Effectiveness." www.oecd.org/document/18/0,3343,en_2649_3236398_35401554_1_1_1_1,00.html.

————. 2007. "Policy Paper and Principles on Anti-Corruption: Setting an Agenda for Collective Action." Development Assistance Committee Guidelines and Reference Series. http://www.oecd.org/dataoecd/2/42/39618679.pdf.

Polgreen, Lydia, and Marjorie Connelly. 2007. "Poll Shows Africans Wary, but Hopeful About Future." *New York Times*, July 25, A6.

Pope, Jeremy. 2000. *TI Source Book 2000—Confronting Corruption: The Elements of a National Integrity System.* Berlin: Transparency International.

Quibria, M. G. 2002. "Growth and Poverty: Lessons From the East Asian Miracle Revisited." Asia Development Bank Research Paper 33.

Roaf, James. 2000. "Corruption in Russia." Paper presented at the IMF conference on Post Election Strategy, Moscow, April 5–7.

Rose-Ackerman, Susan. 1978. *Corruption: A Study in Political Economy.* New York: Academic Press.

————. 1999. *Corruption and Government: Causes, Consequences and Reform.* Cambridge, UK: Cambridge University Press.

————. 2001. "Trust, Honesty and Corruption: Reflections on the State Building Process." *European Journal of Sociology* 42:27–71.

————. 2002. "When Is Corruption Harmful?" In *Political Corruption: Concepts and Contexts*, 3rd ed., edited by Arnold J. Heidenheimer and Michael Johnston. New Brunswick, NJ: Transaction.

Salinger, Lynn, and Dirck Stryker. 2001. "Comparing and Evaluating Poverty Reduction Approaches: USAID and the Evolving Poverty Reduction Paradigm." Assessment prepared for USAID/PPC/CDIE/POA by Associates for International Resources under subcontract with MSI, July 28.

Spector, Bertram I., ed. 2005. *Fighting Corruption in Developing Countries: Strategies and Analysis.* Bloomfield, CT: Kumarian Press.

———. 2006. "Resiliency in Negotiation: Bouncing Back From Impasse." *International Negotiation* 11 (2): 273–86.

———. 2011. *Negotiating Peace and Confronting Corruption: Challenges for Postconflict Societies.* Washington, DC: US Institute of Peace Press.

Spector, Bertram I., with David Duong. 2002. *Handbook on Using Existing Corruption Indices.* Washington, DC: Management Systems International.

Spector, Bertram I., Michael Johnston, and Phyllis Dininio. 2005. "Learning Across Cases: Trends in Anticorruption Strategies." In *Fighting Corruption in Developing Countries*, edited by B. Spector. Bloomfield, CT: Kumarian Press.

Swamy, Anand, Stephen Knack, Young Lee, and Omar Azfar. 2000. "Gender and Corruption." Center for Development Economics, Department of Economics, Williams College.

Tanzi, Vito. 1998. "Corruption Around the World: Causes, Consequences, Scope and Cures." *IMF Staff Papers* 45:4.

Tanzi, Vito, and Hamid Davoodi. 1997. "Corruption, Public Investment, and Growth." IMF Working Paper 97/139.

Tidiane, Sy. 2009. "Senegal Colossus Proves Sore Point." BBC News. November 16. http://news.bbc.co.uk/2/hi/africa/8353624.stm.

UN Development Programme. 2002. *Human Development Report 2002.* New York: Oxford University Press.

UN Development Programme and Global Integrity. 2008. *A Users' Guide to Measuring Corruption.* Oslo, Norway: UNDP.

US Agency for International Development. 1999. *A Handbook on Fighting Corruption.* Technical Publication Series, Center for Democracy and Governance. Washington, DC: USAID.

———. 2005. *Anticorruption Strategy.* Washington, DC: USAID.

Walecki, Marcin. 2004. "Political Money and Corruption." In *Global Corruption Report 2004.* Berlin: Transparency International.

Warrener, Debbie. 2004. *The Drivers of Change Approach.* London: Overseas Development Institute.

Wolf, Thomas, and Emine Gurgen. 2000. "Improving Governance and Fighting Corruption in the Baltic and CIS Countries." IMF Working Paper.

World Bank. 2000a. *Anticorruption in Transition: A Contribution to the Policy Debate.* Washington, DC: World Bank.

———. 2000b. *Helping Countries Combat Corruption: Progress at the World Bank Since 1977.* Washington, DC: World Bank.

———. 2000c. *Making Transition Work for Everyone: Poverty and Inequality in Europe and Central Asia.* Washington DC: World Bank.

———. 2001a. *Diagnostic Surveys of Corruption in Romania.* Washington, DC: World Bank, in association with Management Systems International.

———. 2001b. *World Development Report 2000/2001: Attacking Poverty.* New York: Oxford University Press.

———. 2002. *World Development Report 2003: Sustainable Development in a Dynamic World: Transforming Institutions, Growth and Quality of Life.* Washington DC: World Bank and Oxford University Press.

World Bank Institute and EBRD. 2000. "Business Environment and Enterprise Performance Survey." http://info.wolrdbank.org/governance/beeps/.

Worth, Robert, and James Glanz. 2006. "Oil Corruption Fuels Insurgency in Iraq." *New York Times*, February 5.

Zak, Paul, and Stephen Knack. 1998. "Trust and Growth." IRIS Center Working Paper No. 219.

Index

Also available from Kumarian Press

Fighting Corruption in Developing Countries
Edited by Bertram I. Spector

"A timely review of the progress made during the past decade in the fight against corruption in developing countries. Invaluable lessons are shared by the contributors that enable both government and private sector practitioners to be more effective in combating corruption." —*Stephen D. Potts, Chairman of the Board, Ethics Resource Center*

Corruption is a worldwide phenomenon, but it especially plagues developing countries and those in democratic transition. This timely collection presents a sector-by-sector analysis of the problems that stunt economic growth, distort governance, limit civic and democratic participation, and infuriate the populace.

In stark contrast to standard holistic studies of corruption, Fighting Corruption in Developing Countries argues that examining the issue through the lens of nine key development sectors—education, agriculture, energy, environment, health, justice, private business, political parties, and public finance—will help us to realistically understand the problem and identify concrete initiatives that are likely to have an impact.

The book concludes with practical and policy-oriented suggestions for corruption control that minimize the risk of "recorrupting" forces that often threaten to reverse gains. Students, researchers, and practitioners interested in implementing effective and realistic solutions to fighting corruption will find this book essential reading.

Anticorruption in the Health Sector
Edited by Taryn Vian, William D. Savedoff, and Harald Mathisen

"Provides a breadth of interesting and informative essays on the role of corruption in health care delivery in developing countries and the strategies that have been tested to reverse corruption and thereby increase overall funding for publicly provided health care. It is an invaluable book for anyone who wants to understand the nature of corruption in health care delivery systems." —*Maureen Lewis, Economic Advisor, Research Department, World Bank*

Corruption is a serious problem for both rich and poor countries, threatening international development and eroding confidence in governments. In the health sector, corruption is literally a matter of life and death: facilities crumble when repair funds are embezzled, fake drugs flood the market with corrupt regulators managing supply, and doctors extorting under-the-table payments from patients fail to provide needed care. Most major development organizations have rewritten their anticorruption strategies in the past five years, hinting that reform is within reach. But these strategies pay little attention to incentives and capacity at the sector level. Those preparing to fight corruption in the health sector had very few resources to guide them, until now.

Anticorruption in the Health Sector brings practical experience to bear on anticorruption approaches tailored specifically to health. The contributors, all skilled practitioners, address the consequences of different types of corruption and show how agencies can more effectively address these challenges as an integral part of their development work. Both practitioner and classroom friendly, this book finally addresses a neglected issue that has so much bearing on global health and governance.

Kumarian Press
An Imprint of Stylus Publishing

22883 Quicksilver Drive
Sterling, VA 20166-2102

Subscribe to our e-mail alerts: www.kpbooks.com

Kumarian Press, located in Sterling, Virginia, is a forward-looking, scholarly press that promotes active international engagement and an awareness of global connectedness.